My Old Man's a BUSMAN

Peter Gilbert

AuthorHouse™ UK Ltd.
1663 Liberty Drive
Bloomington, IN 47403 USA
www.authorhouse.co.uk
Phone: 0800.197.4150

© 2014 Peter Gilbert. All rights reserved.

No part of this book may be reproduced, stored in a retrieval system, or transmitted by any means without the written permission of the author.

Published by AuthorHouse   05/12/2014

ISBN: 978-1-4969-7867-7 (sc)
ISBN: 978-1-4969-7868-4 (hc)
ISBN: 978-1-4969-7869-1 (e)

Any people depicted in stock imagery provided by Thinkstock are models, and such images are being used for illustrative purposes only. Certain stock imagery © Thinkstock.

This book is printed on acid-free paper.

Because of the dynamic nature of the Internet, any web addresses or links contained in this book may have changed since publication and may no longer be valid. The views expressed in this work are solely those of the author and do not necessarily reflect the views of the publisher, and the publisher hereby disclaims any responsibility for them.

Contents

Acknowledgements xi
Introduction xiii

Scary Quo 1
My Old Man's a Busman 11
'Back Home' with Bobby Moore 19
On the Radio 28
A Transport of Delight 38
When Elvis Met My Auntie Margaret . . . Twice 48
Getting Ahead in the Movies 63
Nearly Shipwrecked 77
Hazel O'Connor Owes Me a Pint 90
My Second Radio Interview 103
Pop Cricket 107
Ben Elton Made Me Write This Book 132
I Stole Robbie Williams's Underpants 142
Les Adventures de Pierre le Wag à Monte Carlo 152
Shanghaied 166
Tarzan Taught My Mother-in-Law to Swim 177
Rocking Around the Christmas Tree 186
Pop Art 195
Marine Boy 210
My Final Interview 217
Praise for My Old Man's a Busman 222

In memory of Dave 'the Rave' Gilbert, 1935-2013

'Put me on the bus to where the dance goes on forever.'
—The Hamptons, 'London Town'

This book is dedicated to:
Charlie, Jake, Joff, Mum, Netty, Sienna and
lastly (but only alphabetically) Trish.

With special thanks for their help, support and encouragement:
Trish, Netty, Karen (a.k.a. Doc Savage), Dom, Mike M and Dave S.

Acknowledgements

All radio interview content is included with the kind permission of Frank Skinner. References from Mark Radcliffe's book *Thank You for the Days* are reprinted here with the kind permission of the author.

'Margate' lyrics are reprinted with the kind permission of Chas Hodges.

'If There's Anything More' lyrics are reprinted with the kind permission of Laura Catlow.

The author acknowledges the support received from the following, for allowing the use of their (or their clients') names, stories, and references: Beth Chalmers, Ben Elton, Francis Gilson, John Harle, the Macc Lads, Lisa Snowdon, Status Quo, Avalon, Barry Collings Entertainments, the Blair Partnership, ITV Viewer Services—Daytime, McIntyre Entertainments, Money Management UK, Private Secretary to HRH the Duke of York, and Voiceovers Ltd.

Every effort has been made to locate and contact all persons holding any rights to the material reproduced in this work. Where this has not been possible, the author will be happy to hear from anyone who recognises his or her material and will rectify any errors or omissions, amending subsequent editions accordingly.

Introduction

Marine Boy, despite being a two-dimensional 1960s Japanese cartoon character, was one of my earliest childhood heroes.

He lived in an amazing submarine and his friends were a dolphin called Splasher and a mermaid called Neptina. He had underwater boomerangs that could give off electric shocks powerful enough to destroy his enemies' submarines. The hyper-powered propeller packs in his heels enabled him to fly through the water and he could breathe for hours under water by using oxy-gum.

In 1969, what five-year-old would not think that this was cool?

If you've read the above, then I can make one of a number of assumptions.

1. You're one of a select few who are reading a draft copy of what I hope will be a published book.
2. This has been published, and you're actually reading my book.
3. You are a future descendent of mine. Generations of family members having passed down this text as a fairly interesting set of stories and musings from an ancient ancestor—although, perhaps, some of the cultural references may now be obscure. 'Elvis who?'

If the last is the case, then, given the advancements in technology that I presume have been made in the intervening decades and centuries, I'd love to know how you are absorbing this text. A physical book is unlikely (I believe that they, like vinyl and CDs before them, will become obsolete sometime in the twenty-first century, certainly for any new publishing). I prefer to believe that a holographic version of myself has been created and perfectly lip-synced to retell my tales to you, wherever and whenever you choose to bring me to life. You may be on a futuristic (for me), sleek, ultra-high-speed train (I'm writing this on a twenty-first century train), but I prefer to think that you are in a personal hovering space pod while holidaying at La Solar Resort on the moon or that you are living in a hydro-dome under the Pacific Ocean. Maybe, when my holographic avatar is reading out this text, you refer to me as your 'kindled spirit'.

If, however, you are reading this published book as a well-considered choice or purchase in the early twenty-first century, then I thank you. I hope that you enjoy reading it as much as I have enjoyed writing it.

At this point, if you hadn't already guessed, I have to admit that I am a bit of a fantasist. My girlfriend (who might add 'long suffering' before 'girlfriend') can cite many examples of this. On a recent trip to Australia to visit friends and family, we were staying south of Melbourne on the Mornington Peninsular. We were there for only a few days but it was so beautiful with its beaches, olive groves, and vineyards that we never actually made it to the city itself, as we had planned.

While my girlfriend and I were discussing our lack of travel and my fondness for alliteration one day over coffee, we decided that I should be referred to as Peninsular Pete.

Following about ten minutes of chat (nonsense), I had proclaimed myself king (or, at least, mayor) of the peninsula and had been commissioned by a leading travel magazine to write an article about my trip. This article had led me to create a popular blog, the substance of which we then pitched to a producer friend of ours in the United Kingdom, who commissioned a TV show called *Peninsular Pete's Places*. This meant that we would be paid to return to Australia. Another TV series would follow, this one linked with *Phil Spencer's Down Under* to become a joint venture called *Peninsular Pete and Phil's Property Place Down Under*—which would be re-commissioned and inspire further talk of a third series, meaning that my girlfriend and I could take an annual all-expenses-paid trip and then work on writing a book about the series. Life doesn't get much better.

Similarly, my having written only the first couple of chapters (and maybe, if I'm honest, before I'd even started it), I imagined this book as a bestseller featured heavily in WHSmith, Waterstones, and every airport in the United Kingdom, if not the world. Then I saw spin-off books, including (and these will make more sense once you've read more) *The Writing of My*

Old Man's a Busman, The Little Book of Pop Cricket, Great Knockers, and *More Great Knockers,* all leading to global book-signing tours.

The book signings become events in themselves, making celebrities of my friends and family mentioned in this book—as fans travel for miles to meet their heroes and heroines, who are recognisable in T-shirts with their names printed on them. Once a year, we put on an event for charity and fans join us on a journey to tour memorable places from the book. We end up in an arty venue where we do a Q&A and then dance into the night to the tunes mentioned on the top-ten lists in this book, with Dave (D.J Dave mentioned later in the book) on the decks and live performances from artists mentioned such as Laura Catlow and Ben Smith.

Also in the future, I see the game of dice cricket taken up by Hasbro, with online and app versions in development. Pop cricket, initially a radio quiz, is now being adapted for TV. I've appeared on Brekkie TV and have been asked to write various magazine articles and columns.

There is an associated art show and a TV series of the making of the art show. Companies queue to buy the website. I am adapting the book for a one-man Edinburgh show.

I even catch *myself* fantasising sometimes as my mind goes on these mental safaris.

Most recently, I was constructing some ideas for the book based on my memories of the 1970s and of glam rock. The next thing I knew, I had mentally written a complete scenario where I was being interviewed about the book on Brekkie TV (or whatever the current equivalent is) with Melanie Sykes, Des O'Connor, Holly Willoughby, Phillip Schofield, Lorraine Kelly, and Ricki Lake. Suzi Quatro is the other guest.

In my fantasy, we all discuss parts of the book and talk about how true or personal some of it was. Then the others discuss their favourite parts. Holly said how much she'd laughed at the *Harry Potter*–related stuff, while Phil liked the story of my girlfriend discovering my box of singles.

I was then shocked and slightly overawed as Suzi said that she'd read *My Old Man's a Busman* and was delighted to learn that she had been an object of my boyhood fantasy. She was so pleased that I'd written so many nice things about her that she wanted to have me appear as a guest on her next Radio 2 show to discuss my book, my life, and my love of music with fellow guests Frank Skinner, Mark Radcliffe, and Alan Davies.

This type of daydreaming would be fine if I was sitting, relaxing, and having a cup of coffee, but I was driving to a meeting at the time.

Like Mark Radcliffe says of his book *Thank You for the Days*, 'I don't want you to think of this book as an autobiography because that makes it sound much more full of itself than it is [and he's famous!]. . . On the other hand, the odd interesting or funny or embarrassing thing has occurred during my first fifty years.'

And so it is with me, except that I'm not at all famous. I'm just an extra, someone who observes from the outside and occasionally gets a break to do some fun and interesting stuff slightly outside of the norm—or gets to cross paths long enough with people who are in the public eye to make a story out of it. I hope that I'm not alone and that I'm simply reflecting on how ordinary people like me can occasionally experience extraordinary episodes in their lives.

The pièce de résistance that emerged from these mental safaris and fantasies, however, is the original standalone introduction I had written for this book. After he read it, my youngest son asked, 'Did that actually happen, Dad? Have you been interviewed on the radio by someone famous?'

* * *

'That was "Psycho Mafia" by the Fall, and this is Frank Skinner on Absolute Radio. We have in the studio today a young man. Well, I say young . . . I believe that he's nearly the same age as me, but I'm feeling magnanimous—and anyway, I like to give people a lift at this time of the morning. Talking of lifts, I saw the film *Schindler's Lift* last night . . . It was okay, but I thought it went a little bit up and down in parts. Sorry about that, listeners, but I couldn't resist. Anyway, I digress. We have in the studio with us today Pete, an aspiring author who is writing a book about . . . well, I suppose we should ask you that question. Pete—or do you prefer Peter?—tell us a little about this book.'

'I prefer Pete. First of all, Frank, can I just say thanks for inviting me on? I'm a big fan of yours and the show, and I listen to the podcast every week, as I don't usually get a chance to catch the show live.'

'Pete, I'm basking in your praise this sunny Saturday morning, be it that some of it probably relates to my past glories, but thank you for your

My Old Man's a Busman

kindly chosen words. So, back to your forthcoming written words. Let's start with what inspired you to write this book.'

'Well, Frank, I've wanted to write one for ages, years, and have been lucky enough to amass, I think, some interesting and amusing experiences, anecdotes, and celebrity encounters. Now that I'm forty-something and facing a new decade, I thought that I'd better get on with it, as you never know what's around the corner.'

'Like the number twenty-nine bus?'

'Exactly, Frank. And having kids, as I know you have now, it's nice to think that I might leave a legacy—in my case, some words other than those that are maybe written on my gravestone.'

'I agree, and I know what you mean about wanting to leave a piece of yourself for posterity, especially for your offspring—in my case, Buzz. But, surely, everyone has bumped into a celebrity in their time, even some of our Absolute Radio listeners, so what's different about what you have to say?'

'I'm sure that they have, Frank. And I, and most people I know, have celebrity spots that we can talk about down at the pub. But the stories in my book are about the times when it's been more than those brief encounters, a bit more up close and personal, if you like. Having said that, I have included a story about getting Bobby Moore's autograph in 1970, but that's related to the fact that it was my first ever autograph . . . and it was Bobby Moore.

'Also, I have to admit that I'm not averse to getting excited when spotting a celeb. I did have to text my girlfriend—or, maybe I should say *partner,* at our age—a while ago when I was sitting in the same carriage of a train as Lily Allen, although I don't think that she'll feature in the book, as that was literally all there was to that particular encounter, whereas there was a little more to Bobby Moore, if you'll excuse that particular pun.'

'Neither to be ashamed of. I'm sure you know that I like a pun and I also like a little bit of Lily, too, and would probably have done the same thing with my . . . partner. Can I just pick up on your partner reference, though, as I have a problem with this, too? Don't you find it a bit awkward using *partner* or *girlfriend* to describe your . . . how should we say . . . better half?'

'Absolutely, Frank. We often discuss it, my girlfriend—or, should I say *partner*?—and I. *Girlfriend* sounds like something you'd say or write on your pencil case when you are fourteen, probably with a big heart around it, somewhere between Siouxsie and the Banshees and ABBA . . .'

'Now, there's a thought for our Absolute Radio listeners. Carry on.'

'And *partner* sounds like you're trying to hide a secret about your sexual orientation . . .'

'Sorry to interrupt again, but can we say that on Absolute Radio at this time of the morning? Let me just look it up . . . Yes, it's allowed; thank goodness for that. I totally agree with you. We have over two hundred and fifty thousand words in the English language, give or take a few thousand, and not one that describes a . . . let's say . . . middle-life relationship effectively.'

'Yes, Frank, and not too many good options, really. *Squeeze* sounds a bit transient, as well as more than a little derogatory, and *other* or *better half* a bit—dare I say?—common. I certainly wouldn't want to be on the receiving end of either of those in relation to your co-host Emily Dean, for example.'

'Most definitely not. If I called Cath any one of those, I'd be in the doghouse, although not as much as if I referred to her as Wifey.'

'I know what you mean, although I did hear a great one the other day. A guy met his wife on the Internet, and so he calls her Wi-Fi instead.'

'That's marvellous, although, again, we digress. We have more music and guests coming up on Absolute Radio this morning. So, Pete, anything else that you can tell us about your book at this stage?'

'Well, it's part autobiographical and, as I've said, contains some memorable encounters, but it is also fused with observations and, I suppose you'd say, musings about everyday things as well as pop culture and events across the decades.'

'Any stories that you can share with the listeners at this stage, although I know that it's not finished yet?'

'Well, Frank, I got the Hazel O'Connor song "Will You" used in a TV advert, I've invented pop cricket, my auntie Margaret met Elvis, and I once stole Robbie Williams's boxer shorts.'

'Blimey, I'm speechless. Are they all true?'

'Absolutely, Frank. And, each chapter has a relevant list of my top-ten tunes as well as some website and YouTube links, which will make the content come alive for the reader.'

'I'll be honest with you, Pete. I'm loving the sound of the stories and YouTube links, but hasn't the whole top-ten thing been done before?'

'It has, Frank, [with] Nick Hornby being the master, closely followed by Phil Jupitus and Mark Radcliffe, in my view. But I've been writing this book in my head for years, and when I first conceived it, it was always going to include my top-tens, as music is so intrinsic to the stories and my life. So, now that I'm finally writing it, despite what other people have done, [the top-ten lists are] definitely going in. Also, they're obviously different than anybody else's, and so, hopefully, if nothing else, it will remind people of some great tracks that they'd forgotten or maybe encourage them to check out some new or different tunes.'

'Well, good for you. Anything else before we wrap it up? It certainly sounds like a book that we at Absolute Radio are going to enjoy.'

'Not really, Frank. I think at this stage I just need to go and get on with it.'

'So, we could say that at this moment in time you're an open book. Sorry, listeners. So, given that you still have to finish it, will this interview figure in your book at all?'

'Absolutely, Frank. I imagine that this would make a great introduction and be a pastiche of the character Jimmy Rabbitte when he's interviewing himself, resulting in an homage to one of my favourite films, *The Commitments*.'

'Well, thank you for coming in today. We look forward to reading and reviewing your book. As a new "friend of the show", why don't you come back soon and let us know how you are getting on?'

'Well, Frank, thank you. I'd love to come back on the show, maybe when I'm about halfway through.'

'That was Pete talking about his forthcoming book . . . I forgot to ask him what it was called. Thankfully for us here and you, the Absolute Radio listener, he agreed to come back. . . . An homage and a pastiche. What a delicious turn of phrase, don't you think? Do you know I quite fancy a pastiche for lunch now?

Peter Gilbert

'After the news and our next song, we have our main guests, Phil Jupitus and TV's Emma Kennedy, talking about their new book collaboration *I Left My Tent in Nantwich*.

'Talking of halfway through and delicious, I'm currently one finger into a Kit Kat with my tea. Other chocolate-covered wafer biscuits are available. . . . Phil, don't take this as a personal reference to your good self, but here's Half Man Half Biscuit with "Fred Titmus."'

Scary Quo

I was born in Reigate, Surrey, which is now considered middle class, since it is in the heart of the London commuter belt and has the astronomical real estate prices to prove it. But, when I was growing up there in the late '60s and early '70s, in a slightly damp Victorian end-of-terrace house, it was simply my family's home and the town where we lived.

Some famous people have been residents of Reigate: Dame Margot Fontaine, Spike Milligan, André Previn, Alan Minter, Ray Allen, David Walliams, Melvyn Hayes, and Caroline Quentin. I've never met any of these people, but in my sister's class at Reigate Priory School was a boy named Quentin Cook. He, at one point, asked my sister to kiss or marry him (a detail that is lost in the mists of time).

Quentin has undergone a number of name and personality changes, including changing his name to Norman Cook during his time with the Hull-based band the Housemartins and, latterly, with Fatboy Slim.

Whilst not officially a resident, Annabel Lwin, lead singer of the '80s band Bow Wow Wow, is infamously connected with Reigate and, more specifically, Priory Park, where my sister and I went to school with Norm, went for walks at weekends, played on the swings after school, and fed the ducks on the ponds. In 1981, at age fifteen, Annabel was photographed naked in Reigate's Priory Park for a record cover depicting the scene from Manet's *The Luncheon on the Grass (Le déjeuner sur l'herbe)*. Her mother alleged that she had been the victim of exploitation of a minor for immoral purposes and therewith instigated a Scotland Yard investigation, presumably into the band's manager. The photograph can be seen on the cover of Bow Wow Wow's 1982 vinyl EP *The Last of the Mohicans*.

Back in the late '60s, Mum stayed at home and looked after us kids. Dad was a bus driver for London Transport.

Despite the fact that we were far from well off, we did, as far back as I remember, have a car. Some of our family lived quite a few miles away and didn't drive. I think the fact that Mum and Dad were both only children (we kids had no uncles, aunts, or cousins) meant that keeping in touch with the immediate family we did have was important to them—and, therefore, we needed a car. That said, we probably could have gone on the bus for free.

I'm not sure if it was planned this way, but our house in Reigate was on top of a hill, meaning that Dad could always bump-start the car down the hill in order to save on fuel and extend the life of the battery.

'Every turn of the key takes seven miles out of the battery' was a familiar phrase heard in our house. It was a neighbourhood spectacle, Dad pushing the car by the steering wheel to get it going, then running along, jumping in, and starting it once it had gained some momentum and was rolling down the hill.

I'm sure that the neighbours watched this daily event from behind their curtains, secretly hoping that one day he'd mis-time the run so that the car would carry on down the hill with my dad futilely chasing it. But, to my knowledge, that never happened. It would definitely have won £250 from the producers of *You've Been Framed* had anybody had camcorders, video cameras, or even mobile phones in the late '60s.

I vaguely remember that the first car our family had was a black Ford Prefect. After that, we had a grey Austin Cambridge, which seemed enormous at the time. We still had the Cambridge in 1971 when my brother was born. I remember how put out my sister and I felt when his carrycot sat full-length—there were no seat-belt laws in those days—on the seat between us, requiring us to squeeze in and squash our legs against the door. We were used to the luxury of space when there were only two of us on the once seemingly endless expanse of backseat.

The '60's and '70's offered plenty of things—other than the potential horror of a runaway car and a squished dad—to scare us kids. Many of these things were broadcast into our living rooms. Some of them are as follows:

- Berg from the TV series *Belle and Sebastian*

Berg always seemed to be grumpy, angry, and shouting at Sebastian. A constantly shouting adult figure was enough to scare any young child in those days. This daytime black-and-white programme about a young boy and his pet Pyrenean Mountain Dog, Belle, sometimes had very sad storylines and had a most haunting French theme tune sung by the child star of the series. To this day, I can hardly listen to it without welling up.

- The Morlocks from the 1960s film version of H.G. Wells's *The Time Machine*

I remember watching this at a very early age and being terrified when Rod Taylor, who was playing the time traveller H.G., was fighting with and trying to escape from the Morlocks, who were trying to stave in his skull with wooden clubs.

It seems incredible to me now that I'm able to have this memory, because in our house, as far back as I can remember, anything remotely scary, such as a Western, was turned off, as my parents had deemed it inappropriate. In those days, my sister and I only had a vague idea of what a Dalek was.

- Witchy Poo from *H.R. Pufnstuf*

Jack Wilde, who had become famous for playing the Artful Dodger in the film version of *Oliver,* plays Jimmy, a child swept away to a fantasy world after a storm at sea. He has a magic talking flute called Freddie, which the evil witch, Witchy Poo, is always trying to steal from him. Jimmy is helped by H.R. and his friends, who are giant, colourful, foam-costumed characters. Think of the *Banana Splits* on speed.

Witchy Poo, brilliantly played by the actress Billy Hayes, maniacally rode around on a broomstick-like vehicle called the vroom broom and spent every episode trying—with her henchmen, Orson Vulture, Seymour Spider, and Stupid Bat—to steal the flute. She was the one who lured Jimmy to the island in her enchanted boat in the first place. Looking back, I see it as a ridiculous kids' programme. But at the time, it seemed to prey on the fear of being moved away from the safety of home and then being chased by evil.

- The dwarf from *The Singing Ringing Tree*

Although the dwarf was by far the most frightening character, jumping up and down in rage on a cave roof when things went wrong, most of the programme's characters were frightening, including the prince who had been turned into an evil bear and the weird fish that kept turning up in the lake by the cave. This show seems, in retrospect, to have been an East German attempt at psychological warfare. Did East Germany produce this TV series and subsequently sell it to the United Kingdom with the aim in mind of scaring children of the next generation so effectively that they refused to appear from behind their sofas? Did any TV executive in the United Kingdom actually watch the show before it was aired on TV? The same, though, could be asked about *Paulus the Gnome*.

- The Titans and their extraordinary fishy submarine (speaking of scary fish)

Those bug-eyed monsters that chased hero Troy Tempest and his WASP (World Aquanaut Security Patrol) buddies in the brilliant Jerry Anderson puppet/animated TV series *Stingray*. Equally scary in the '60s was another of his creations, the Mysterons, who were the invisible baddies in the series *Captain Scarlett*.

Their familiar deep-voice introduction at the beginning of each episode saying 'This is the voice of the Mysterons' was terrifying. Baddies are bad enough, but invisible ones?

- *Escape into Night*

    My vague memory of this programme is that it's about a girl in bed (maybe bedridden) who drew pictures of her house with bars at the window. Whatever she drew came true in her dreams, usually bad things and the stuff of nightmares. In a million years, the show would never feature in CBBC's schedule again, although somehow *Teletubbies* and *Mr Blobby* made the schedules.

- *Doctor Who*'s Daleks, arguably the scariest thing on TV back then

    The Daleks were especially frightening when they shouted '*Exterminate*' at the doctor. What was it about those spotty giant tin cans that could not even go up steps that had us so much more terrified than the Cybermen, or any other of The Doctor's adversaries—or, in fact, most things? In actual fact, back then, just the theme tune would have my sister and me hiding behind the sofa or running out of the room.

But, in some ways, all of the above pale into insignificance when compared to the show that our parents actually paid for us to see (TV licence aside)—the one that in 1968, in cinemas across the land, pricked at the very core of what scared us most, preyed on every child's deep-seated fear, and gave cause for every adult to repeat the warning not to talk to or take sweets from strangers: the Child Catcher from *Chitty Chitty Bang Bang*.

Watching the film again now, it's difficult for me to imagine how frightened all of us children were when we watched an evil, ugly, despicable character sniffing out children from their hiding places. He sniffed them out with his unfeasibly long nose, enticing them into his horse-drawn caravan of wonders with sweets and lollipops. Once they were in his caravan, he flicked a switch, which transformed it from a colourful and visually wonderful vehicle into a prison cage. Once the children were in the cage, the despicable, ugly man with the long nose then rode off to imprison them in the bowels of a castle, to be enslaved forever. Okay, so, maybe it's not that hard to imagine.

There were many other warnings featured in my childhood, the effects of which lasted well into my teenage years or even adulthood, such as this, oft quoted by Dad: 'Don't go too near the swans. One flap of their wing can break a grown man's arm.'

This was obviously a sensible warning when we were feeding the ducks on the lakes in Reigate Park at the age of four. But even now, whenever I see a swan, I expect it to come at me with wings akimbo and a disconcerting focus on my upper limbs.

'The downbeat of a swan's wings is powerful enough to drown you if it's sitting on your chest.'

Now, instead of retaining a child's unquestioning wonder when I heard this particular 'pearl of wisdom', I was a fully grown adult and therefore did question the statement's validity. If this was true of swans, then I'm sure that YouTube would be full of clips with titles such as 'Swan Attacks!'. The papers would run headlines like 'Man found drowned after deadly swan encounter', and I would definitely have seen, in the TV listing, Channel 5's *When Swans Attack!*

That said, I'm still petrified of falling into a pond or lake populated by the Queen's birds. However, the fear of being taken by the child catcher was often fed to us by our parents.

'Don't wander off or you may get taken.'

'Hold hands or you may get lost.'

'Don't talk to strangers. They may carry you off.'

'Don't go off with anyone telling you that they want to show you their puppies' (one I'd obviously want to ignore later in life).

And, of course, the classic 'Don't take sweets from strangers.'

All of these were designed to keep us safe from harm and get us to behave, but they also had the effect of scaring the living daylights out of us.

My first encounter with anybody who could remotely be described as a celebrity was when I was four years old. I can remember it as if it were yesterday. I was petrified, but not in a star-struck, legs-turned-to-jelly, brain-turned-to-mush sort of way that makes one's tongue grow in the mouth so that one can only drool and babble incoherently. I was far too young to have this type of reaction to anybody who appeared in the world media. Instead, I was genuinely afraid for my well-being.

My Old Man's a Busman

The nearest town to Reigate was Redhill, where we often went shopping on a Saturday.

As we walked down Redhill High Street that day, Mum and my sister ahead and I walking beside Dad, I suddenly felt the pavement shudder and rumble beneath my feet.

I say 'felt' because this was not a sound. It was something more akin to what happened in the scene from *Jurassic Park* when the characters are in a jeep for their first encounter with a dinosaur and feel the footsteps of Tyrannosaurus rex.

Nobody else seemed to notice, but I distinctly remember feeling very uncomfortable. Then I could *hear* heavy footsteps, too, getting closer and closer. I wondered what on earth was happening.

I remember turning and seeing the largest and possibly the strangest man that I had ever seen running towards us.

At this point, you have to understand not only that I had had a fairly conservative upbringing, but also that people who were featured on TV, on the programmes that we children were allowed to watch, were middle-of-the-road mainstream singers such as Max Bygraves, Andy Williams, and Val Doonican, all of whom were still featured in the charts and were therefore a point of reference for us when it came to music and celebrity. Basically, the celebrities to which we kids were accustomed were ageing men in jumpers.

What was coming towards me, like an express train, was a young, very tall man with very hair long like a girl's. He was dressed completely in denim (jeans, shirt, and jacket) and wore large, heavy, noisy boots.

It was not the image of anybody I'd seen before. As he was running full pelt towards us, I could see that he was looking directly at us. In my mind, he was obviously mad. That, given that I'd received so many warnings and been taken to see *Chitty Chitty Bang Bang*, made me certain that he was about to snatch me and carry me off.

As I held my dad's hand a lot tighter, expecting him to pick me up and carry me into the nearest shop for safety, I saw and heard the madman bellow out a single word as he bore down on us: 'Daaaaaaaaaaaaaave!'

My dad turned, slightly startled by somebody shouting so loudly at him, but as he turned and looked up at the man, to my utter amazement, my dad said, 'Hello, Roy!'

It turned out that Roy was a regular passenger on Dad's bus, one who would spend the entire journey standing up at the front, chatting to Dad about music.

Dad and Roy talked for a few minutes. Having been introduced to Roy, I looked up at the strange, tall man, who nodded at me before he bounced back up the street and out of our lives forever.

Dad explained, as we continued up the road, that Roy played in a pop group that was recording an LP. He told me their name but only being about four years old and being used to hearing the names Elvis and Buddy in relation to music, *Status* and *Quo* were just two strange sounding words to me.

Roy Lynes, a keyboard player, was one of the early members of Status Quo, having joined the group in 1964. The album they were recording was *Pictures of Matchstick Men*. The single of the same name was released in November 1968, reaching number seven on the UK charts. It was, unfathomably, the band's only US hit, reaching number twelve.

The single 'Pictures' was a reflection of the psychedelic-inspired pop of the time, which probably explains its success in the United States. This was followed up by 'Black Veils of Melancholy', which was a universal flop and was the catalyst for the band's change in musical direction. However, my dad's friend Roy wrote its B-side, 'To Be Free'.

Even my girlfriend, who claims to hate Status Quo's music with a passion, recently heard the song 'Pictures of Matchstick Men' for the first time. Not realising that it was Status Quo, she was moved to ask, 'What's that? I've never heard it before. It's great.'

After I convinced her that the song was actually by Quo, she then told me that Francis Rossi's (an original and current member) daughter went to the primary school next door to her secondary school in Purley, Surrey, when she was about thirteen.

On the occasions when Francis went to collect his daughter from school, he would park outside of my girlfriend's classroom's form-room window in what she remembers as a dark-coloured Range Rover.

Having a doddery, old, deaf, and partially sighted teacher, the girls would sneak out of the window and go over to chat with Francis. My girlfriend remembers that he was always very smiley, cheerful, and happy to chat. It was the height of the girls' day or week, chatting to a real life rock star, even if he was a parent. In one of those cases of pure coincidence, my girlfriend's teacher's name was Mr Gilbert.

For me, the first track that hints at the real sound of Quo, the one we all know and love, is 'Down the Dustpipe', released in 1970. We had to wait until the release of *Piledriver* in 1972 to hear their more familiar sounds on tracks like 'Paper Plane'. Their seventh album, *Hello,* released in 1973, gave us 'Caroline'. 'Down Down' followed a year later in 1974. It was the long, hot summer of 1976 before we heard 'Wild Side of Life', at which point Roy had not been part of the line-up for over six years.

Roy left the band just before they reached the height of fame and fortune in the '70s and '80s. He only played on the first three albums. My mum remembers that he left the band because, since he was slightly older than his bandmates, he felt that he had other responsibilities, especially after falling in love with a woman while on tour with the band in New Zealand. She was expecting their baby.

Roy now lives in Australia and fronts the band Statoz Quo. He subsequently played with the original band when they toured Australia.

Despite this, I imagine that there must have been many a time for Roy, as a musician, if nothing else, when he regretted not playing on era-defining tracks such as 'Caroline' and 'Down Down', performing in packed stadiums with the rest of the boys, where grown men don their double denim, put their thumbs in their belt loops, and head-bang like it's 1975.

Peter Gilbert

My Top Ten Scary Songs

'The Monster Mash'—Boris Pickett and the Crypt Kickers
'Angie Baby'—Helen Reddy
'Devil Woman'—Cliff Richard
'Something for the Weekend'—The Divine Comedy
'Black Magic Woman'—Santana
'Horror Show'—Laura Catlow
'The Devil Went Down to Georgia'—The Charlie Daniels Band
'They're Coming to Take Me Away, Ha-Haaa!'—Napoleon XIV
'Wicked Annabella'—The Kinks
'I Put a Spell on You'—Screamin' Jay Hawkins

Things to Check Out

On YouTube:

- The Morlocks (1960)
- *H.R. Pufnstuf* intro
- Child catcher from *Chitty Chitty Bang Bang*
- 'Pictures of Matchstick Men'—Status Quo

Elsewhere:
As It Occurs to Me—Richard Herring podcast series
www.myoldmansabusman.com

My Old Man's a Busman

My early years were defined by two things: music and comedy. Music always seemed to fill our house via the radio, TV, or records. Nothing better fused it together with comedy than Dad's playing 'A Transport of Delight' by Flanders and Swann, a song about buses.

I can remember Dad singing along to it and laughing at the lyrics. Through repetition, I discovered that it was very different from other songs we listened to. This one was about buses. It had catchy lyrics, and I was able to sing along to some of them, too, although probably only the 'ding, ding' at first. Some of the lyrics are as follows.

- 'When you are lost in London and you don't know where you are'
- 'That big six-wheeler scarlet-painted, London transport, diesel-engined, ninety-seven-horsepower omnibus'
- 'Hold very tight, please . . . ding, ding'

I can't think of any songs about people management, brands and shops that my kids would have tuned into because the lyrics had anything to do with their dad's work. The nearest example is from Laura Catlow's song 'If There's Anything More': 'We work in telesales and IT, in admin and libraries. We sell sweets and work in cafés. We're shop assistants and police ladies.'

My dad played the bus song so often at home that it's simply in my psyche and part of my childhood. I used to sing it to my kids when they were in the bath. Whilst, like me when I was young, they did not get all the words, I taught them to do the 'ding, ding' at the end with precision timing.

Even now, 'A Transport of Delight' is on a playlist in my car. On long car journeys, the kids often pick it as a singalong. This sort of music is banned when my girlfriend is in the car, however, as she thinks it is a crime to bring up the children on such rubbish. She cannot believe the 'ding, ding' story. Even worse for her is that my eldest, at five years old, knew all the words to Lonnie Donegan's 'My Old Man's a Dustman' and she nearly cried when her daughter asked that we play Chas and Dave's singalong CD in the car.

Whilst buses aren't up there with love, sex, and break-ups, the bedaffodilled Morrissey gave us the poetic line 'And if a double-decker bus crashes into us' in 'There Is a Light that Never Goes Out'.

It's also difficult to beat, from 'Beer & Sex & Chips 'n' Gravy' by the Macc Lads, 'Cleaned my teeth, put on my best clobber. Tonight's the night I'm going to knob her. Vauxhall Viva's covered in rust, but you can't shag a bird on a twenty-nine bus.' Also in contention are the little-known lyrics 'Put me on the bus to where the dance goes on forever' from the Hamptons's song 'The Best Thing about London Town'.

Comedy also came from TV—notably, from sitcoms. *On the Buses* was one of Dad's favourites, for obvious reasons. When it was screened on TV in the late '60s and early '70s, it was deemed far too rude for us to see, but we'd occasionally get to see a snippet or sneak a peek.

The four main characters, as I remember, were the driver, Stan; his conductor, Jack; the bus inspector Blakey who was the baddie of the show, always miserable and who only ever seemed to say his catchphrase 'I hate you, Butler'; and Stan's sister Olive.

In total, over seventy episodes were produced and shown on TV between 1969 and 1973. The show was a weekly fix for Dad (talk about a busman's holiday). It was so popular that there were some spin-off films in the early '70s. The first of these was *On the Buses* in 1971. When the show aired on a Saturday morning straight after children's TV, I thought that some nostalgic, good old-fashioned British comedy would be a good addition to my kids' education. I'm no prude, but it wasn't long before the content had me scrambling for the remote control in order to switch channels.

The opening sequence shows Stan and Jack ogling a young woman who is straddled on the front of a bus with her skirt barely covering her

My Old Man's a Busman

decency. Reference is made to sex maniacs; Stan and Jack both help another large-breasted woman adjust the ticket machine strapped to her chest; and there are no fewer than twenty sexual references and innuendos . . . all in the first three minutes.

I don't remember the TV programme being like that. It's no wonder that Dad loved it so much and that we children were sent to bed when it came on.

Over the years, we children were subjected to many bus-related jokes. My favourite is this one:

Paddy and Murphy, a little worse for wear after the pub, decide to steal a bus from the local bus depot to get home.

> Paddy says to Murphy, 'I'll keep lookout while you get the bus.'
>
> After waiting ten minutes and having heard much revving of engines, Paddy decides to see what's going on. He goes into the yard to find that Murphy has moved two buses and is reversing a third.
>
> 'What the feck are you doing, Murphy?'
>
> 'Well, Paddy, these three are blocking the number twenty-three, which is the one we need to take.'
>
> 'You're a fecking idiot, Murphy!'
>
> 'Why's that, Paddy?'
>
> 'We'll just take the number eighteen and walk from St Barnabas Street.'

The word *bus* usually conjures up an image of a red (or scarlet, according to Flanders and Swann) London bus—and probably a double-decker. This is partly because that is the imagery that appears on many pictures and tourist items related to London and the United Kingdom. But my dad drove a green bus.

In those days, things were much simpler and more clearly defined.

Sean Connery was James Bond, John Pertwee was Dr Who, Ron Ely was Tarzan, London buses were red, and buses everywhere else were green. That's just the way it was. Those were the rules.

These days, the world has gone mad.

Seaside buses are often yellow. They may also be white or blue. Their colour is often indistinguishable, as they're covered in the latest film advertising. Driving in Canterbury, Kent, recently, I found myself following a bright pink bus. Heresy.

My brother-in-law Tom also worked for a bus company, pretty much all his life. It's a bit of a family tradition. My dad, my brother-in-law, and I, later in life, all worked for a bus company. Thanks to Tom, I got my first job, for which I'm eternally grateful. Although, in hindsight, I wish that he had worked for a record company or radio station.

Back in 1970, however, work was a lifetime away for me. Life was simple. A visit to the sweetie shop after school was as good as it got. Little did we know, however, that life as we knew it was about to change forever.

In December 1970, in the Chocolate Box sweetie shop opposite our school, we could have been buying Orangeade Spangles, Sherbet Dib Dabs, Jazzies, sweet cigarettes (now called candy sticks in order to be politically correct), Catherine Wheels, Curly Wurly bars, Parma Violets (my sister's favourite), sherbet lemons, strawberry laces, Smarties, Pink Panther bars, love hearts, and love hearts printed with football team names for the boys (I've yet to find anyone else who remembers these. Although I think that they were short-lived, they definitely existed), Black Jack, and fruit salads (of these last two, one could buy eight for a penny—which, at the time, was a big handful of sweets for a child).

Sometimes, at home time on school days, Dad would be driving the bus from near the school to the bottom of our road. We would get a lift home for free if the inspector (Blakey) was not around. This was a rare treat, indeed. It was a double treat if it was sweetie day, as well.

Our sweetie bubble was just about to burst, though, because, unbeknown to us kids at the time, our generation's D-Day was around the corner, waiting to teach us an early lesson: that nothing lasts forever.

Our parents' D-Day had been the end of World War II on 6 June 1944, but ours occurred when decimalisation came into force.

My Old Man's a Busman

Forget today's inflation, unless you live in Zimbabwe. Within the space of twenty-four hours in February 1971, one new penny suddenly reduced the number of Black Jacks in our eager mitts to four. The price jump was too much for my seven-year-old mind to grasp. It just seemed unfair.

A series of public information adverts on TV, which seemed to run every five minutes, tried their best to educate us by saying, 'A sixpence is two and a half new pence. Decimalisation.' There were other variations on this theme.

Max Bygraves, a parents' favourite of the 1950s and 1960s variety-show era, even released a song called 'Decimalisation', which is the equivalent of Ant and Dec's releasing a song about the Euro today. The song was all about this new monetary system. Its lyrics taught us that there was going to be 'A hundred new pennies now to every pound,' that 'Five new pennies are like a shilling,' and that 'Ten new pennies is a two bob bit.'

The song, unsurprisingly, didn't even get into the chart's top thirty and, therefore, didn't appear on *TOTPs* (*Top of the Pops*), as it was called in our house. *TOTPs* was the most popular music show on TV at the time. It gave the weekly chart rundown and showed all of the biggest hits and bands of the day.

Former Beatles member George Harrison topped the charts at number one with 'My Sweet Lord' on our D-Day, 15 February 1971. This was nine days before my brother was born. He was a decimalisation baby.

Whilst the government's brainwashing 'Sixpence' infomercial was memorable, it could never compare to the best ad of 1971 and, perhaps, ever: the Brooke Bond PG Tips' chimpanzee's 'Removal Men'.

Brooke Bond had been using chimpanzees in their ads since the late '50s, pairing them with film heroes of the day, such as cowboys and Ben-Hur, but with the chimps' acting to a voice-over commentary. In the '70s, the ads showed the chimps lip-synching to a script, which gave us the legendary ads still talked about (and still receiving YouTube hits) five decades later.

The ongoing question of which is the best ever Brooke Bond chimp ad is much debated between my friend Dave and me. We often engage in long, heated, debates using dodgy French accents, but it's always in good humour. For Dave, it's the chimps' 'French Bike Race' ad, which includes the lines, 'Avez-vous un cuppa?' and 'Can you ride tandem?'

Peter Gilbert

My choice is different, although it's from the same campaign. I prefer the ad showing the father-and-son removal firm carrying a piano down the stairs. That wins it for me every time, especially given its nearly immortal end lines.

> Son (at the bottom of the stairs with the piano on his foot): 'Dad, do you know the piano's on my foot?'
>
> Dad (sitting at the piano): 'You hum it, Son. I'll play it.'
> ♪♫...♪♫...

In hindsight, I imagine that there may have been issues of animal cruelty. Also, I'm sure that conditions were far from perfect back then. Yes, we now know from research that chimps appear to be smiling when they're scared, not when they're happy. But back in the day, we were kids and simply saw chimpanzees who were dressed as people doing and saying funny things and drinking tea. Brilliant.

The year 1971 also introduced us to a new TV show, this one featuring a gang of kids and a bus. It was called *Here Come the Double Deckers.* We'd previously seen Cliff Richard, in the film *Summer Holiday,* touring the world on a double-decker bus—which, of course, we watched every time it was on TV (there were no DVDs, Freeview, Sky Movies, or digital streaming back then), but this was a weekly TV programme made for and aimed at us.

The show featured a gang of kids in London who had a secret hideout behind a fence. Part of their 'hideout' was a London double-decker bus kitted out with all sorts of weird and wonderful gadgets and gizmos. Each week, the gang got up to all sorts of hijinks, fun, and mischief, including chasing robbers and riding around in a homemade hovercraft. With today's proliferation of choice and channels, it's almost impossible to describe the excitement that one Saturday children's TV show could bring. Everyone wanted to be part of that gang.

Get a bunch of forty-something (maybe going on fifty) Brits together today, and they will talk about *Here Come the Double Deckers* for hours, with the men reminiscing about how they fancied Billie (a girl), and with women remembering that, as girls, they fancied Scooter. Eventually, during these conversations, everyone ends up singing the memorable theme tune.

Much later in life, although not as part of a kiddie gang (which had more innocent connotations then), I worked with two companies that used double-decker buses as part of their brand awareness campaigns. One was converted into a living space with a working kitchen and a luxurious lounge; the other was outfitted with every conceivable piece of the latest technology. So, not only was I able, in part, to eventually live the dream, but I also ushered the family association with buses into another century.

Peter Gilbert

My Top Ten Bus Songs

'The Double Deckers' (theme song)—Cast of *Here Come the Double Deckers*
'There Is a Light that Never Goes Out'—The Smiths
'Beer & Sex & Chips 'n' Gravy'—The Macc Lads
'A Transport of Delight'—Flanders and Swann
'Magical Mystery Tour'—The Beatles
'Rudie Can't Fail'—The Clash
'At the Zoo'—Paul Simon
'National Express'—The Divine Comedy
'Bus Stop'—The Hollies
'Summer Holiday'—Cliff Richard

Things to Check Out

On YouTube:

- Decimal coinage, new system, 1971
- 'Tour de France' PG Tips advert
- PG Tips' Mr Shifter
- *On the Buses* film opening titles

Elsewhere:
www.myoldmansabusman.com

'Back Home' with Bobby Moore

On a particular day in May 1970, Dad's bus was not passing by the school at home time (maybe the bus inspector was around), so there was no bus trip home. Since Mum could not drive, that meant that we children had to walk home.

We'd not gone far, only a hundred yards or so, when a few of the other boys started running towards some men in suits who were walking towards us.

England's football team, on their way to Gatwick Airport, en route to Mexico and a World Cup competition, had stopped in Reigate, Reigate—my town—for a walkabout.

In 1970, the M25 (London Orbital Motorway) didn't exist. Only a couple of short sections of the current route were complete, which meant that anyone travelling from the west and heading for Gatwick would usually pass through Reigate on the A25. Looking back, I have no idea why they stopped there, as it's only a few miles from the airport.

This fact, however, was irrelevant to us football-mad boys, as we believed that our town had somehow been singled out by these footballer legends who were our heroes.

I had been too young to remember the 1966 World Cup, but Bobby Moore was a hero to us and a legend to our parents. After all, four years earlier, he had lifted the World Cup, football's greatest prize, at Wembley Stadium. He was clean-cut and popular with Dad, unlike the new breed of player exemplified by George Best and Charlie George, whom my dad considered to be long-haired show-offs.

I remember seeing some of the other boys going up to the groups of players to get their autographs. I begged Mum to find a piece of paper quickly so that I could, too. I was becoming anxious as the precious seconds ticked by while Mum rummaged around in her handbag. I feared that the players would stop signing and leave before I managed to make it over to them.

Finally, after what seemed like an eternity, Mum produced, from the depths of her bag, a small, used, brown-window envelope and then handed it to me, saying, 'Sorry. That's all I've got—and I cannot find a pen.'

I grabbed the envelope and ran over to where the players were. I waited behind a couple of older boys who were talking to Bobby.

When the boys finally moved on to Gordon Banks, the goalie, I found myself standing before the great man himself, holding a crumpled, used envelope and no pen. I can only presume that more-savvy and better-prepared kids constantly carried around notepads and pens so as not to look quite so pitiful in front of their football heroes.

I don't actually remember any words being spoken between us, but I do remember that Bobby Moore looked down, took my envelope, asked one of the other players (whose name I wish I could recall) if he could use his pen, and then signed my envelope for me. 'There you go, son,' he said. Well, I like to think that he said something along those lines.

Immediately after that, the players stopped signing, waved, and made their way back to the coach. So, I guess I was really lucky. A few more seconds of Mum's hunting in her bag and I'd have missed that memorable moment.

The delay did, of course, mean that I didn't get anybody else's autograph. At the time, however, I didn't really care, as I had the best. Looking back, though, I think that an autograph from Gordon Banks or Geoff Hurst would have been good, too.

There must be something about Reigate and famous footballers, as the town was George Best's home in his later years.

Singing 'Georgie Best superstar wears frilly knickers and a Playtex bra' to the tune of 'Jesus Christ Superstar' was very amusing to many schoolboys in the early '70s. When *Jesus Christ Superstar,* written by Tim Rice and Andrew Lloyd Webber, was first launched as a rock musical, Playtex bras were often advertised on TV. The original blasphemous parody was simply to sing it as 'Jesus Christ Superstar wears [fill in the blank]', but somewhere along the line, the words 'Jesus Christ' were unilaterally changed to 'Georgie Best'.

I'm not sure why George Best became the subject, as any footballer or star of the day who had the correct number of syllables in his or her name could have been substituted. In fact, sometimes we did make a substitution. But Georgie, whose name had to be extended to fit, anyway, was the one whose name we all used to chant. Maybe it was because, at the time, he was the first footballer to have achieved celebrity or superstar status because he appeared in TV ads in addition to being famous for playing football. George Best was a forerunner to David Beckham.

Beckham has suffered even more humiliation, however. His relationship with Victoria, or Posh Spice, as she was known then (as part of the girl band the Spice Girls), became public knowledge. Fans of the opposing team would chant to the 'bread of heaven' refrain from the hymn 'Guide Me O Thou Great Redeemer'. 'Does she take it, does she take it, does she take it up the aaaaaaaarse? Does she take it up the arse?'

While this was very amusing, it was probably highly embarrassing for Victoria, sitting with her parents watching her then-boyfriend play.

Unfortunately, like England did in the 1970 World Cup campaign, I lost something, too. Whilst they lost the title that year, I lost the envelope with Bobby Moore's autograph on it somewhere along the way. I have a stash of memorabilia now. Every time I look through it, I wish that I still had that autographed envelope. It would definitely never have gone on eBay.

Brazil won the 1970 FIFA World Cup, as it was officially known. The Brazilian team, featuring Pelé (who was playing in his fourth and final World Cup), is often regarded as the greatest World Cup team ever. Also, the 1970 tournament is often thought of as the best tournament ever. Brazil had won all six games to make it into the finals, had won all six qualifying games during the televised finals, and had beaten Italy 4–1 in the final. (England was beaten 3–2 by West Germany in the quarter finals. Sound familiar?) As this was their third World Cup title, Brazil was allowed to keep the Jules Rimet Trophy permanently.

With Brazil 1–0 up, thanks to a Pelé goal, Italy equalised, but then Brazil went into overdrive. Italy never really got a look in and so, for the rest of the match, were on the receiving end of a football master class, culminating in Brazil's fantastic fourth goal.

Peter Gilbert

That gold Jules Rimet Trophy had been used since 1930. It was originally called Victory but was later renamed in honour of a former FIFA president. While it was replaced in 1974 by the less romantically named FIFA World Cup Trophy, which is still used today (currently held by Spain at the time of this writing), the Jules Rimet was nostalgically remembered twenty-six years later in the build-up to the 1996 European Championship campaign by Frank Skinner and David Baddiel (and the Lightning Seeds), with their 'Three Lions' anthem. 'Three lions on a shirt, Jules Rimet still gleaming, thirty years of hurt, never stopped me dreaming.'

Although England didn't win in 1970, The team did have a number-one hit with the record 'Back Home', which was released as the official England team song and began the tradition. Subsequent English squads and football clubs recorded songs to celebrate their having reached major tournament finals.

The England team failed to qualify for the next two World Cup finals. And although the teams did release records in 1982 and 1986, they did not reach the coveted number-one spot in the charts (let alone in a World Cup or European Cup tournament) again until 1990, when the squad, featuring the rapping John Barnes, topped the pop charts with the New Order collaboration 'World in Motion'.

The song that had started it all, 'Back Home', was also used as the theme tune for Baddiel and Skinner's BBC mid-'90s football/comedy TV programme *Fantasy Football League*, over which Frank Skinner presumably had some influence, as he is quoted as saying that 'Back Home' was the first single that he had ever purchased himself with his own money.

Personally, I remember very little about the actual televised tournament in 1970, as I didn't have that much interest in it at the time. I do remember that, to Dad, it was a big deal. It was football. It was a World Cup. England was playing, and England was the title-holder, having won the title four years before (in 1966) at Wembley Stadium.

I may not have been that interested in the tournament itself, but in May 1970, there was only one 45" vinyl single I wanted to buy: 'Back Home' by the 1970 England World Cup Squad, with Bobby Moore and Gordon Banks as vocalists. I pestered Mum day and night and each time I heard it played on the radio. Finally, one day after school, Mum took me into Woolworth's and bought it for me. It was the first record I ever owned.

I couldn't wait to get home, and so I virtually dragged my mum from Woolworth's back to our house in anticipation of being able to hear the song . . . again.

Now, Dad had a rule about B-sides. Whenever we bought a record, he made us play the B-side first. This was because, in his opinion, there had been some great B-sides in the past. Left to our own devices, he said (and he was probably correct), we would simply play the A-side to death and never discover the joys found on the reverse side, B-side, or flipside.

And so it was that, after having lost my record-buying and—ownership virginity, I got home only for Dad to insist that we play the B-side first. I was frustrated. I didn't care about the flippin' B-side; I just wanted to hear the song that we kids sang in the playground, the one that began with clapping and then went into the team's singing 'Back Home', a rousing, uplifting anthem about how the team plans to give their all for everyone who is watching and cheering back home.

'Back home, they'll be thinking about us when we are far away . . . and we'll give all that we've got to give for the folks back home.' Unfortunately, as we can see in hindsight, they did not give enough.

The B-side, also sung by the team, is called 'Cinnamon Stick'. The song begins, 'Sweet as sugar, twice as nice, cinnamon stick, cinnamon stick, see that twinkle in her eyes. Cinnamon stick.' After this, the tempo increases as the song goes into declarations of love, etc.—nothing to do with football or the World Cup. Dad, I was right not to want to play it.

Also, like most men, Dad liked all of his records (and tapes) labelled, catalogued, and put into alphabetical order (something that is unfathomable to many women). He was not computer-literate and so had thousands of bits of paper listing all the tracks, their running lengths, and whether they were slow, medium, or fast tempo piled up around his vast collection.

Sometime in the early '70s, Dad stopped driving a bus and began to drive a laundry van. This job entailed collecting and delivering people's laundry, as some people still didn't have washing machines in their houses and chose to have their clothes washed/laundered in this way, saving a trip to the launderette. Other people were just well off enough to send their laundry out. There was a specific delivery route for each day of the week, and each parcel of washing had a label on it. These labels were coloured to identify the day of the week (e.g. green for Monday, blue for Tuesday, etc.)

and bore printed numbers to identify the owner and his or her address. Sometimes, there were spare reels of these labels lying around.

One day, Dad arrived home with two rolls of tickets, one for me and one for my sister. She and I met these with overenthusiasm.

For reasons now lost to the mists of time, these tickets were allocated according to colour. The green labels, which had *A* numbers printed on them—A1, A2, and so on—went to my sister. The red labels, with *B* numbers on them, came to me.

These were to be used for cataloguing our music collections. Then, as is the case now, the 'Back Home' single is number B1 in my vinyl collection. The corresponding red ticket is stuck on the top left-hand corner of the record sleeve.

My collection was stuck in the loft and hidden away in cupboards for years. When I recently moved, I unveiled my prize collection of vinyl in front of my girlfriend. What I had anticipated to be a magical moment of reverence and nostalgia, as we thumbed through my singles collection, became a moment of almost derisory hysteria.

My girlfriend physically recoiled when she saw the tattered, battered yellowing file dividers in the box denoting where each alphabetical-order section of artists or groups started. Having followed Dad's own system, I filed groups beginning with 'The' under the main name (e.g. the Rubettes under *R*) and filed singers by surname, always. So, Elvis Presley is filed under *P*.

When my girlfriend plunged her hand into the box (failing to start at *A* and then systematically work through the strict alphabetical system, as any normal bloke would do!), the first single she pulled out was by the Glitterband (she had obviously delved into *G*). She quickly dropped it back into the box . . . with her eyes raised to the heavens and while giving a disapproving tut.

The next one she pulled out, however, was my virgin purchase: my lovingly preserved (with an almost pristine B-side) single, nestled in its original blue sleeve: Pye Records ref. 7N17920, 'Back Home' by the 1970 England World Cup Squad. My girlfriend exclaimed, 'Oh, for God's sake!' Then, as she was about to vinyl-crackingly plunge the record back into the box, her eye caught the flash of red in the corner, carrying a now slightly faded 'B1'. Not usually known for uttering profanity (unless absolutely necessary), she turned and calmly but menacingly enquired, 'What . . . the f*** . . . is that?'

Unfortunately, despite the fact that my girlfriend and I are close in age, her record collection is full of much cooler artists such as T-Rex (her first), the Clash, and Siouxsie and the Banshees, leaving my collection looking forever in her eyes like 'crap'. (I am conveniently ignoring the fact that her collection includes David Cassidy.)

We're still together, although my girlfriend is somewhat concerned about where my tendencies may manifest themselves in the future. I have had to swear an oath not to encourage either my or her offspring to label and catalogue . . . anything.

I tried to lighten the mood by telling my girlfriend that I knew that I was mildly CDO. When she responded, slightly condescendingly, by telling me that it was actually OCD, I replied by saying that I knew that—but that I liked to keep things in alphabetical order.

I think my comic delivery must have been slightly off that day, given the reaction I got.

Since then, I've realised that it's just one of those differences between the sexes. Many friends and colleagues have told me about similar arguments they'd had with their female partners—even some about prize collections of European beer bottles. To display or not to display them? I have also heard about rows inspired by the man's insistence on sorting CDs into order—and even about whether or not the CD collection should be on display. Really?

A recent example was when a friend, after having purchased new tech equipment for his home, including a top-of-the-range server and TV interface, decided to upload all of the family's DVDs onto the system. Because he is male, this, of course, meant that he would catalogue them. To my delight, he asked for my help.

After days of loading all of them, the day—well, evening—when we would categorise them finally arrived.

We had a couple of beers before deciding how we should approach it: create a file first and start adding films to it, or create all of the files at once, just in case we changed our minds? Having settled on the latter, we then had to decide what to call the files. Would we go by genre, or would we file them alphabetically by title? (We'd already dismissed listing them by director, thinking that that was going a bit too far. Surely, we'd face ridicule from his wife and be accused of being sad gits.) Would we need sub-files or subcategories? Daft question.

As the evening went on, so did the debates. Should *The Blues Brothers* be categorised under *B,* comedy, musical, or musical comedy? Is *Ferris Bueller's Day Off* a kids' film or a comedy—and, regardless, should it be filed under *F* for 'Ferris' or *B* for 'Bueller'? Was *Watch with Mother* a kids' film or a nostalgic film? *La Dolce Vita*—black-and-white, '60s, foreign language, or subtitled? And *Kill Bill:* action, foreign language, or foreign language as a subset of action?

When it was time for me to go, I think my friend and I had actually thought of about twenty file titles and had scribbled numerous lists, but we had not actually got around to putting any films into files. We were pleased with our efforts, though, which had taken a little over four hours.

Before leaving, I went to say goodbye to my friend's wife (the kids were long to bed) and tell her about our progress.

'I wondered what you two were doing in there. You shouldn't have wasted your time. I've already done it.'

'What? What do you mean, you've done it?'

'I've filed all of the films. I did it this afternoon and thought you'd see.'

'You can't have done. There's hundreds. How many did you do?'

'All of them.'

'You can't have done all of them. It would have taken you hours.'

'It didn't. It took about an hour.'

'How did you do that?'

'It was easy. I did what you said to do: set up the files and dragged the films into them.'

'Yes, but what files did you set up?' my friend and I shouted, almost in unison.

'The obvious ones,' she said to her husband. 'Yours, mine, and the kids'.'

My Top Ten Football Songs

'Blue Is the Colour'—The Chelsea Football Squad
'Ossie's Dream (Spurs Are on Their Way to Wembley)'—Tottenham Hotspur Squad, featuring Chas and Dave
'Leeds United'—Leeds United Football Club
'You'll Never Walk Alone'—Gerry and the Pacemakers
'Back Home'—England World Cup Squad
'Three Lions'—Baddiel and Skinner, featuring the Lightning Seeds
'Bonnie Scotland (We Have a Dream)'—Scotland World Cup Squad, featuring Gordon Sinclair and fans
'Nessun Dorma'—Luciano Pavarotti
'World in Motion'—New Order
'The Referee's Alphabet'—Half Man Half Biscuit

Things to Check Out

On YouTube:

- George Best, 1960s 'Fore' TV ad
- World Cup 1970 final

Elsewhere: www.myoldmansabusman.com

On the Radio

I was brought up in a very musical household, not with Mum and Dad playing Brahms recitals on the piano and cello every evening, but simply with pop music—and loads of it. It seemed to be a constant in my early life, either via the radio in the kitchen, which was permanently tuned to Radio 1, or from the playing of records. We used to joke that Dad was so into his music because his initials were D.J. But, whatever; it was infectious and had an immediate and long-lasting impact on us kids.

Mum and Dad were from a generation where relatives would get together around the piano and have a sing-song, however our home-tutored music education had more to do with the age that *they* were when rock'n'roll changed the face of music in the late '50s.

Neither of my parents played an instrument, although Dad was extremely accomplished at the air guitar and air drums. He used to tell tales of himself and his mates in the late '50s. They'd get together at his house to play their latest record. My dad was apparently known as Dave the Rave. Dad and his friends would 'play' along to the records by creating and then beating on or twanging instruments, which they made from anything lying around. Dad was usually on the table drums, which meant that he tapped or drummed his fingers on the table in time to the drumming on whichever record was playing. The boys called themselves the Smelly Sock Club, as they would hang a used pair of socks nearby whenever they got together. And they say that today's youth are strange.

Somewhere exists an old reel-to-reel tape of their band, with my dad's friend Stan singing and with Dad on drums—well, drumming his fingers on a table. Maybe I should convert it to a WAV or MP3 file and send it to Simon Cowell. DJ Bus and the Conductors could be the next big thing.

Up until the time when I was nine years old (which is when we left Reigate), we lived in an end-of-terrace, three-storey Victorian house with a kitchen and a dining room downstairs, a lounge and my bedroom on the first floor, and two bedrooms and one bathroom on the top floor. This house had an outside toilet, leaving me with less than fond memories of being sent outside in the cold and the rain to the tiny brick building, which, in addition to being home to the loo, was home to many spiders.

We did have an inside loo, too, but I have latent memories of the guilt that I felt for breaking it, apparently shortly after we had had it installed.

With a typical four-year-old's curiosity, and perhaps because I had been influenced by the Andrex puppy ads on TV, I decided one day to see how much toilet paper I could unravel along the length of our upstairs hallway and back again. Then, I flushed it down the toilet. I remember taking great delight in rolling out the paper on the floor and seeing how far along the carpet I could get it to go with each push.

Not surprisingly, though, once I had inserted this mass of tissue into the bowl and flushed, adding water to it, the toilet overflowed into the bathroom. My parents were furious.

I was told that I had broken the toilet, that it would have to be replaced, and that, as punishment, I must use only the outside loo for a week. I hated spiders. I don't think I ever recovered from that experience.

I must have been in my thirties when Mum finally confessed that the toilet had simply been blocked—but that she and Dad had told me that it was broken in order to scare me into not doing the same thing again. I have often thought that, given people's modern-day penchant for litigation, I could take it up retrospectively with the European Court under the Child Cruelty Concerning Broken Toilet Untruths Act, or some such similar act.

When not upstairs breaking toilets or in the outside loo avoiding spiders, I and my sister would be in the kitchen. Whether Mum was preparing a meal, cleaning, doing the washing, or washing up, the radio would be on, tuned to the relatively new Radio 1, which first broadcast in 1967.

At weekends, Ed 'Stewpot' Stewart would be playing kid-friendly records like 'Sparkie the Magic Piano' and 'Puff the Magic Dragon' by the Seekers on *Junior Choice,* his write-in request show. The theme tune was 'Mornington Ride', also by the Seekers. On the occasions when I hear that song—'Rockin', rollin', ridin', all along the bay'—it takes me straight back to our kitchen in Reigate.

The dining room was predominantly used for meals and for the big treat: watching TV. My earliest memories of television were of the test card, which appeared on the screen for most of the day. Also, we would probably have stared at the girl with her clown doll for a good five or ten minutes whilst waiting for our daily weekday dose of *Watch with Mother*.

Today, with 24/7 TV, Sky Movies, Freeview, Netflix, et al., it's difficult to imagine a world where TV shows only aired for a few hours a day. Plus, the programmes were in black-and-white. It was so exciting when there was actually something to watch.

Watch with Mother was aimed at preschool children and was an early forerunner to *CBeebies*. It was broadcast daily for fifteen minutes. A different programme from the *Watch with Mother* stable was shown each day of the week. The ones I remember watching the most are *Andy Pandy, Pogles' Wood, Tales of the Riverbank, The Herbs, Camberwick Green, Trumpton, Bizzy Lizzy,* and *The Flower Pot Men*.

Kids love character names that rhyme or have alliteration, presumably because they are easy to remember (or, at least, adults appear to think so). There are many examples in the kids' and adult arena alike: Reed Richards in *The Fantastic Four;* the Green Goblin, one of Spider-Man's arch-enemies; and Pepper Pots from *Iron Man*. As kids, we had many, including Andy Pandy, a boy puppet who appeared in his eponymous TV show along with his teddy and his friend Looby Loo. While most anything on TV seemed good to us back then, the show was never my favourite. I remember that I was always a bit disappointed whenever it came on (we never knew in advance which programme would air until it came on), especially given that I'd already sat and watched a black-and-white still image of a girl and a clown for ten minutes.

Our perennial favourites were *Camberwick Green* and *Trumpton*, although, as I learned after participating in debates similar to those we had about PG Tips' chimpanzee TV ads, *Camberwick Green* simply went a nose in front, for a couple of reasons.

First, the excitement quotient was double on days when *Camberwick Green* aired. Not only were we surprised that it had come on, but also we were happy to see a different character appear from a music box at the beginning of each episode. Episodes were at least a week apart, and each episode was based on a different character. Imagine the fun and excitement we had in guessing which character would jump out once that music box appeared.

Second, one of the characters was called Peter. Maybe not so surprising is that he was a postman.

That said, *Trumpton* featured a character called Windy Miller who, whilst his name neither rhymed nor was alliterative, did live in a windmill. Whenever he went into the windmill, he first had to negotiate the sails as they turned. They actually went around quite fast (it must have always been very windy in Trumpton), which meant that Windy had to dash between them and avoid getting hit in order to get through his door. It was thrilling to watch.

Another of my clear early TV memories includes being wakened and taken downstairs in my pyjamas to watch the first moon landing in July 1969. Unfortunately, the magnitude of that event was lost on us kids, who were so young. I remember thinking at the time that the images were very fuzzy and jumpy, often difficult to make out, and that whole thing was a bit slow and boring.

I did get a sense that something very important was taking place, though. Why else would our parents have wakened us in the middle of the night and allowed us to be downstairs watching TV?

On the first floor of our house was a second living room, which we called the lounge. This was the 'best' room. While occasionally, at weekends, we'd be allowed in there to listen to music, the room was mainly used only when guests came or, most exciting, when it was Christmas. That's where Santa would have left our presents.

On Christmas, my sister and I would always find our stockings filled with nuts, an apple or orange, and a tube of Jelly Tots, Fruit Pastilles, or Smarties. A plastic sack containing my and my sister's presents would be positioned next to our special glittery Christmas name card, which always made us feel a wave of excitement and get 'butterflies' in our stomachs when it emerged each year from the Christmas box.

Looking back now, I see that it was simply a piece of white card with our names written on it in gold glitter. Mum had written our names in glue, covered the card in cheap glitter, and then shook off the excess to leave the glittery names behind. To my sister and me, however, it was magical, evoking images of the Christmas fairy.

When it came time to bring down the Christmas box from the loft and put up the decorations, this is what we looked forward to most: seeing our glittery name card, which meant, of course, that presents were on the way.

At the time, my sister and I never questioned it, but these cards bore the names Tinks and Wag, even though our names are Janette and Peter, respectively. My great-uncle and great-aunt, Stan and Lily, whom we visited regularly in Peckham, South London, had given us those nicknames when we were tiny. They had stuck.

My sister's nickname was Tinks, a shortened version of Tinkerbelle (as in, 'you're our little Tinkerbelle'). Mine was Peter Wag because my parents thought that I was, or behaved like, a little wag (a scamp).

Maybe it was inevitable, then, when my brother came along a few years later, that he would get a nickname, too. We never imagined at the time that he would be stuck with his nickname forever.

There was no TV in the lounge, just a sofa, a sideboard full of records, and a record player. On those special occasions, at weekends, when we were allowed into the room to listen to music with Mum and Dad, there was no chance that 'Puff the Magic Dragon'—or any other song that we'd recently heard on the radio—would be played. Just Mum and Dad's music.

We spent hours of our early childhood listening to Elvis, Buddy Holly, Cliff Richard, Bill Haley, Frank Sinatra, Herman's Hermits, the Animals, Gilbert O'Sullivan, and many, many more.

And that was it. We'd simply go to the lounge and listen to music, as if attending a concert. While it was not quite a Victorian recital atmosphere, we were encouraged to sing and play air instruments along to the songs. This is the reason why I still know every lyric to dozens, if not hundreds, of old songs, and also why I am able to play a whole range of air instruments, including guitar, keyboards, drums, trumpet, harmonica, clarinet, trombone, and sax—embarrassing my better half, especially now that her daughter plays air guitar with me. AC/DC's 'Whole Lotta Rosie' is one of our favourites. 'Twang, twang, twang, twang, twang, twang, twang, twang, twang, twang.' Angus!

A few years before Dad sadly passed away to that record shop in the sky, we were chatting about music and wondering how far back I actually remembered hearing a record on a radio. These are the sort of conversations we have in our family.

My sister can recall all of the telephone numbers and car registrations that we've had down through the years, probably because she has been asked to recite the list at so many times at family gatherings. It has become a bit of a party piece. It's rock'n'roll at our parties.

'What was our phone number in Reigate?'

'Four-six-eight-two-seven.'

'What was Uncle Stan's phone number in Peckham?'

'Six-three-nine-four-four-two-eight.'

'What was the registration number of the DAF?'

'L-P-H-four-eight-one-K.'

During the conversation about how old I was when I first remembered hearing something played on the radio, my dad said something along the lines of, 'Well, I remember you and your sister singing along to "Two Little Boys" and "I'd like to Teach the World to Sing", so it must have been before those.'

Once a statement like that was made in our house, the gauntlet had been thrown down. It was only a matter of minutes before the Bible—well, the music bible, which in our house was *The British Book of Hit Singles*—would make an appearance. (This, of course, was before the days of the Internet.)

The idea of this particular challenge was that Dad, using a mix of his musical knowledge and references to 'the bible', would pick records from various months and years when I was young to see how far back I could remember.

The objective was to identify the first songs I remember that were played on the radio. This is to be distinguished from just *hearing* something on the radio, as I may have heard early hits years later. What I had to do was close my eyes and take myself back in time to re-experience the feelings, smells, and sounds to know that I was really remembering hearing the songs on the radio at home, probably in our kitchen.

Dad predominantly used the reference section at the front of *The British Book of Hit Singles*, so the majority of the songs were all number-one hits—the ones that I'd have been most aware of as a child because they were frequently played on the radio. It is useful that this section lists the precise date when a record made it to number one. So, it is accurate within a couple of weeks (given that the songs would have had airplay before reaching number one).

Dad started around December 1969, as he knew that I definitely remembered 'Two Little Boys', partly because my sister and I used to sing along to it, as we knew all the words at the time when it was number one.

My yes songs (i.e. the ones I could categorically remember hearing on the radio) were as follows, placed here in descending chronological order.

'Lily the Pink'—The Scaffold, December 1968

This song has a special place in our family because Aunty Lily had 'pink' hair. To us children, it looked just like candy floss. It never even crossed our minds that it wasn't her real hair colour, as we had never heard of a pink rinse.

Also, this song was played so much at home that the repetition could have clouded my memory of when I first heard it. So, it didn't win, although that's a moot point since my dad and I went back way farther than that, ultimately.

'I'm a Tiger'—Lulu, September 1968

This song is so repetitive and catchy that it was easy to sing along to. Also, on TV, there was a video of Lulu singing at a zoo, with tigers in the background. Whenever I recall seeing her singing this song, I see her make a paw/claw movement with her hand each time she sings the word *tiger* in the chorus. My sister and I aped that gesture.

'Those Were the Days'—Mary Hopkins, September 1968

This song had been Ireland's Eurovision Song Contest entry, so we had seen it performed on the TV.

'Excerpt from a Teenage Opera'—Keith West, August 1968

This song was often referred to as 'Grocer Jack' because that name is repeated in the lyrics. It probably appealed to us because kids sang the catchy chorus.

'Congratulations'—Cliff Richard, April 1968

Cliff was my sister's favourite before her David Cassidy period. She made me sing along to this one. This was Britain's entry for that year's Eurovision Song Contest.

'Cinderella Rockefella'—Esther and Abi Ofarim, February 1968

This was number one in the charts on my fourth birthday. To this day, I cannot explain why this song sticks in my mind. I can even remember its accompanying video (or maybe it was Esther and Abi Ofarim performing live). It's a bizarre pop song. Maybe that's why it is so memorable? It was a one-hit wonder.

'Puppet on a String'—Sandie Shaw, April 1967

This song was that year's entry for the Eurovision Song Contest, so we saw it on TV. I also saw Sandie Shaw perform this tune with Jools Holland at the Winter Gardens in Margate many years later, in 2011.

'I Was Kaiser Bill's Batman'—Whistling Jack Smith, March 1967

This song was yet another one-hit wonder, which isn't really surprising, given that there are no lyrics, just whistling. Still, it's very catchy. Since my sister and I couldn't whistle, we used to 'do, do, do, do' along to it.

My dad and I went through about fifty songs that day. I'm satisfied that it was a fair test.

Other contenders included the following:

- 'Fire Brigade'—The Move
- 'Jennifer, Juniper'—Donovan
- 'I Can't Let Maggie Go'—Honeybus
- 'Little Arrows'—Leapy Lee
- 'Simon and His Amazing Dancing Bear'—The Alan Price Set
- 'Ha! Ha! Said the Clown'—Manfred Mann

It was a really close call. I'm sure that my sister and I do-do-do-do-do'd along with Whistling Jack (I still can't whistle), so 'I Was Kaiser Bill's Batman' was probably the first one I had heard played on the radio. I know for sure that my family would have watched the Eurovision Song Contest on TV and that I would have heard the song played dozens of times on the radio back then, so I was compelled to declare 'Puppet on a String' by Sandie Shaw as the official winner of 'the first song that I can ever remember hearing on the radio' contest.

My Top Ten One-Hit Wonders (they may have had others but only one that anyone really know)

'99 Red Balloons'—Nena
'Mambo No. 5'—Lou Bega
'Venus'—Shocking Blue
'Spirit in the Sky'—Norman Greenbaum
'Cinderella Rockefella'—Esther and Abi Ofarim
'Excerpt from a Teenage Opera'—Keith West
'I Can't Let Maggie Go'—Honeybus
'Radar Love'—Golden Earring
'Hocus Pocus'—Focus
'Black Betty'—Ram Jam

Things to Check Out

On YouTube:

- Trumptonshire tunes—Windy Miller
- 'I'm a Tiger'—Lulu
- BBC One test card

Elsewhere:
www.myoldmansabusman

A Transport of Delight

In July 1973, we left Reigate in our relatively new, Natiola-coloured, variomatic-engined (which means that the colour was bright red, the engine was turned by a giant elastic band, and the car was very uncool) DAF 55 car and headed for a new life on the south coast.

DAF was and still is a Dutch brand, better known for its quality trucks than its cars, the latter being, in my opinion, underrated and misunderstood, especially by secondary-school classmates:

'Oi, Gilbert, your old man drives a tosser's car.'

Mum and Dad's oldest friends lived in Hythe, which is situated on the shores of Southampton Water. We regularly visited them on the holidays and had fallen in love with the area, which is surrounded by beaches and the New Forest. House prices were significantly lower, which meant that my parents would have some spare cash while Dad found a new job. Because my sister suffered badly from asthma, a condition not helped by our slightly damp Victorian terraced house, it was decided during one visit to Hythe that we would move there permanently.

I remember that it all happened fairly quickly, as Mum and Dad had booked a summer holiday in Poole, Dorset, that year, virtually down the road when compared to Reigate. They would not have done this if they'd already planned the move. I think that this must have been the most spontaneous and risky thing that my dad had ever done in his life.

That said, the holiday to Poole gave us the opportunity to discover Sandbanks. Back then, we didn't think of it as millionaire's playground, even though it was one of the most expensive real estate areas in the world and was home to the rich and famous, such as Harry Redknapp. It was simply a stunning beach in a most beautiful area. I still love to visit whenever I can.

My Old Man's a Busman

Following that holiday, we were regular visitors to Sandbanks on summer weekends. It was only about forty miles away. With petrol at thirty-five pence per gallon (seven pence per litre) back then and with money tight, it was a relatively inexpensive day out. It was even cheaper when we'd leave at the crack of dawn so that we could park for free on the road instead of paying to go into the car park.

Our routine was always the same: up at 6.30 a.m.; leave at 7.00 a.m. sharp. We'd then be parked up before 8.00 a.m. to ensure that we got a spot in the free parking section on the road. Dad would never pay for car parks if he could help it. We would walk miles rather than pay.

Sandbanks tended to get busy quickly since it was a popular summer destination. Dad would become indignant if someone else beat him to the prime parking spot nearest to the beach. Hence, our early start—to prevent Dad's indignation. On arrival, we'd walk around for a while until the baker opened at 9.00 a.m., at which time we'd buy fresh rolls for lunch and then head straight to the beach.

Great days! Still, it could be cold on the beach at 9.00 in the morning.

In the early '70s, the news was full of strikes, inflation, unrest, three-day weeks, and power cuts. Even after we had moved, we kept candles on hand in the new house, a three-bedroom bungalow, for the inevitable power cuts. I remember hearing on the radio, and then telling Dad, that petrol might even go over fifty pence a gallon one day. He told me that it would never happen.

Hythe itself is a lovely village on the edge of the New Forest. It boasts a marina on the shores of Southampton Water, giving great views of the big cruise ships as they make their way up and down that stretch before docking in the port. It has a long pier that stretches out to the ferry, which carries people across to the city of Southampton. It is also only a few miles from the local beaches Calshot and Lepe, which offer stunning views of the Isle of Wight. Because of these things, it was a lovely place to grow up.

Although it has fewer famous people to its name than Reigate, Hythe can boast of T.E. Lawrence (*Lawrence of Arabia*), Bruce Parry (of *Tribes* TV fame), and the best of all, if you ask me, Sir Christopher Cockerell, inventor of the hovercraft, whose autograph I obtained (and subsequently lost) following a dare that I wouldn't go knock on his door and ask for it.

Those were more innocent days. Daring someone to happy-slap Cockerell and record the incident on a mobile phone was decades away.

I wish now that I could recall more of that day. I do remember that Cockerell politely asked me to step in while he searched for a piece of paper. What I could see inside was like something out of a film about a mad historian, as there were books and papers strewn everywhere. These were more innocent times. I didn't think it at all odd that an old man living on his own had asked me to 'step inside' and wait. I was just dismayed that, once again, I was an unprepared autograph hunter.

My adult self would have stayed and asked loads of questions about how Cockerell had come up the idea of the hovercraft and what it felt like to see his invention every day out of his window. His house overlooked Southampton Water. At the time, there was an hourly hovercraft passenger service between Southampton and the Isle of Wight, which he would have been able to watch. Unfortunately though my primary-school self was only interested in the prize: winning the dare and getting back to my friends as fast as I could to tell them that I had won and could prove it.

The hovercrafts were noisy as they buzzed between the twin island destinations of Southampton and Cowes, but they were much faster than the car ferries they were competing against. Hovercrafts also ran between Portsmouth, farther down the coast, and Ryde, on the westernmost point of the island. They still do. But the real deals were the huge ones that carried cars as well as passengers between Dover in Kent and France.

The introduction of the quieter and more stable hydrofoils, which sat above the water, brought about the demise of the hovercraft (which could not run in high winds, as it would be blown sideways). As with the iconic Concorde aircraft, it was a sad day when hovercrafts were finally taken out of service and were no longer part of the traffic on Southampton Water.

It's still a thrill for me to see those marvellous machines in action. At the time of this writing, they were still in service between Southsea and Ryde. Luckily, I have friends in Southsea. When I visit them, I get to see the hovercraft 'take off'—rise up on its giant skirt of air and launch into the sea, aided by its giant propellers. It is a must-see attraction.

When, as a boy, I was taken to see the hovercraft, one could practically walk up and touch it as it stood waiting to 'launch'. But now, unless you are actually boarding, you have to stand behind large Perspex panels, meaning that you can look but not touch. There are, however, small gaps between those panels. If the conditions are favourable, with wind blowing hard off the sea, you can position yourself just to feel—as the mighty machine rises, backs down the slipway, and launches into the sea—the spray on your face as it is thrown back by the giant propellers.

Today, I can still revel in that boyish wonder for a few seconds before my kids, bored, say, 'It's just a boat, Dad,' and we have to move on to the amusement arcade on the next pier down.

The technology of the hovercraft spawned other inventions such as the electric hover lawn mower Flymo, which sold itself because it was easier to push around than manual or other electric mowers, although it didn't have a bag or tray and therefore left the grass cuttings on the lawn. In 1978, Qualcast, which made electric mowers that did collect the grass, ran a TV ad campaign showing a Flymo owner raking his lawn long after the Qualcast owner had finished his similar-size lawn. It ended with the line, 'It's a lot less bother than a hover.' One execution involved a yokel, whose dialect made it sound like, 'It's a lot less bovver than a hover.'

It was just one of those campaigns that pricked the collective consciousness, so much so that in 1981, when the post-punk band Tenpole Tudor had a top-ten hit with the song 'Swords of a Thousand Men', people would often say, 'Swords of a thousand men? Now, *that's* a lot less bovver than a hover.'

Mum still lives in the area, so my kids get to enjoy thrills from my own childhood, such as seeing the big cruise ships up close and racing the train up the pier. The pier is 640 metres long, so now I leave the racing to the kids. But the challenge when we lived there was to leave just after the train that was taking passengers to the awaiting ferry and to run, trying to beat the train to the end of the pier, also saving oneself the train fare.

Moving counties (Surrey to Hampshire) also meant moving to a new school system. When I was at school with Fatboy Slim at Reigate Priory, it was a middle school. Students attended for two years between infants' and grammar or secondary education. So, I'd left the first year of middle school and gone into the third-year primary school, or year five in today's system. Very confusing.

Another anomaly arising from the different education policies between Surrey and Hampshire Counties was that the Surrey system started foreign language classes early. I learnt one year of French in my first year at middle school. Hampshire—or, more specifically, Hythe County Primary School—didn't start foreign language classes early, so, there, I did the first year of French again in my third year of primary school and the second year of French in my fourth year of primary school (which is year six today).

In 1975, I moved onto secondary education at Noadswood Comprehensive School. It turned out that not all junior schools in the area had the same policy.

Hythe County Primary School was the only school in the area that taught French—and so the whole thing started again. My French language skills were going to go one of two ways.

Unfortunately, I was so bored with French that, by the third year of secondary school (or year nine), when we hit new, harder stuff, I just gave up. If I recall correctly, I achieved 23 per cent in my end-of-year exam and therefore dropped French for the final two years, which were the fourth and fifth years (or years ten and eleven in the current system).

Later in life, I bitterly regretted the decision, especially considering that I was lucky enough to spend four consecutive years on a trackside yacht in Monaco, watching the Formula One Grand Prix.

'Monsieur Lafayette marché le long de la rue avec son chien blanc' is not much bloody use when trying to get a beer in the packed-out trackside Rascas Bar in Monte Carlo on the night before the big race.

Living near the coast, we were all much more aware of the RNLI (Royal National Lifeboat Institution) and the dangers of the sea. But back in 1968, prior to the *Decimalisation, Decimalisation* infomercial campaign, the department that made government information films released a cartoon featuring two characters: Joe and his ample-bodied, ice-cream-licking wife, Petunia. They informed all of us that the coastguard, like the other three emergency services (police, ambulance, and fire brigade), could be contacted by dialling 9-9-9. They said that if you saw ships or people swimming that were in trouble, then that's what you should do.

Maybe it was a sign of the times—the Swinging Sixties, peace and love, etc.—that we received this message in such a cheery way, with spotted hankies, ice cream, and deckchairs. The zeitgeist of the era could also be the reason why, in the early '70s, what with Britain's strikes, power cuts, and general unrest, the people of the Government Information Department were churning out films to scare the living daylights out of us.

Each new film highlighted for parents and kids another way in which we could be killed or, at least, seriously harmed if we did not keep our wits about us.

In 1973, messages such as 'Don't play with matches,' 'Always tell your mum,' and 'Stoves are dangerous' were delivered by a cartoon boy who interpreted them from the 'babblings' of a ginger cat called Charlie (in the same way that the characters Sonny and Sandy were the only humans able to understand the clicking of Skippy in the tale of the Antipodean bush kangaroo and Flipper the Dolphin respectively) in a series of information films called *Charlie Says*. But from 1971 to 1975, a frightening series of films warned us of much darker dangers: leaving glass on beaches (the images showed that simply running on a beach can rip your feet to shreds and put you in hospital for weeks), playing in fridges (they will suffocate you to death), playing around 'dark water' (i.e. ponds, lakes, and so forth; they will kill you, as you will slide down into them from a muddy bank and drown), flying kites near pylons (which will kill you by way of electrocution), playing in a field and not hearing the combine harvester bearing down on you (you will be chopped up into little pieces and killed), and—arguably the most frightening to all eleven-year-olds in 1975—*rabies* (every dog and cat in the land is trying to kill you).

We did get a respite in 1974 when the Government Information Department released a film advising people not to leave rugs on a polished floors, as 'it can be dangerous. Throughout the early '70s, we had the Unigate Milk Company's *Humphrey* ad campaign, which threatened that stripy straws would steal our milk if we didn't drink it.

In 1975, the gentler Green Cross Code Man reminded us, 'Always use the Green Cross Code, because I won't be there when you cross the road. Stop, look, listen, think.'

These films were intended to create maximum tension and fear, which made facing the Daleks seem like a doddle in comparison.

The early to mid '70s would have been a low point, given the constant inducement of fear, had the period not also given rise to the glam rock movement.

The year 1973 was arguably the heyday of glam rock, with the charts and *TOTPs* filled with artists and groups such as Mud, Wizzard, Sweet, Slade, Suzi Quatro, Gary Glitter, Alvin Stardust, the Rubettes, and Marc Bolan's T-Rex. It was also the heyday of the 7" vinyl single, since, to reach the coveted number-one spot or even to get into the top ten in the charts, bands and artists had to sell hundreds of thousands of records a week.

Compare this to the late nineties and early aughts (or noughties), when tens of thousands sales can get an artist or a group to the top of the chart. In April 2006, Gnarls Barkley reached number one with 'Crazy', having sold no physical singles at all. They achieved this by way of 31,000 downloads. Mika's 'Grace Kelly' 'topped' this achievement in 2007, with sales of just 30,500.

Bill Haley must have been turning in his grave. In 1957, he and his Comets reached the top spot in the UK charts with 'Rock Around the Clock', having chalked up sales of one million singles.

The glam movement came on the back of the Osmond vs. Cassidy era. During the first years of that decade, most every teeny girl's heart was divided between Donny Osmond and David Cassidy on both sides of the Atlantic. Even we lads were not averse. Donny Osmond's version of 'Why' became B2 in my singles collection. My sister was a massive David Cassidy fan. Her love and devotion was so strong that when my dad teased her, referring to him as David Custard, she would run crying to her room.

My dad didn't use the nickname exclusively to annoy my sister. Anyone in the media with a remotely similar-sounding surname, such as Jacques Cousteau, the TV marine biologist, was fair game. A Sunday afternoon was incomplete without an episode of *The Undersea World of Jack Custard*.

I've subsequently learned that my girlfriend was also very much a part of the David Cassidy camp. She and her friends would play, pretending to kiss David, pretending to marry David, pretending to be in David's TV show *The Partridge Family,* and pretending to meet David when he came off the plane. This last was inspired by the news footage of people engaged in mass hysteria when this American heart-throb made a trip to the United Kingdom.

It's almost impossible now to describe the hysteria surrounding these artists. With the diversity of music and media today it's not quite the same.

My Old Man's a Busman

At the height of his fame in the early '70s, David Cassidy's fan club reputedly had more members than Elvis's and the Beatles' put together. In addition, the edition of *Rolling Stone* that shows Cassidy 'naked' on the cover is still, over forty years on, the bestselling issue of that magazine ever. The hysteria surrounding David and Donny was followed by home-grown tartan talent from Scotland, the Bay City Rollers, at about the same time that the glam movement took hold.

At this time, there was, of course, other music being played on the radio and featuring in the charts, namely a wave of hippy folk, including luminaries such as Neil Young, America, and Stills and Nash. Closer to home were the likes of Deep Purple and Jethro Tull. But even with the onslaught of British pop talent on radio and TV, the then-contemporary pop music certainly didn't feature at home or in school.

Personally, I remember that glam bands dominated the charts at Christmastime, but history shows that only Slade and Mud—in 1973 and 1974, respectively—achieved number one with all the other great classics of the period, including the perennially loved and played 'I Wish It Could be Christmas Every Day' by Wizzard, were simply pretenders to the throne. Slade were preceded in 1971 by another Osmond, Jimmy, with the novelty song 'Long-Haired Lover from Liverpool', while 1975 was dominated by the enigma that was Queen's 'Bohemian Rhapsody'.

The United Kingdom has always had an affinity for the novelty record, especially at Christmas. My generation can trace this tendency back to 1968's 'Lily the Pink' by the Scaffold and to 1969's 'Two Little Boys' by Rolf Harris.

The year 1971 gave us Benny Hill's 'Ernie' ('he drove the fastest milk cart in the West'). Following Jimmy Osmond's hit in 1972, we had a break for eight years, giving more credible songs a go—until St Winifred's School Choir pulled at the heartstrings of most women over thirty-five years of age in the United Kingdom with the sugary-sweet (or sickly sweet, depending on your viewpoint) 'There's No One Quite Like Grandma' in 1980. The year 1982 gave us Rene and Renata's 'Save Your Love', followed in 1983 by the Flying Pickets' acappella version of 'Only You'.

Two decades of dominance by the Spice Girls and Simon Cowell's stable of TV talent-show winners almost saved us from all the novelty trash developed since that time. But for the British, it's simply in our nature to support novelty trash. As a nation, we incredulously voted with our hard-earned cash, in 1993 and 2000 respectively, for the two worst songs ever, *Mr Blobby* and *Bob the Builder*.

Among the songs banned from radio over the years because of their lyrics (not including the more obvious contemporary offerings that contain four-letter swear words and direct references to sexual and violent acts), Johnny Ray's 1954 'Such a Night' was a bit too racy; the Kinks' 'Plastic Man' contained the word *bum*; and Elton John's 'The Bitch Is Back' contained the word *bitch* (obviously). Maybe radio should have a policy of banning crap records, as well.

Top Ten Transport Songs

'Down in the Tube Station at Midnight'—The Jam
'Last Train to Clarkesville'—The Monkees
'Big Yellow Taxi'—Joni Mitchell
'Calling Occupants of Interplanetary Craft'—The Carpenters
'Brand New Cadillac'—The Clash
'The Banana Boat Song'—Harry Belafonte
'My White Bicycle'—Nazareth
'Mystery Train'—Elvis Presley
'Rocket Man'—Elton John
'The Rock Island Line'—Lonnie Donegan

Things to Check Out

On YouTube:

- Isle of Wight hovercraft *Solent Express*
- Concorde takes off from Bournemouth Airport

Elsewhere:
www.myoldmansabusman

When Elvis Met My Auntie Margaret . . . Twice

My relationship with Elvis Presley began when I was very young. His music has been a constant in my life as far back as I can remember.

Elvis was a regular part of our lounge concerts at home in Reigate. Back then, I looked forward to listening to his early hits from the '50s, such as 'Jailhouse Rock' and 'Blue Suede Shoes', which would have been played if Dad had chosen, as they were fast and up-tempo songs. If Mum had her way, then we'd be more likely to hear slow songs, like 'Are You Lonesome Tonight?' and 'That's When Your Heartaches Begin', both of which Dad hated, as they included spoken-word sections. If there was one thing that Dad hated even more than not playing the B-sides of records, it was talking on records. He would go as far as putting his hands over his ears and making daft noises to drown out the sounds when those bits came on—much to the annoyance of my mum, who was trying to enjoy the song.

Of course, there are exceptions to every rule. 'Old Shep' was one such exception. It had absolutely no talking in it, but Dad hated it even more than the other songs because it was very slow and had schmaltzy lyrics. The song had been a hit in the charts, but it was also allegedly the first song that the young Elvis had ever performed in public at a singing competition at the annual Mississippi–Alabama Fair and Dairy Show in Tupelo in 1945. He stood on a chair to reach the microphone.

Reports of subsequent events show that Elvis won second prize, which was $5 and free rides at the fair. But Elvis's own recollection years later was that he only achieved fifth place and, worse, was reprimanded by his mum for going on some of the more dangerous rides.

From an early age, I knew all the words to 'Old Shep' (as well as all of the other songs mentioned). It's definitely in contention for the top sad song of all time. It tells the story of a man who had a puppy since childhood. As a man, he has to shoot the dog because it had gotten old. Worse still, he has to do it whilst the dying dog is looking up at him.

Heart breaking.

Elvis had a way of putting real emotion into a song so that it tugged at the heartstrings. That's why 'Don't Cry, Daddy', 'Separate Ways', and 'My Boy' are contenders for that list of top ten sad songs, too, although these songs are, for me, an acquired taste, like earthy red wine and olives—a passion that develops with age. Back then, I was only really a fan of Elvis's early '50s music.

In the mid '70s, Radio 1 featured a weekly battle of the bands which pitched two artists or groups against each other, such as the Rolling Stones vs. the Who (the 1990s equivalent of Blur vs. Oasis). Listeners would write in with their votes. The results were read on air at the beginning of the following week's show. Such was Elvis's status at the time that, when it came time for his turn, the show went out as Elvis of the '50s vs. Elvis of the '60s. It didn't even pitch him against the Beatles.

I find it strange, then, when some say that Elvis 'the King' Presley really only 'ruled' for two years, between 1956 and 1958 (before he went into the Army) when he exploded onto the music scene and changed the face of music forever, upsetting parents and the establishment alike because he was a white man performing black music.

After that period, some say, Elvis's music was never the same. They allege that his career after that point was focused on churning out second-rate movies and soundtracks, leaving the way open for the Beatles, the Rolling Stones, and other recording artists of the day to take his place.

History shows, however, that—regardless of anyone's opinion—this actually wasn't the case. In the United Kingdom alone, between 1959 and 1963, Elvis had twelve number-one hits, including one that featured talking in the middle: 'Are You Lonesome Tonight?'

After that, even I, a massive fan, have to admit that things became a little lean vis-à-vis his chart-topping success, as Elvis only reached the number-one spot two times more over the next five years: in 1965 with 'Crying in the Chapel' (another slow song that Mum loved and Dad hated), and in 1970 with 'The Wonder of You'—although 'In the Ghetto' and 'Suspicious Minds' had both reached number two in 1969 and Elvis had enjoyed fifteen more top-ten hits before once more reaching the coveted number-one spot in the British chart, following his death in August 1977, with 'Way Down'.

I admit that I sound like an Elvis geek. I am an Elvis geek. But what's most unusual about this fact is that, under normal circumstances, peer pressure and 'survival instincts' would have knocked my musical tastes right out of me, given that it was imperative at school, if one didn't want to be ostracised, to keep up with what was being played on the weekly *Top of the Pops* and what was in the top forty—and definitely not listening to the music our parents liked.

However, my constant 'brainwashing' at home and my being influenced by a lad at school named Robbie managed to keep my passion alive, although at times it was tough.

Robbie looked like a young Elvis. He was obsessed with the man and his music because his dad, who also bore a striking resemblance to Elvis, albeit a slightly older version, was also a massive fan who had brought him up on little other than Elvis's music.

Robbie's obsession for Elvis's music, combined with the fact that he was quite a cool character at school, fuelled a little gang of Elvis fans and inured us not to turn our backs on our idol when, all around us, others thought that Elvis was a has-been, an old-fashioned musician, or a musical 'dinosaur'. However, Robbie's social status could not save the rest of our reputations.

I was an Elvis-loving choirboy (the boys at school had found out about that, too—more details in the following chapter) who was ferried around in a DAF 55 car. The girls were hardly lining up.

I wasn't Elvis-obsessed to the exclusion of other music. Thanks to my parents, I had an eclectic appreciation of old music: Buddy Holly, Roy Orbison, Lonnie Donegan, Herman's Hermits, the Beatles, the Animals, and Fats Domino, to name a few. None of this changed how others perceived me at school, though. Because of peer pressure and my genuine love of most music, I was into glam rock and other chart acts from the early '70s, such as Queen, ABBA, ELO (Electric Light Orchestra), and

My Old Man's a Busman

Status Quo—and even punk rock when it hit us in 1977 (which helped my social status a little bit).

There weren't many kids listening to the Boomtown Rats, the Sex Pistols, ABBA, or Elvis on back-to-back on tapes in 1978, but I was doing it . . . and I still do.

My mix tapes (now MP3s) are usually themed and named and are often punctuated with surprise songs for the listener. The songs I choose are known for being tenuously linked, although they are linked in my head. They all make perfect sense if you do enough research and get all of the references.

Of course, in my eyes, Madonna and Elvis go together. She did 'Like a Prayer'; he, 'Crying in the Chapel'. There is an obvious link between the two songs. You may have to work a little harder for the explanation if the Clash, Donna Summer, and Catherine Jenkins appear on the same playlist, but there is always a reason for it.

Like my namesake Peter, the one who denied that he knew Jesus, I tried to keep my association with Elvis as quiet as possible at school so as not to attract undue attention. Unfortunately, Robbie was loud and proud, and so I got much stick about it from my peer group, purely because I was associated with Robbie. As if that wasn't bad enough, one day I made the proverbial (and literal) schoolboy error, which will live with me forever.

It was the summer of 1978, the last weekend in August, the last week of the school summer holidays, and we, the Elvis fan 'gang', had been to a twelve-hour back-to-back Elvis movie bonanza marking the anniversary of his death at a cinema in Southampton.

With our illicit (we were thirteen and fourteen years of age) cans of lager and packets of cigarettes (you could smoke in cinemas and theatres back then) sneaked in under our jackets, we had spent the whole day watching Elvis movies, concerts, interviews, and movie outtakes.

It may sound sad now, but, at the time, our little gang were in our element. Away from the prying eyes of our peers, we could, for a moment in time, sing along to every word and enjoy the experience of being 'the world's biggest fans'. After all, we had taken part in a twelve-hour fan fest, not wanting that event, or day, ever to end. However, all good things, as we know, do end. When that one finally did, we used our hard-earned pocket money to purchase our T-shirts and tin badges, and then we sang happily all the way home.

The following Monday was the first day of the new term back at school. It was hot.

In September 1978, while punk swept the nation and every parent hated Johnny Rotten of the Sex Pistols and anyone else who had anything to do with the punk movement, the charts actually reflected that era's disco/pop music, featuring the likes of Donna Summer, Bacarra, ABBA, Kate Bush, Boney M, and the Bee Gees—and, seemingly, every song from the musical *Grease*. No Elvis in sight.

At some point midway through an afternoon lesson on that first day back at school, amidst the heat and in a cramped classroom of sweaty teenagers, both befuddling my brain and compromising my ability to think rationally, I removed my jumper. It was only a matter of seconds before someone pointed at me and shouted to the whole class, much to my horror and utter embarrassment (which remain to this day), 'Look at Gilbert. He's covered in Elvis badges.'

In an act of secret support and solidarity for the King following our twelve-hour vigil, I had pinned six badges of Elvis to my school shirt.

I went beetroot red. I felt even hotter. I felt sick. I was mortified that I'd been caught. This episode was up there on the embarrassment scale with the stories of people whose mums caught them masturbating.

As quickly as I could, I removed the badges, but time seemed to stand still as my clammy, sweaty fingers removed them one by one, all under the watchful and slightly pitiful gaze of the teacher. Then the chorus started up.

'Gilbert loves Elvis. What a tosser.'

'Gilbert is Elvis's bum chum.'

'Gilbert. What a joey.'

I tried to ignore it, although my face was getting hotter and hotter whilst I stared straight ahead at the blackboard. Mercifully, the teacher had gained control of the classroom and was about to restart the lesson before I heard the final insult: 'Spazzer!' said one of the girls whom I secretly fancied.

Only another year to go at this school.

Thank God that nobody found out about my Elvis moments at home. Whenever we went to the beach, usually Sandbanks, I would take a cassette player and go for long walks along the beach, listening to hours of Elvis music. I also had fantasy Elvis concerts.

I had tacked a giant poster of Elvis, from his concert *Aloha from Hawaii,* to my bedroom wall. The poster had come from the soundtrack LP that Mum had bought. I'd sing along for hours to his music, pretending to be Elvis in concert and singing to 'my' fans in Hawaii or Vegas. I have to admit that sometimes, when I am alone in my car, I still do this.

All of this would have been fine if my schoolmates had found out when compared to what is quite possibly my worst Elvis geek crime ever.

During an early '80s poetry writing phase (so, now, I was an Elvis bumming, DAF passenger, choirboy, and poet tosser) when I was in teenage love with and felt angst over a girl called Suzanne, I'd written some prose composed entirely of Elvis song titles. I had titled it *One Broken Heart for Sale.* It included sixty-two unbroken song titles. At the time, I'm sure I thought that it was award-winning. But now . . . ?

So, given that I was such a massive but not-so-much-in-the-closet fan, imagine how I felt on the day when I (at that time, a teenager) found out that one of Mum's best friends, 'Auntie' Margaret, who lived a few doors up from us in Hythe, had actually met Elvis.

Auntie Margaret wasn't our real auntie. We called her 'Auntie' out of an imposed mix of 'respect for our elders' and familiarity. The rules for us kids was not to call adults by their first names because it was impolite. Under normal circumstances, we kids had to use the relevant personal title, such as, in this case, 'Mrs' Margaret (maybe Dad had watched too much of *The Basil Brush Show,* where Basil, a puppet fox, referred to his human friend as Mr Roy). But if the person was a close friend or long-term acquaintance of our parents, then we were allowed to use the 'Auntie' or 'Uncle' title. It was nice for us children since we didn't have any real aunties or uncles, because Mum and Dad—unusual, given their generation—were both only children.

This particular spelling of *auntie* (with an *ie* at the end) was also important to us, as it denoted a younger person, as opposed to *aunty* (with a *y* at the end), which we used to describe our blood-related aunts, such as our beloved, candy-floss-haired Aunty Lily, who was my dad's real aunty by marriage (so actually our Great Aunty). Please don't confuse this with 'Aunty figures' that appear in young boys' fantasies, wherein a boy is with an older woman, a friend of his mum's, or even his own friend's mum. This type of auntie would take a teenage boy 'in hand' or 'show him the ropes'—think Stifler's mum from the *American Pie* films.

So, one day, while we were sitting in our kitchen, Mum just came out with it, completely out of the blue, as if she was telling me what she had bought at the shops that day. How could Mum, who had made me the fan I was, who was still playing Elvis records, who saw Auntie Margaret virtually every day—how could she have overlooked, for all of these years, the monumental fact that Auntie Margaret had met Elvis?

This is how I heard the conversation: '[Blah de blah, blah de blah] Sainsbury's . . . Oh, did I tell you? Auntie Margaret actually met Elvis in Germany.'

'*What?*'

After I had hotfooted it up to Auntie Margaret's house, leaving a trail of dust to rival the Roadrunner's, I learned that what my mum had said was true—and so I found myself sitting in Auntie Margaret's house, looking through albums of photographs of her with Elvis, and listening to her stories.

In late 1956, Auntie Margaret had been a devoted fan since the age of fourteen (in early 1956, she could not decide whether she was in love with Elvis, Bill Haley, or Dickie Valentine). At sixteen, she had been a voluntary worker at the Elvis Presley fan club offices in London, opening mail and responding to the thousands of UK fans.

When she turned seventeen, Margaret got her mum's permission (because her friend was twenty-one, her mum thought that the friend was mature and grown-up and would look after young Margaret, keeping her out of trouble) to travel to Germany, on the off chance of meeting her idol.

Having travelled to Bad Nauheim, close to the Ray Barracks in Friedberg where Elvis was stationed (all the two young women knew was that Elvis had rented a house in the town), Margaret and her friend spent hours wandering around until they stumbled upon a group of people hanging around outside a particular house, which turned out to be the one.

They had waited there for hours, not even knowing if Elvis was due back that day. As they were about to leave to return to their hotel in a nearby town, a car pulled up. Out stepped 'the King'.

Margaret remembers thinking at the time that it was very much like being in a dream. Her absolute love, idol, and hero was getting out of a car a few feet in front of her. As an adult, she thought she was mad to have made that trip. She had been a girl of seventeen in the mid '50s, travelling with a girlfriend across Europe on the off chance that Elvis would actually be at the house in Friedberg—and facing a million-to-one chance of catching a glimpse of him.

Although Elvis was tired, telling them he'd spent the day on jankers (tedious tasks or chores usually dished out as punishment for a minor misdemeanour, like coming back late from leave or having a non-immaculate uniform), Margaret remembers him as 'wonderfully courteous, polite, and generous, spending time with all the fans that were there, signing autographs and having individual pictures with everyone'.

More than that, Elvis actually spoke with her. He was amazed that she and her friend had travelled all the way from England to see him, and he said that he'd love to visit their country one day, which, unfortunately, or allegedly, never happened.

It is well documented that Elvis did set foot in the United Kingdom during a stopover at Prestwick Airport, Scotland, in March 1960, en route from Germany to the United States, but it's also rumoured that, two years earlier, in 1958, he had spent a day in London with British pop music's answer to Elvis Presley: Tommy Steele.

While Steele never publically affirmed that there was substance to the rumour, theatre producer Bill Kenwright supposedly revealed Steele's secret to Ken Bruce on his Radio 2 show in April 2008.

Kenwright claimed that 'Elvis flew in for a day, and Tommy showed him round London. He showed him the Houses of Parliament and spent the day with him.'

This had allegedly come about following a phone call Presley had made to Steele.

The following day, Kenwright said to the reporters that he was not sure it was a good idea to have told the story.

To add to the intrigue, or conspiracy, Steele, fifty years after the event, felt the need to go on public record when he wrote to the *Daily Mail* newspaper and said, 'It was two young men sharing the same love of their music. I swore never to divulge publicly what took place, and I regret that it has found some way of getting into the light. I only hope he [Elvis] can forgive me.'

And that should have been that: an ageing pop star with no relevance to the kids at the time made a statement about something that may or may not have happened fifty years earlier involving another has-been, and a dead one at that, who had no real relevance to the kids of the day.

However, given people's modern-day obsession with celebrity and trying to make a buck off the rich and famous—and in a ridiculous act that is up there with Somerset's Wookey Hole, when it challenged its geographical and geological rival, Cheddar Caves, to a contest concerning which had the biggest stalactites—press officers employed by Stagecoach, the company that owned Prestwick Airport, issued a statement requesting proof, photographic or otherwise, of the alleged meeting between Presley and Steele, stating, 'Until such proof is provided, we will continue to describe our property, Prestwick Airport, as the only place in Britain where Elvis Presley ever set foot, and [we[will not be removing the marker, photographs[,] and special lounge at the airport which relate to this claim.'

In a final twist to the story, conspiracy, cover-up, or wheeze, Lamar Fike, a former member of Elvis's Memphis Mafia, who reportedly lived with Elvis at the time, has since posted a claim that it was he, not Elvis, who visited London with Tommy Steele that day.

So, what are we supposed to conclude?

Hundreds of thousands of British fans have been wrongly disappointed for over fifty years. Also, did Elvis, in fact, visit Britain? Tommy Steele, after having spent a whole day with Elvis and subsequently agonisingly apologising for letting out his fifty-year-old secret, had been duped and did not know the difference between the biggest icon on the planet at the time (arguably, ever) and one of his security men. Elvis did spend the day in London . . . and no one recognised him?

Really?

With each passing year, it seems increasingly unlikely that we'll ever know the truth or whether the Prestwick Airport staff will dejectedly turn up for work one day, knowing that their claim to fame has been overturned.

It's probably more likely that we'll find the answer to the UK music scene's other famous secret—not what happened to Richey Edwards of the Manic Street Preachers on that fateful day by the Severn Bridge, but who was singing on the 1981 Christmas hit 'The Hokey Cokey' by the Snowmen: Ian Dury, Jona Lewie, or A.N. Other?

After about an hour chatting with his fans that day in Friedberg, Elvis's housekeeper called him in for dinner. The group drifted off towards the railway station, chatting excitedly about their amazing, once-in-a-lifetime experience.

Then, in what can be likened only to a movie plotline, the two young women—who hadn't gotten far—met a woman pushing a girl in a wheelchair. She asked Auntie Margaret if she knew where Elvis's house was. They got chatting about what had happened that evening. After Margaret told the woman and the girl where the house was, she and her friend went back with the pair. The other girls and women in the group had continued on into town at that point.

Margaret remembers this:

> The lady knocked on the door, and the housekeeper answered. The lady explained that they had travelled a long way and asked if it would be possible for the girl to get Elvis's autograph. The housekeeper said that Elvis was not available right now. We then heard Elvis call out and ask who it was. The housekeeper disappeared. Less than a minute later, Elvis appeared again and had pictures taken with the girl. He must have been tired, having had his dinner interrupted and already spending an hour with fans, but he still took time out to see her. It was magical, fantastic.

The photos are amazing. Not many fans have one-on-one pictures of themselves with Elvis in their memorabilia boxes (not even Cliff Richard met Elvis when he travelled to the same house in 1958), especially ones taken outside of the United States—although it would be great if one turned up one day. Imagine, a picture of a friend or girlfriend in front of the Houses of Parliament in 1958, where you can just make out Elvis and Tommy in the background, pointing up at Big Ben.

The real shame, of course, is that one day, sometime in the not too distant future, no one will care. My kids were impressed when they met Margaret (we're not quite so formal now) and saw the pictures, because they'd heard about Elvis from me, but I'm sure that when they are earning, they'll not be spending their hard-earned cash on Elvis memorabilia, not even a picture taken in London. And *their* kids will most likely ask, 'Elvis who?'

Elvis recorded hundreds, if not thousands, of songs during his incredible career. Who knows what he may have achieved if he had lived longer. Among songs from all of the genres that he covered, including the classic songs he recorded over the years, Auntie Margaret, when pushed, says that her favourite track is still his 1958 number-one hit, 'Jailhouse Rock'.

'I just remember how gorgeous we all thought he was and how excited we were with his music at the time. I love hundreds of his songs even now, but this is the one that takes me straight back to that time when I was a young girl.'

To this day, the publicity shot of Elvis for the film *Jailhouse Rock* is one of the most iconic images of Elvis's early career.

Of course, as well as being a singer, Elvis was also an actor who appeared in over thirty films. Although, for the most part, these films were vehicles to produce a soundtrack—and latterly, documentaries of his concerts—some of those album soundtracks were his most successful.

The soundtrack album for *G.I. Blues* in 1960, a movie celebrating Elvis's Army life and his return to the United States following active duty, entered the US Billboard album chart at number one. It remained number one for ten weeks and stayed in the chart for one hundred and eleven weeks. It was the most successful album of Elvis's entire career, measured by weeks in the chart. The 1961 *Blue Hawaii* soundtrack was the biggest-selling album during Elvis's lifetime, selling two million copies in the first twelve months of release and spending twenty weeks at number one in the Billboard chart.

I would personally place Elvis's films into three categories:

1. The First Four

Love Me Tender (although Elvis only sang one song in this), *Loving You, Jailhouse Rock* (Auntie Margaret's favourite), and *King Creole*—reportedly Elvis's favourite—are all great movies full of memorable chart hits.

2. The Concerts

These are for diehard fans only, especially those who attend a twelve-hour fan fest. *Elvis,* his 1968 comeback special, is my favourite, although *Aloha from Hawaii* shows Elvis at his white-jumpsuit-wearing best. Sometimes not categorised as a film, the televised concert in 1973 was reportedly watched by over 1.5 billion viewers.

3. Everything Else

The rest of Elvis's films were pretty formulaic: boy meets girl, boy fights another boy over a girl, boy sings enough songs to release an album and keep the studio in contract fodder.

The better of the rest includes, in my opinion, *G.I. Blues, Blue Hawaii,* and *Speedway* (co-starring Nancy Sinatra). The worst is *Harem Holiday* (which I watched with a neighbour, 'Auntie' Marjorie, since Dad was watching the football, which took priority).

If you've been reading this book (and haven't for some bizarre reason flicked to this chapter first), you have noticed a trend in the top-ten lists at the end of each chapter and may well be expecting a revelation of my top ten Elvis songs at the end of this one—maybe forecasting that it will include 'Old Shep'. If this is the case, then, unfortunately, you will be disappointed.

I really struggled to put together all of the chapter-ending top-ten lists. Given the vast array of songs and artists available from my collection and my memory, it's been tough to decide what to leave out. I've had no shortage of options, and I have wrestled quite a bit with trimming the lists before making a final decision. I saw no need to put any song I didn't know on the list. Nor did I include a song just because it had the word *green* in the title . . . or whatever.

Maybe if I had included a chapter featuring a yodelling story, I would have realistically only been able to come up with two songs before having to add others as fillers: 'I Remember You' by Frank Ifield, and the brilliant Dutch prog' rock rhyming song 'Hocus Pocus' by Focus.

As an example, for the comedy and Christmas lists, I scribbled down the songs that came naturally to mind, the ones I definitely wanted to include, before even looking into the vaults. Each list had about thirty tracks—which grew. I then spent hours agonising over each choice, imagining a *Desert Island Discs* scenario where I'm forced to make a short list for a radio programme.

However, when it comes to Elvis, it simply isn't possible for me to name his top ten songs. I could have cheated and done my top-ten Elvis albums or movies, but even that would have been difficult and against the spirit of the exercise.

The reality, of course, is that, to the reader, it doesn't really matter. Whatever goes down becomes unquestionable fact, and the lists are only evidence of my personal opinion, anyway. So what if I list 'Old Shep' or 'Blue Suede Shoes' and they're not my real favourites? But it does matter to me because if, in one of my fantasy interviews, I was asked about the songs on my lists, I would want to talk about them honestly and passionately. If I couldn't do that, then, in some way, I would be cheating myself *and* the reader. That said, it does take a bloody long time to do it properly.

There's an episode of *Star Trek* I remember, one of the proper ones with William Shatner as Captain Kirk, where something takes over the computer that runs the *Enterprise*. Eventually, Spock gives it a maths equation to solve. The problem is so hard—impossible, in fact—that the computer goes mad and eventually destroys itself (or leaves).

That's how I felt when faced with this task. So, in the interest of not driving myself insane, I've gone for providing a top-ten lists of songs written about Elvis instead. This was marginally easier, although I still started with twenty before I thinned the herd.

The Elvis legend and corporation live on in many guises. One of these is a great Elvis impersonator, Jim 'the King' Brown, who has covered some more contemporary songs under the title *Songs that Elvis Should Have Done*.

Many of these can be viewed on YouTube. Some of his songs, such as 'Sweet Home Alabama', are definitely worth a look, but the best (in my opinion) is AC/DC's 'Whole Lotta Rosie', which shows Jim Brown singing in sync with footage of Elvis in concert. Fabulous.

Long live the King.

Peter Gilbert

My Top Ten Songs Inspired by 'The King'

'Real Good-Looking Boy'—The Who
'Elvis Isn't Dead'—Scouting for Girls
'There's a Guy Works Down the Chip Shop Swears He's Elvis'—Kirsty MacColl
'Calling Elvis'—Dire Straits
'Advertising Space'—Robbie Williams
'King Rocker'—Generation X
'Singing with the Angels'—Suzi Quatro
'A Century of Elvis'—Belle and Sebastian
'Walking in Memphis'—Mark Cohn
'King of the Mountain'—Kate Bush

Things to Check Out

On YouTube:

- 'Are You Lonesome Tonight?'—Elvis Presley (laughing version)
- 'Heartbreak Hotel' (1968)—Elvis Presley (hilarious performance)

Elsewhere:
www.myoldmansabusman.com

Getting Ahead in the Movies

I'm sure that most of us have been told, at some point in our lives that we look like somebody famous. I'm no stranger to this. I've been told on more than one occasion that I look like Martin Clunes. Once, in a club in Cheltenham, someone said, 'You look just like the bloke with the ears off the telly.'

Others remark on my face's resemblance to Clunes's sometimes vacant expression. Most recently, though, people (including my girlfriend, niece, and sister) have said that I look like Greg Davies. While I have to admit that I can see a slight resemblance when I look at certain pictures of him, apparently it's the mannerisms we use and the way we speak that are very similar.

People have pointed this out to me more frequently as Greg has become more famous. I guess that I'm going to have to put up with it, accept that there is an element of truth to it, and learn to take it as a positive. It could be a lot worse. As a child who had buck teeth, people were previously more likely to say that I looked like Bugs Bunny.

For those who are not familiar with Greg, he is a comedy actor who does stand-up and appears in comedy shows such as *Cuckoo* and *Man Down*, but he is probably most famous for his role as Mr Gilbert (the headmaster) in *The Inbetweeners*. That's two Gilberts mentioned so far in this book, not counting my relatives. The first mention appears in the 'Scary Quo' chapter.

Greg is 6'8" and was once described by his friend and fellow comedian Rhod Gilbert (no relation—and he does not count as a third Mr Gilbert, as he is not pertinent to the story) as looking like Rik Mayall in a fairground mirror, which he does. And which is probably why Rik plays Greg's character's dad in *Man Down*. Pity for me, then, that the show's producers weren't looking for somebody to play his somewhat shorter brother.

Until the day arrives when I am cast in a TV role, maybe in time for the next series, my claims to fame in the world of performance are somewhat limited.

I was a member of the local church choir. As this was in the '70s (i.e. whilst I was at secondary school), it was off the scale in terms of being uncool. Anyone who found out simply regarded me as a tosser, making my attempt to be popular with the girls a futile one, unless they were in the choir, too.

What was I thinking?

Whilst we did some non-choiry things, such as putting on productions of the popular Bible-based musicals *Joseph and the Amazing Technicolor Dream Coat* and *Jesus Christ Superstar,* they did not help my cause when, despite my best efforts to cover my tracks, my classmates eventually found out.

'Singing in a frock tonight, are you?'

'Singing with the gay boys' brigade, are you?'

Even my girlfriend—who, over thirty years later, has heard me merely refer to this period of my life—teases me for 'liking a good musical'.

But, of course, we did have to do proper choir things, like sing in church on Sunday and sing at weddings and special events, all of which required dressing in a full 'gay boy' robe.

Looking back through a different lens, I think that the highlight for me was singing in Winchester Cathedral. At that time, I was head chorister and had been nominated to sing a solo version of 'Over the Wings of a Dove'. I don't think it was a brilliant performance. I was no threat to Aled Jones, but Mum was proud. She has embarrassed me by mentioning this fact to a number of my girlfriends over the years. I'm sure she still has a copy of the song on cassette somewhere, saving it for at least one more toe-curling outing.

The details of the Winchester Cathedral event are unforgettable, but the day is burnt in my memory for another reason. It was May 1976. Southampton, against all odds, had beaten Manchester United 1–0 in the Cup final. Unfortunately, because of the Winchester 'gig', I was on a coach at the time and was only to hear the commentary on the radio.

Around the same time, I had formed a band consisting of my sister, Mark from over the road, Lesley from down the road, and me. We were all members of the choir but were desperately trying to eliminate the uncool connotations that came along with it. Perhaps we had also been influenced by the 1976 glam rock music extravaganza *Never Too Young to Rock,* which featured Mud, the Rubettes, and the Glitterband—all chart-filling bands of the day. But the film is truly dreadful, I learned when I looked at it again all these years on.

Given that we could all sing a bit, you may be wondering why this book isn't about how we rose to fame, married each other (Lesley and I, obviously), split up, took drugs, partied hard, had various celebrity partners, re-formed on a wave of nostalgia, and enjoyed minor chart success four decades later with a greatest-hits release—especially since you know that we actually did play a 'gig'. We worked hard and practised all summer for it, too.

I, obviously aspiring to be the songwriter (long before realising that this was the most lucrative role in the band), penned the 'famous' song 'Rockin' Man', which I would perform.

Thankfully, no recordings of this song exist. But if you had had the misfortune of hearing it, I'm sure that you would have recognised it as vaguely familiar, given that it was heavily influenced by (some would say 'plagiarised') Elvis's 'Blue Suede Shoes'.

'You rock like this, you rock like that, you kick your heels, and then you jump back. I'm the rockin' man . . . Oooh! I'm the rockin' man . . .' Thankfully, I can't remember any more.

So, with a potential number-one single under our belts, our band just needed a few more songs. I can't remember any other tunes from the set list, except for 'Billy, Don't Be a Hero' by Paper Lace, which we included for a couple of reasons, as follows:

- I had the single (B4 in my collection) and therefore knew the words.
- Lesley, who had a great voice, was good at the song's female interlude, 'Come back and make me your wife.' However, when it came to the big day, Lesley was on holiday, and so my sister sang it instead. Our group performed as a trio.

On the big day, we had a venue, an audience, a rider, and instruments—but the O2 it wasn't.

Venue

Mark's garage, with some bunting strung around and with ladders and so forth moved to the back and sides to make some room for the three stools.

Audience

Mark's mum and dad, who obviously thought that this was the start of something big, and my mum and Auntie Marjorie from over the road.

Rider

A packet of crisps and a can of Coke each, provided by Auntie Marjorie.

Last, here are the details of the band, whose name has unfortunately been lost to the mists of time.

Lead vocals: Yours truly, complete with a stool to perch on and a skipping-rope handle to serve as a microphone (I didn't need a real one in a single-car garage).

Guitar and backing vocals: My sister, Netty. She couldn't play guitar at the time, so she simply strummed randomly away on a cheap practise guitar of Mark's. Netty has since taken lessons and plays the bass.

Backing vocals and tambourine: Lesley. However, and unfortunately, we had neither Lesley nor her tambourine on the big day.

Drums: Mark. I say that he played drums, but he didn't actually own any. Instead, he used an array of washing-up bowls and pans, plus wooden spoons for drumsticks, like a three-year-old would do—although Mark split them all, playing like Keith Moon.

All these things considered, we sure did entertain people.

Despite the band's obvious failings on the big day, I still blame Lesley for our lack of success and fame. If she'd have made that gig, then our band might have rewritten pop history.

I also performed in a school production of the play *Alice,* a hybrid of the C.S. Lewis books *Through the Looking Glass* and *Alice in Wonderland.*

As I had only been one of the backing singers in the choir productions a main part still eluded me. I had played various chorus, crowd, and extra parts, including a photographer and one section of the Jabberwocky's body. While the latter may sound exciting, nobody could see me, as I was underneath a costume very similar to a Chinese dragon.

I appeared in a school production of the play *Noah* as a character known as 'the common man'. Whilst I actually got a review in the local paper, I've been back through the Old Testament a few times since then and cannot find one mention of that particular character in the story. I'm not sure whether it is because my character was apparently dreamed up or because he dies at the end of act one in the play that I halted my acting 'career' at such an early point.

This performance nearly didn't happen, as the teachers were in the middle of an industrial action and all extracurricular activities had been cancelled. The local paper, the *Totton Times (a now defunct publication)* ran a piece about it.

> Noah Braves the Flood
>
> The Hampshire Education Authority's severe restrictions on the use of schools for evening activities struck a hard blow at the groups of children and staff who had given up so much of their spare time rehearsing plays and musical performances for the winter season.
>
> Many shows were stopped dead in mid-rehearsal time. Very few, due to the advanced stage of preparation they were in, with regard to rehearsals, costume making, and scenery building, were granted some small respite from the Authority axe.

> So it was that 'this winter of our discontent' was made, for just one evening, glorious at Noadswood Comprehensive School by a performance of *Noah*.

What a start! The paper was on our side and had quoted Shakespeare in the review. So, what about the performance itself?

> The obvious enthusiasm of the cast, unleashed from the official constraints, conveyed itself to the audience who enjoyed the show immensely. Sets were simple, but were complimented by often ingenious costumes and appropriate lighting and sound effects which were impressive.

And the actors—more specifically, me?

> 'The first drops of the coming flood were to strike down the common man, presented with considerable savagery and conviction by Peter Gilbert. The drama of his going was the highlight of the production . . .'

In hindsight, it was probably a good move when I exited my stage career after receiving that review.

After all of the cast's hard work, we only got to do one performance—and that was marred by administrative errors. The *Totton Times* had misspelt the name of the girl playing Selia, and so Julie went in as Judy. Plus, the school secretary, who was responsible for the programme, typed my name incorrectly, so it went down in school, publishing, and acting history that 'the common man' was played by Pater Gilbert.

My 'momentous' achievements, however, pale when compared to my appearance in a 1979 film—one that, at the time of writing, can still be purchased on Amazon.com. Called *Follow You Follow Me*, the film is also listed on IMDb.com, described thusly.

> *Follow You Follow Me* is a British (rather) short film (35 minutes) from 1979. It's a story about two schoolboys (teenagers) that despite coming from different socioeconomic circumstances are best mates. Joseph is the shy boy of the

owner of a factory and Peter is the self-confident and outgoing son of the common factory worker.

Their friendship is in danger as there's an upcoming conflict at the factory involving their fathers, who both sees the boys reflecting the other part, and not wanting them to see each other anymore. I don't think that's very uncommon, that parents want to choose the friends of their children, not realising that they have their own personalities and preferences.

This is a rather realistically made film where I think you both get a realistic view of life in England at the time, and a good story without any real twists. It's just a plain story about friendship between two teenage boys, no more, no less.

A friend from school and choir, Francis, who was known as Franny, had been cast in one of the lead roles by a producer friend of his family. Kids from our school and youth club were used as extras in a variety of scenes, including a fight scene and a scene set in a disco. The fight scene was filmed on a Saturday outside of our school, although the crew could have saved themselves the trouble by turning up most school days and filming the scuffles that took place outside of the school gates at home time.

The disco scene, filmed in our youth club hall, was my first experience with the reality being different from what one sees on-screen. I refer to this as a Nutsey Beach moment.

On the River Test, which runs from Basingstoke to the head of Southampton Water in Hampshire, is a bend in the river, near Totton, which has a shingle bank known locally as Nutsey Beach. Local kids go there to paddle, rope swing, throw stones, meet up, and generally lark about.

My friend Richard ('Dickie') had told me about the place. As a kid, he had regularly played there with his mates. For me, regarding Nutsey Beach, Dickie had conjured up romantic images of *Swallows and Amazons* meets *The Lost Boys,* describing *Peter Pan*–style adventures played out on sweeping sands and wide turbulent waters—always, of course, under summer's blazing sun and brilliant blue skies.

Dickie and I did not meet until we were in our twenties, but we instantly hit it off, given our joint passion for old TV shows and music. We would often lose hours talking, over a few pints of real ale, about *Casey Jones, The Flashing Blade, Catweazle,* and *White Horses*—and debating the 'ultimate' soundtrack for whatever topic or era we'd decided to discuss that day.

Dickie, to whom I am eternally grateful, also encouraged me to cultivate an appreciation for a wider range of music. I'm not sure why, but he was an avid collector of classical CDs. Whilst we were much more likely to be hunting out and playing the more unusual 'In the Year 2525' by Zaeger and Evans, 'Creeque Alley' by the Mamas and the Papas, or 'Casual Conversations' by the Eagles, occasionally he would slip some Vivaldi or Bach into the mix—their more popular or recognisable compositions that had been used in TV ads. I slowly began to appreciate how these could sit alongside other songs I loved. More important, they could add another dimension to a playlist or mix tape.

Many years later, not having yet experienced it, I went to see this magical, mythical place, Nutsey Beach, for myself.

Admittedly, it didn't help that it wasn't 'flaming June'. It was March: dull, cloudy, and a bit chilly. Also, I wasn't a kid. I was an adult, but I still had visions of coming across an exotic Ganges River Delta–type vista.

Having walked through the woods and across the field, I saw the 'mighty' river, which was barely a few feet across and had sloping, muddy banks covered in reeds and weeds.

It took quite a while of wandering along the banks for me to realise which bit was the famous beach I'd heard so much about. It turned out to be nothing more than a bend in the river, where the stones that were carried along the bottom collected and left an area just about big enough for two people to stand on.

What an absolute disappointment. From that day on, I have categorised anything that turned out not to be what it was built it up to be, either in reality or in the mind, as a Nutsey Beach. Examples include the following:

- Any of the last three *Star Wars* films, but most definitely the long-awaited number four, by which I mean *Episode I: The Phantom*

Menace. The potential disappointment one may experience when viewing this movie is brilliantly captured in the 2009 film *Fanboys*.
- The film *Return to Waterloo,* written and directed by Ray Davies, whom I think is a songwriting genius. Consider the lyrics to his 'The Village Green Preservation Society', which includes references to 'the Custard Pie Appreciation Consortium', 'virginity' and 'strawberry jam'. I could go on. Shangri-La.
When I heard that Davies had written and directed a film, I ordered it straight away and couldn't wait for it to arrive. I was so looking forward to seeing it. A musical film written by Ray Davies: what could possibly go wrong? It arrived. I watched it within minutes. It was awful.
- Tizer. I hadn't drunk it for nearly thirty years. Once I tried it again, I found out that they'd changed the formula (and probably taken out all of the bad things that had once made it taste good).
- Finding out that Whistling Jack Smith—or, more precisely, the guy who 'performed' under that name on *Top of the Pops*—neither whistled on the track or was really Jack Smith.
- The member of Boney M who appeared to be singing but did not actually sing the songs.
- *The Coral* by the Coral from 2002 and Ted Nugent's *Cat Scratch Fever* from 1977. These are two albums I had bought for one standout track and with the hope that the others (or, at least, some of them) would be as high quality as the title track or the singles. Unfortunately, both of these fell woefully short and are therefore categorised as Nutsey Beach albums.
- Marmaris, Turkey. In 1982, it was beautiful fishing village featuring a harbour, islands in the bay, and a few bed and breakfasts. They were thinking of building a hotel. Having seen it in a brochure recently, a mass of hotels, I'm going to campaign to have it renamed. I'm told that it even has 'a strip'. I'm also told that a trip to Hawaii would probably also be equally disappointing.

So, having turned up at the youth club to take part in the film's disco scene, I had no idea at the time that in films, the music has to be added at the editing stage and is not played at the time. I had thought that I'd turn up and simply lark around and chat to girls whilst dancing to some loud music, but actually, the cast spent the morning rehearsing by dancing and chatting to loud music and then spent the rest of the day acting, dancing, and pretending to chat . . . in silence.

I don't think that those of us there danced to the title track, 'Follow You, Follow Me', by Genesis. Looking back at the film, I think that the production crew must have used most of its budget on securing the rights to use that song.

With the heyday of the glam era truly over, the late '70s charts were a smorgasbord of punk, disco, glam hangover, early new wave, hits from the movie *Grease,* and the odd novelty song. We were probably pretending to dance to the likes of Hot Chocolate, ABBA, Kate Bush, Gary Numan, Blondie, Donna Summer, *Grease* hits, and Brian and Michael (although 'Matchstalk Men and Matchstalk Cats and Dogs' is not that easy to dance to, even when you can hear it).

Franny is well versed in this sort of thing now. Instead of pursuing an acting career, he became a successful TV production manager with a string of high-profile programmes to his name, including *That Mitchell and Webb Look, Jam and Jerusalem, Little Britain, The Thick of It, Absolutely Fabulous, French and Saunders, Whites,* and, more recently, *The Only Way Is Wessex.* In *Follow You Follow Me,* he played Joseph, the wimpy, posh character whose father owns the factory. At the beginning of the story, his character is best friends with Peter, the working-class, leather-jacketed, cool, tough, confident, gets-the-girl, Fonzie-like dude—who was nothing like this Peter at the time . . . or since.

The role of Peter was played by a proper drama-school child actor, Stephen Bratt. In an example of life imitating art, my namesake did get the girl: mine.

At that time, I had somehow managed to get myself a girlfriend (probably as she went to a different school). She had managed to get herself noticed at the castings and was chosen to play a girl that Peter gets off with. This included a scene where the two had to snog outside of the disco. As if that wasn't humiliating enough, I was an extra in the scene and so had to stand around and watch take after take.

Stephen Bratt must have been a better kisser than I. Or, maybe the fact that he was an actor who was playing a tough guy was the reason why my girlfriend found him more attractive than me, a choirboy who was driven around in a family DAF car.

I've focussed on improving my snogging technique since then. I must have been successful, as no girlfriend since has, to my knowledge, left me to get off with an actor.

I have no idea, given the role that he played, how Franny became the poster boy for the film. Maybe it was his angelic choirboy look. Whatever the case may be, there he is adorning the cover of the video/DVD and all other images promoting this 'epic' (thirty-five-minute) film.

Jealously is an ugly word. Whilst all of this did happen a very long time ago, it would fair to say that I was not overly upset to see Franny's image being used instead of Stephen's, the supposed star. Nor was I upset to find, in Stephen Bratt's IMDb filmography, that *Follow You Follow Me* was the last thing he was credited for.

Before *Follow You Follow Me*, Bratt's credits include an episode of *All Creatures Great and Small* in 1978 and *Play for Today* in 1979. I begrudgingly agree not to scoff at this last one as this TV series launched many of today's great actors' careers, including Anthony Hopkins, Ben Kingsley, Helen Mirren, Julie Walters, Ian McKellern, and Emily Dean (who played Amy Redman in a 1978 *Play for Today*) of 1981's *Day of the Triffids* TV series fame (where she played the part of young Susan). Dean is also co-host of *Frank Skinner's Absolute Radio Show*, deputy editor of *In Style* magazine, and a podcast presenter.

So, Stephen didn't get the career. Nor did he get the girl—well, not for longer than a week, as I won her back. I say 'won'. When Bratt left to go back to drama school, my girlfriend took me back after her 'celebrity' fling with him. It didn't last between us, though. It couldn't have, as things just weren't the same after she had dumped me for Bratt.

You will not find my name in the credits of *Follow you Follow me*, as, yet again I was a lowly extra (unless my IMDb application to be credited as 'schoolboy', alongside Michelle Packer and Francesca Beckerleg's credits for 'Girl', has been accepted and implemented) and many of the scenes in which I appeared had been cut from the final edit.

The back of my sister, Netty's head survived the disco scene. In it, her '70s hairdo appears in full cinematic glory. Thankfully, the footage of me

Peter Gilbert

in this scene had been cut. I have tried working on my dancing technique (as well as my kissing) since then, but I haven't had as much success.

My big part, one that was not in the original script, was to skim stones into the sea at a local beach with Franny and Mark (from the band). I think it was going to be used at the beginning of the film to show Joseph's character as happy and enjoying time with school friends, as a juxtaposition to the troubles that would soon follow. However, this scene was also cut, probably since none of us could skim more than two or three bounces. I imagine that the footage wasn't very good and the three of us had exaggerated a little in an effort to get more celluloid time.

I'm better now at skimming stones, although I'm not up to Olympics standards like the people I see effortlessly skimming ten-plus bounces that seem to go on forever towards the horizon. If I had been able to do that, it would have gotten me in the opening shot or the closing credits, whether from behind or in silhouette.

I don't know if skimming stones is exclusively a British thing, but, if so, we should lobby the Olympic Committee to include it as a sport, as the Olympics already permits events that may or may not be sports. Most of these fail to gain people's general interest. Others seem to have been included as a favour to certain nations.

While we're at it, we should probably try to get the following included in the Olympics:

- Throwing pebbles at drinks cans on the beach or on a post—from a seated position . . . and with a fag on
- Flipping beer mats off the bar and catching them in ever-increasing numbers
- 'Snatching' twenty-pence pieces off one's upturned elbow in ever-increasing numbers
- If you're a child of the '70s, space-hopper racing

That said, we could simply combine the Olympics with the classic '70s TV game show *It's a Knockout* and have competitors in giant foam costumes trying to carry buckets of water up grease-filled slides and onto revolving platforms. This would be much more entertaining than dressage and synchronised swimming.

If you watch the 8.21-minute abridged clip of *Follow You Follow Me* on YouTube, which I recommend over purchasing the full-length version, then you will see half of a person's face, mine, appear for a split second to the right of Joseph's bullying aggressor. This occurs for three seconds at exactly one minute and thirty seconds into the clip. Watching that film again now is a window into my adolescence, my youth captured on celluloid, as it was all filmed in and around Hythe. The house used for Joseph's family home was my girlfriend's house. The cross-country race was filmed on a New Forest path near the school where we were regularly forced to submit to an acceptable form of child torture in winter's sub-zero temperatures. Seeing the school and youth club brings back memories of that week's filming and my many happy years growing up there.

That said, despite the fact that *Follow You Follow Me* was made two years later than *Star Wars,* it's no *Star Wars.*

Peter Gilbert

My Top Ten Movie Songs

'Sweet Home Chicago'—Jake and Elwood Blues (John Belushi and Dan Aykroyd) (*The Blues Brothers*)
'I Wanna Be Like You'—Lois Prima and Phil Harris (*The Jungle Book*)
'Time Warp'—Richard O'Brien (*The Rocky Horror Picture Show*)
'Try a Little Tenderness'—Andrew Strong (*The Commitments*)
'Please, Mr Jailer'—Rachel Sweet, featuring Johnny Depp (*Cry-Baby*)
'You Never Can Tell'—Chuck Berry (*Pulp Fiction*)
'Bang (My Baby Shot Me Down)'—Nancy Sinatra (*Kill Bill*)
'Dueling Banjos'—Eric Weissberg and Steve Mandel (*Deliverance*)
'Old Time Rock and Roll'—Bob Seger and the Silver Bullet Band (*Risky Business*)
'Banana Splits'—The Dickies (*Kick-Ass*)

Things to Check Out

On YouTube:

- Sophos Red Nose Day Space Hopper Race
- *Follow You Follow Me* film, 1979

Elsewhere:
www.myoldmansabusman.com

Nearly Shipwrecked

I spent my first two years of the 1980s 'studying' A-levels at a sixth form college in Totton, Hampshire. Pursuing women, alcohol, nights out, beach parties, and socialising took a toll on my final results. After that, university was not a viable option for me.

The college in Totton was standalone, unattached to a school and as such a hybrid of the two. Whilst the dress code was relaxed; basically we could wear what we wanted, students had to attend the college for the full day, not just when we had lessons. This often led me to bunk or skive off, as I had quite a lot of free time. On Wednesday afternoons, which were designated for sports, I and my mates often skipped college after lunch and travelled into Southampton to the cinema. My physical education report card for my first year at college simply read 'elusive', although I maintain that my wider education was enhanced by the watching such '80s classics as *The Blues Brothers, Smokey and the Bandit, Any Which Way You Can, Stripes, Porky's, The Cannonball Run,* and *Breaking Glass*.

When not in lessons, we students were very tribal. The student population could be divided into four distinct groups, each inhabiting a specific area of the college, mostly within the assigned student block.

- The swots, whose habitat was the main building's library. Rarely were swots found in the student block.
- The heavy-metallers, who were easy to spot with their long, greasy hair and in their black Saxon or AC/DC T-shirts. These people were often found in the downstairs rec room that housed the Space Invaders machine.
- The smokers (to my shame, I was among this group), who were found in the absolutely disgusting smoking room which housed a

couple of benches, a few plastic chairs, and an old grey carpet that was hardly recognisable, given the thousands of fag burns it had accumulated over the years (we rarely used ashtrays).
- Everybody else, who mainly hung out in the canteen.

The areas and groups were very distinct. But, because every group included some part-time smokers, my group was the most transient. The smoking room was small, designed only for the occasional visitor, but it would be standing-room-only and completely fogged at mid-morning break.

Because we were students and were therefore not always in a position to buy a full packet of cigarettes, we played out various scenarios at any one given time. If a person was lucky, or feeling flush, then he or she would be smoking a favourite cigarette or the brand in vogue at the time, probably Marlboro or Marlboro Lights. If a person wasn't so lucky, then he or she smoked whatever was affordable, which probably was not Marlboro, as they were a bit pricey. Still unluckier people bought a single fag from somebody else when they didn't have the money to buy their own pack. People who didn't have enough money for their own pack but who did have enough to buy more than one cigarette from somebody else would club together and get a whole packet to share with the group. This was called the communal pack.

Some people managed to 'bum' a fag off a mate for free (or with a promise to repay at another time). Sometimes, somebody brought a packet of Sobranie Cocktail cigarettes back from holiday. These were very rare and were branded as 'girlie fags', but one never turned down a free smoke if somebody else was feeling flush and dishing them out.

Lyrics from 'It Must Be Love' by Little Man Tate brilliantly sums up smoker culture: 'Don't get me wrong. You weren't the first girl that I ever kissed with tongues. But you were the best. You let me touch your chest coz I saved you twos on my last cigarette.'

I reinvented myself at college, neither radically nor consciously, but somehow I became a different mix of people. I had slightly longer hair, wore jeans and cowboy boots, was developing a sense of humour (if not musical taste), and was suddenly and surprisingly no longer 'a tosser'. Even more surprising, I received attention from girls, even from some who had been previous schoolmates.

During that period, I hung out with like-minded, floppy-haired, new romantic types and listened to the sounds of bands such as A Flock of Seagulls, Japan, the Associates, and Depeche Mode. I also penned some prose and poetry. At the time, I thought my writings amazing and fit for publication. In hindsight, I see them as expressions of typical teen angst, or, more accurately, as up-oneself drivel—worse than the Elvis piece I had written.

Here is an example:

> Unanswered Questions
>
> She sits there, listening, concentrating.
> What thoughts are going through her agèd mind?
> Nobody knows, and, if nobody asks, nobody ever will.
> Dark, secret thoughts?
> Happy, joyful thoughts?
> Thoughts of the future, thoughts of the past?
> Imaginative, silly?
> Cruel or kind?
> Nobody knows, and, if nobody asks, nobody ever will.
> She stops, looks.
> Thoughtfully, she rises and then leaves, never to be seen again.
> What was she thinking as she left?
> Nobody knows, and, if nobody asks, nobody ever will.

I can't remember what made me write this, although I'm sure that it wasn't a deep and meaningful concern about young people's lack of respect for what the elderly have to offer. I was more interested in writing what amounts to short, punctuated prose and being creative with punctuation. Then somehow, somewhere, it becomes a poem and is deeper, more meaningful.

But, then again, if nobody ever asks . . .

I don't think I'll ask anyone who is educated to appraise this poem (although I'm quite impressed with my younger self for using the *è* in *agèd*). The 23 per cent I received on my French exam is a bad enough record of my academic failure. That said, at least two academic doctors will read this book whether it is published or not. One of those people is my good friend Karen Savage. Her brilliant moniker is therefore, Doc Savage.

Having left college with some GCSE A-levels but with no real career plan or desire to continue my education, I took an opportunity to work as a crewman on a boat based in Marmaris, Turkey—one that made private-hire trips for tourists around the Turkish coast and over to Rhodes in the Greek islands.

I'd done some sailing around the Solent and on Southampton Water whilst living in Hythe and knew that my sea legs were okay, having frequently 'survived' force-eight winds and rough seas in a small yacht.

Being a crewman was a great life experience for the six months it lasted. I met so many varied and interesting people, as boat life tends to be very cosmopolitan, with crews, partners, and hangers-on from a variety of nations all socialising together.

It also presented a great opportunity to people-watch, although, unfortunately, when I do this for concentrated or protracted periods of time, I do apply gender or national stereotypes, even when the people are out of their natural habitats.

On the boat, I noted that Scots, especially those from the east coast, tended to be dour. I think that this is partly due to the weather, but apparently it's deeper than that. In Scotland, there's a phrase that sums it up: 'You'll have more fun at a west coast [of Scotland] funeral than at an east coast wedding.'

I know quite a few Scots, Yanks, and Italians—and, of course, some of them do buck the trends I'm about to note. If you observe people enough, you will recognise some of these stereotypes.

- Turks are friendly; Greeks, arrogant.
- Italians are stylish; Germans, organised.
- Americans are loud.
- The French are creative in the kitchen.
- Scandinavian women are blonde, cute, and fun to be around.

Some women aren't very good at reading maps. My girlfriend will object to this, as she is actually a very good map reader, but she is an exception. It's incredible, really, as you can put women in an unfamiliar department store and they'll find the soft furnishings or lingerie department in about thirty seconds without looking at a store guide or asking anyone for directions. But give them a map . . .

Girls don't play much on the beach or in the pool. Give a group of lads a ball, an inflatable, pebbles, and a drinks can, and that's three days of games and competition sorted. But when was the last time you witnessed any of the following?

- A group of girls skimming stones in the sea or on a lake or pond
- A group of girls breaking out the netball on the beach and passing it around for half an hour before eventually rigging up a makeshift goal
- A group of girls using the upturned inflatable as a goal, with one of the group defending it as though her life depended on it
- Bored girls spending an hour throwing pebbles at an empty drinks can to see who can hit it the most times or, better still, knock it over

The best example of stereotypical behaviour I saw was when I was on holiday in Menorca. The resort I was staying in was frequented by Brits, Scandinavians, and Germans. As creatures of habit, everyone had their favourite spots around the pool. After a few days, I was used to seeing the same people and observing their routines, habits, and dress sense.

Brits wore swim shorts. Scandinavians wore tight, fairly large swim trunks. One particular German man wore tiny, tight Speedos, or budgie smugglers, as they are sometimes called.

People who dress in entirely inappropriate clothing, not just swimwear, fascinate me. Either they think they look great or else, worse, their partners and loved ones endorsed their look. The budgie smugglers, any clothing item in luminous pink, matching clothes, or knitwear bearing images of wolves were, at some point, appraised in front of the mirror, a partner, or a friend and were given the thumbs-up.

As the German guy was given to strutting around the pool, pointing often at his kids and barking orders at them, the Brits gave him the unsurprising nickname Adolf. We exchanged knowing looks whenever he appeared.

There was a pool toy—a large, pump-action tube—for sale in the resort shop. It was a bit like a giant syringe in that it fiercely squirted water across quite a large distance. Seemingly, every kid at the resort had one. Kids love a weapon. This one was simple, fairly safe, and effective.

I and my resort-mates had had no discussion nor had made any collective agreement about this toy. But the kids who had them seemed to have so much fun. As the week went on, more and more of the toys appeared. At around 3.00 p.m. every day, unprompted and unarranged, a mass water fight broke out in the pool.

Maybe the particular day I'm thinking of now was hotter than the others, but, for some reason, more dads were in the pool. Perhaps our inner big kids had finally gotten the better of us. When the silent alarm went off at 3.00 and the water fight broke out, the dads joined in and, of course, took over.

At the start, it was every man for himself, with lots of shouting and gun and water jet noises, as well as kids shouting to their dads to give the toys back. But in less than a minute, a scenario began to play out.

Things were getting a bit rough, mainly because of the Brits. Most of the Scandinavian dads took themselves and their kids over to the side of the pool. Once this happened, the other dads started to form two distinct groups: the Brits and the Germans. Again, nothing had been said, but years of brainwashing and stereotyping had kicked in. We had weapons, and this was war.

As we advanced on each other, we Brits focussed our attention on 'Adolf', who had taken front and centre and clearly saw himself as the leader, pointing at and barking orders to his newly formed troops.

By the time the German and I were a few feet from each other, he was being ferociously bombarded by the jets of a dozen British 'weapons'. As he took a few hits square in the face, he ducked down below the water's surface to avoid the attack.

Not wanting to waste our ammo by firing at the water, we turned our attention to the rest of the German group, whom, up to that point, we had largely ignored. But now we were close enough for them to retaliate by blasting us in the face.

Suddenly, 'Adolf' popped up out of the water right in front of us and started blasting all of us with water, shouting, 'Die, Englanders, die!'

It was something straight out of a Hollywood war movie. We couldn't retaliate because we were laughing at him. What a twat!

To make matters worse for 'Adolf', as he turned back to his 'troops' for support, he found that they were already heading out of the pool. As he spun back around to face us, he saw that we were leaving, too. He was left standing in the middle of the pool, pretty much on his own, being watched by the mums. The kids, having retrieved their toys from their dads, were now advancing on 'Adolf', and so he sloped off to his 'bunker', probably muttering to himself, 'All Brits abroad are racist and uncouth, wearing football shirts as their evening attire and seeking out English pubs showing football on the TV.'

The water fight didn't become a daily event. It was just one of those 'of the moment' things, but it was great fun and reminded me that stereotypes may have some basis in fact.

As I recovered on my sunbed, it took me back to my days on the boat. Being part of the crew can be very tedious. While anchored in a bay for three days, sheltering from a storm, I read more books than any time before or since.

I also learned to play backgammon. I remember being 143 to 127 games down during one particularly long siege and literally dreaming of nothing but backgammon moves, as I had done little else but play the game for twelve hours solid.

Books are not readily available at sea, and English language books weren't readily available in non-tourist countries such as Turkey in the early '80s. Therefore, it was always a treat when I got to a new port or when new boats arrived, because I could swap books with other crewmen. I'd read pretty much every genre going: political thrillers, fantasy books, historical novels, detective stories, autobiographies, and even the odd Mills & Boon. Such was my desire to relieve the boredom at times.

Of course, it's not all socialising, playing games, reading, and scrubbing decks. The open sea also has its dangers. A couple of episodes from my time at sea will stay with me forever. Both happened early in the trip while we were sailing the boat from Malta, where I had joined it, to Turkey.

The first was during a night watch on the first leg of the journey from Malta to Crete. Crew members were doing solo shifts of four hours on and four hours off during the night. To relieve the boredom of pointing the boat in the right direction in the dark, we used pass the time by chatting to other boats' crews on the radio.

This particular night, a very heavy fog came down. While I was swapping jokes and chatting about favourite bands with a Swedish radio operator, who was on a cargo boat sailing out of Greece, all of a sudden—as in a ghost-ship story—a large fishing vessel appeared out of nowhere, sat seemingly yards in front of me, and disappeared back into the fog almost immediately.

I'm sure now that the vessel had not come as close as it may have seemed in the middle of the night in the fog, but it was big and tall and therefore seemed bloody close to me. I had to crane my neck to see the lights at the top of the cabin. That's close.

Apart from being in an aeroplane at forty thousand feet, trust me, nothing gets the adrenalin pumping more than a 'near miss' in the middle of the night, in the middle of the Mediterranean Sea, on deck . . . on your own.

Once I'd composed myself, I said farewell to the Swede and put a call out to try to contact the ship concerned. They answered almost immediately. It had transpired that they—I learned from the person speaking a combination of very limited French and English schoolboy vocabulary—had picked up our boat on their radar but had calculated that they would not hit us, given their current course. So, the ship had simply kept going. When I asked why they had not sounded their horn, at least, to alert our small ship of their presence, I heard raucous laughter over the radio.

'Were you scared, English?'

Very fucking funny.

The second incident occurred on the next leg of the journey, between Crete and Rhodes.

We used an on-board device called the LORAN-C to plot our course and then navigate by means of GPS signals. It was an old-fashioned satnav. A new addition to the boat in Malta, the LORAN-C was essential, given that we would be sailing in open sea and at night. However, like many males, the skipper didn't think it was necessary to read the thick manual that came along with the device. We'd use good old trial and error during

My Old Man's a Busman

some daytime sailing first, he determined. Sure enough, as with a new DVD player or TV, we got it worked out.

After one entered coordinates into the LORAN-C, it planned a course. As we sailed, it told us in which direction to steer to keep on course.

Refusing to read a TV manual may mean that a person spends a frustrating hour trying to programme the remote's first button with BBC One. Or, a person takes a few days to get the hang of using all the menus available on current TVs. But that's about it. A ship's navigational equipment should be taken a little more seriously.

We set sail for the day and night trip between Crete and Rhodes. This time, I had the second night-watch shift, which I preferred, as I'd get to see the sunrise, which was always stunning and genuinely awesome at sea. I use *awesome* correctly here, unlike my kids, who describe kicking a stone down the road in a straight line as 'awesome' or 'immense'.

Throughout the night, the LORAN-C kept indicating that I should steer south to keep on course. I found this odd because, usually, my sense of direction and ability to keep on course were pretty good. Still, every time I checked the screen, it showed that I should steer a little more south.

Having helped set the course, I knew that we'd be passing a large island to our right (starboard) sometime in the early morning. My eyes were peeled, trying to catch a first glimpse of its outline against the horizon. The sun began to rise, making the sky less jet black.

While I could see nothing to my right, I became aware of a large cloud bank looming up on my left. Over the next half hour or so, I could make out that it was large and close, which was odd because, weather-wise, it was relatively calm. Usually with clouds comes wind.

There was still no sight of the island to my right. As the first rays of the dawn's sun appeared over the horizon, it became clear to me why. To my left (port), perfectly silhouetted against the sky, was not a large cloud bank but a very large and very close island with a rocky outcrop. We were heading straight for it.

I'm not sure if the pink wispy strands in the sky that morning were high clouds silhouetted against the breaking dawn or, more spiritually, strands of Aunty Lily's pink-rinsed, candy-floss-like hair streaking across the sky as she looked out for me. Had the sun come up five minutes later, or, rather if we'd arrived five minutes earlier, then we would have sailed straight onto the rocks in the darkness, which would have been somewhat less than ideal.

So, having finally composed myself after the trauma and also suffering a sense of defeat similar to the one that men who finally have to refer to a map on a car journey (pre-satnav)—after having protested half a dozen times that they know where they are or after having said, 'It will be okay once we get to the next junction, as I'll know where I am'—suffer, I got out the LORAN-C manual.

It turned out that the device needed at least three GPS signals to give an accurate reading. When it did not have those three signals, then the LORAN-C showed a small indicator on its screen.

We went back to look on the screen that I'd been using for the past four hours.

'Oh yes, there it is,' the skipper said helpfully.

So, we'd been sailing through the night relying on a navigation device to keep us on course. The device had given inaccurate readings because it lacked a signal and therefore had been directing me to keep steering farther south, meaning that we ended up on the exactly wrong side of the island by morning.

In all situations, one should try to find a positive or, at least, a lesson. This incident provided me with both. Despite having nearly been dashed on the rocks in the early hours, I could at least console myself by realising that my instincts and sense of direction had indeed been correct. However, I learned that one should not always rely on technology. I'm sure that many satnav users and anyone connected with the Apollo 13 space mission would agree.

After all of this excitement, the trip ended and I returned home. I now needed a job. After all, Marlboro Lights wouldn't buy themselves. I'd had a great experience, one that I would not have traded for the world, but my college peers all had a six-month head start on me with regard to employment and earnings.

As luck would have it, Tom had a vacancy in his office at the National Bus Company in Eastleigh, Hampshire. And so my family's association with buses continued.

'Hold very tight, please . . . ding, ding.'

My Old Man's a Busman

Whilst I'm eternal grateful for this start on the corporate ladder, the job was no glamour gig. I was not 'master of the road' but more fourth assistant in the office, more lowly than I would be when, a few years later, I met Robbie Williams.

The job was very monotonous, but I was very eager and willing . . . and earning. I have much for which to thank Tom, but I thank him especially for giving me my first break into work that is difficult to get. I think that I repaid his faith with my hard work and a strong work ethic that has stayed with me since.

After a few months, I had saved enough money to start learning to drive and to be able to book a holiday with my girlfriend at the time. Life was looking good.

That first holiday was to what was then Yugoslavia but is now Croatia, a beautiful country with a stunning coastline. This was where I met the first of two people who had famous cousins.

My girlfriend and I went by coach from London to Croatia and back, an experience not to be repeated (I had returned from Turkey to London the previous year in the same way and should have learnt my lesson then). We camped for two weeks in the blazing heat, another experience never to be repeated.

The upside was that this was before the Euro and before the global depression, so, with the exchange rate at the time and with the campsite's giving an ever better rate if you spent money on-site, we ate and drank like kings and also had enough money left over to treat ourselves to a day trip to Venice, an experience that is definitely to be repeated.

Since we had gone on that holiday with another couple, we were fairly insular and self-sufficient on the coach ride there. We pretty much ignored everybody else on the first day. Setting off on the second day, we were delayed by the inevitable late arrival of two couples. They annoyed us, especially since they arrived on the coach waving, smiling, and offering insincere apologies and talk of the alarm's not going off.

As the coach was fairly full, these two couples sat in the seats in front of and behind the four of us. We chatted with them from our seats and were soon drawn in. From that morning until we arrived back in London two weeks later—and beyond—we were an inseparable group.

One of the couples, Mick and Lou from Sheffield, introduced me to the music of the B-52s. Mick was a massive fan and, as it turned out, the cousin of Glen Gregory from Heaven 17.

Heaven 17 were a Sheffield band who had a massive international hit with 'Temptation' in 1983. Subsequently, have regularly toured on the wave of '80s revival concerts. More latterly, the band appeared at festivals, such as the one at Glastonbury, to perform their original hits. In 2010, they made a tongue-in-cheek cameo appearance in a TV ad for a Sheffield-based broadband provider.

Coincidentally, my girlfriend is the biggest fan of the B-52s. She has been 'forever'. Because of this, she has trouble believing that I had not lost my B-52s' 'virginity' until 1982. Their signature track, 'Rock Lobster', had been released in 1979.

Born out of the post-punk era and arguably the creators of new wave, the B-52s had a sound that was, and still is, a unique mix of dance and surf music, but with quirky lyrics, often in their trademark call-and-response style. 'Wig', from the album *Bouncing Off the Satellites,* which was released in 1985, perfectly highlights this.

> What's that on your head?
> A wig.
> Wig, wig, wig.
> Fred's got a wig.
> Cindy's got a wig.

And so on. One Saturday not that long ago, having been putting it off for weeks, we performed the chore of weeding the front drive. We live in a small country cottage. The gravel drive to the front very quickly fills with weeds and grass and looks awful. We decided that the only way to get through this chore was to blast out some tunes at the same time.

As I bemoaned my lot, gathered the tools, and started to pry out the pesky weeds, the track '52 Girls' blasted out of the iPod speaker, followed by the rest of the B-52s' *Wild Planet* and *Bouncing Off the Satellites* albums on shuffle.

There are many worse ways to spend a couple of hours on a Saturday.

My Top Ten Songs about the Sea

'Sailing'—Rod Stewart
'Wipeout'—The Safaris
'Come Sail Away'—Eric Cartman (voiced by Trey Parker) of *South Park*
'Beyond the Sea'—Bobby Darin
'Seaside'—The Kooks
'The Ocean'—Led Zeppelin
'Yellow Submarine'—The Beatles
'Albatross'—Fleetwood Mac
'Blue Bayou'—Linda Ronstadt
'Seven Seas of Rye'—Queen

Things to Check Out

On YouTube:

- 'Rock Lobster' (official video)—The B-52s
- 'Temptation' (1983)—Heaven 17
- New Marlboro Man commercials

Elsewhere:
- www.myoldmansabusman.com

Hazel O'Connor Owes Me a Pint

After leaving college and having no real sense of purpose, other than to start earning some money, my early career jobs included stacking and filling at a supermarket, doing administrative work in the office of a bus company, performing administrative tasks in another office for a company that produced rubber (some of which was used in the production of condoms), and finally, before landing the job that would define my early career, enjoying the freedom of life on the open road as a rep, driving around the south of England and selling chocolates to small shops.

Because I was reasonably successful at this, the company had me sell chocolates to bigger shops—and then to even bigger shops and chains of shops. Ultimately, as often happens in a career, I found myself back in an office, this one the London head office of Terry's of York, which manufactured chocolates such as All Gold and Chocolate Orange.

Although pleased with her son's career to date—I work for a good company that produces nice products, and I earn a decent salary and have access to a company car—there was a price that Mum had to pay for my success, as I have always been brand-loyal to the companies I have worked for. This meant that on Mother's Day, for quite a few years, Mum had to forgo her beloved box of Black Magic chocolates and put up with a box of Terry's All Gold. Even though her face did light up—'See the face you love light up with Terry's All Gold,' as the advert goes—I don't think that I ever really converted my mum to Terry's, truly turning her away from 'the dark side'.

I still buy chocolate oranges today (as well as Pepsi-Cola, Nestlé cereals, and Microsoft products, as I subsequently worked for those companies, too, and they effectively paid my salary and kept me in a job).

This period also signalled the start of my work travels. Other than driving around the south of England in a car, which at that time consisted of journeys to and from the Terry's factory in York, later jobs would require me to make trips to other places in Europe and to the United States.

Before I travelled much, it always seemed very glamorous to stay in a hotel and not have to pay one's own way. Whilst travelling can be glamorous, spending three nights in a row in different hotels near to a motorway is not.

On more than one occasion, I've had to vacate my room in the middle of the night, in the rain and cold, for a false fire alarm—probably caused by somebody in a no-smoking room who was trying to sneak a crafty fag out of the window. On another trip, a Glaswegian hooker propositioned me in the early hours.

Now, whilst this may conjure up images of me, much worse for wear, staggering back to my hotel in Glasgow in the early hours, it actually happened at 6.00 in the morning as I was leaving the hotel, suited and booted with a suitcase in tow and heading for the bus stop to get to the airport for an early flight.

I'm not in the market for a prostitute in the first place, but certainly not at 6.00 a.m. on my way out, which I clearly was, and definitely not when the woman in question was probably on her way home after a night's 'work' and was looking for a quick last order. I can also assure you that she was no Julia Roberts in *Pretty Woman*.

I do have a confession to make about hotels. I'm a compulsive taker of the freebies, particularly coffee, tea, and the bathroom lotions and potions. I say 'compulsive'; my girlfriend says 'obsessive'—especially when I've been away for four nights and come back with armfuls of 'contraband' or when we're abroad on holiday and she catches me sneaking these things into my suitcase. She has now imposed a 'not when we're on holiday' rule.

I do, however, have a few points to make in my defence:

- I follow a strict code of conduct.
- I only ever take what is in the room. I consider these items bought and paid for (even if not by me personally). I have never stolen from the maids' trolley, although I will admit that doing this is

very tempting, especially when I come out of my room and there it is (the service trolley), all alone and unattended.
- I never take the sugar or milk. I cannot explain why I imposed this rule on myself, other than to say that I subconsciously think that the milk will go off, even though the long-life milk will probably outlive me. I also think that the sugar packs will burst and get into everything in my suitcase, even though the same thing could happen to the coffee sachets I take.
- I don't take the shower caps.
- I don't take (as much) from small, independently run hotels. The number of items that I take is based on the status of the hotel. Therefore, I take pretty much everything from a large chain, but only the odd item from an independently run establishment.

I donate all of the swag to a homeless drop-in centre near my house. Very grateful for it they are, too. I therefore consider myself not to be a thief or compulsive, but simply a modern-day Robin Hood.

I have stayed in hundreds of hotels, good and bad ones. There are always things that annoy me, however. One particular thing, above all others, drives me insane.

Yes, the current vogue practise not to provide a centre light can be a pain when I am trying to find my memory stick in the bottom of my bag. The dreary and bland artwork is lazy, depressing, and uninspiring. Charging guests for using the Internet in modern times is incredible. The perpetual absence of a knife and butter near the toaster can infuriate me. Yet, these are all forgivable. The inadequate amount of complimentary milk left in my room to make my tea and coffee with is not forgivable.

Of course, I can ask for more milk—and it is usually freely given. I can even ring down to reception and have milk bought up to my room. But who has unilaterally decided that a thimbleful of milk constitutes enough for one cup—or, worse, one mug—of tea?

I know how many cups of tea, coffee, or hot chocolate are in various packets and sachets offered by hotels because I generally take them all. But there is hardly enough milk provided to service one decent cup. It's not like the milk will go off anytime soon. Is hotel management worried that people will steal the milk?

Every day, millions of hotel rooms around the world are serviced by staff members who drink coffee and tea. I presume that sometimes these rooms are checked by supervisors, managers, hotel managers, and, on the odd occasion, hotel chain directors, whom I'm sure also stay in the rooms. So, it astounds me that not one person in this whole industry, apart from me, looks at that little bowl of packets and pots and thinks, *Hmm, not really enough milk there.*

At this particular time, which was in the early '90s, I had been promoted to Terry's head office in London, working in the sales department. A colleague, Chris, worked in the marketing department and was the brand manager for All Gold.

Being a brand manager meant that Chris was responsible for liaising with all of the agencies that came up with our products' packaging, promotions, advertising, etc. In light of this, I experienced a Nutsey Beach moment on my first day of working in the office.

Like many people, perhaps, I had envisaged that the people working in the marketing department would be all about drawing boards and coloured pens—creative types sitting around and designing stuff, surrounded by piles of rejected, crumpled-up pieces of paper.

I had no idea that they effectively read research and then wrote briefs for dozens of other agencies' employees to sit around, with their drawing boards, pens, and Apple Macs, designing stuff. What a let-down! When walking around the marketing department, all I saw was people sitting at their desks, typing, just like we did in my office.

Having worked closely together on a number of projects, Chris and I chatted fairly regularly. One Friday, whilst we were having a chat by the coffee machine, Chris told me that his team was having trouble with the latest All Gold advertising campaign. Our marketing director was unhappy with all of the music proposed by the agency.

I couldn't quite believe what I was hearing.

'So, our advertising agency, with all of their resources, can't find a song?' I asked.

'Nope. Not one that anyone is happy with, anyway.'

How could I resist? What a gift. It was as if Chris had thrown down his glove and challenged me to a duel.

'If I can come up with the music, will you get it heard?'

'But you haven't really got time, because the agency people are coming back again early next week.'

'But if I crack it over the weekend, will you get Alex [the marketing director] to listen to it?'

'Of course, but you won't get any recognition or payment if it gets used. We'll just give your ideas to the agency.'

'Okay, you're on.'

Payment didn't matter to me. I was simply convinced that I was able to come up with the right song or piece of music to use for the ad. That in itself would give me such a great feeling that it would be payment enough.

Secretly, though, deep down, a part of me couldn't help naively thinking that if I did crack it, somewhere along the line I would surely get a name check or at least some sort of recognition, even if only in some internal communication or newsletter.

By the end of the day, Chris had given me the VHS of the advert to take home. As we left the office, I said, 'I'll have it cracked for you by Monday morning, so set up a meeting with Alex.'

I jumped into the car, desperate to get home, my head already spinning with ideas, when a thought suddenly struck me. In my excitement, I'd forgotten that my brother and his girlfriend were coming to stay that weekend, which would seriously limit the time I would have to work on finding the right piece of music—unless, of course, I could get my brother excited about it, too.

My brother and I are close. All three of us siblings are. But, because my brother is seven years younger than I, we had not always been close. For the first few months and years of his life, he was the baby. Starting when he was the age of five, he was simply the annoying little brother who wanted to be around me a lot, whether I wanted him there or not. Then, he became a stroppy teenager. The big change occurred when we could finally legally go to the pub together as equals. Since that time, we've never looked back.

Throughout that time, there has been one constant: his nickname. Which is Joff. *Joff* is derived from my brother's christened name, Jonathan, and is much more than a nickname.

For as long as I can remember, everyone in our family has called my brother Joff. We still do to this day. I cannot remember ever having written

Jonathan on anything in connection with my brother. He has and always will be Uncle Joff to my kids, who, until fairly recently, did not know what his real name was.

When Joff left school, he followed Netty. *Netty* is a more simply explained derivative of my sister's christened name, which went from Janette to Nette to Netty. Joff's nickname followed him to his job working in a bank. His name badge there had 'Joff' printed on it. Now that he's a director, he does go by the name Jonathan at work. But to everybody else, including our parents, he has always been Joff.

As with all folklore, my family tells different versions of the story explaining how Joff got his nickname. One version, an incorrect one, has it that when our brother was born, my sister and I could not pronounce his name properly, as it was too long.

My mum relates this story, but, if she thought about it sensibly, she would remember that when Joff was born, Netty and I were age eight and seven respectively, meaning that we were quite capable of a reasonable level of speech, even pronouncing words with three syllables. We could say 'choc-o-late', 'Cur-ley Wur-ley' (that's four syllables), 'shoe-lace-es', and, therefore, 'Jon-a-than'.

The true story is that Netty and I, purely engaging in childish wordplay, would change the sounds of the syllables around, for example, from 'Jon-a-than' to 'Joth-a-nan' and then dropping our t's and h's to 'Jof-a-nan', which was then shortened to Jof. For reasons I cannot explain, the final spelling was J-O-F-F. All of this had happened over a fairly short period of time. It was just one of those things that stuck.

Despite his having been born seven years after I was, Joff also had the passion for music and a knack of learning song lyrics instilled into him at an early age. Therefore, once he arrived at our house for the weekend and was apprised of my situation at work, he became an eager and equally willing participant in the 'All Gold Ad' challenge.

He and I managed to talk of nothing else that evening or during our meal. The women, our respective partners, realised that they were not going to get any other conversation or holiday planning out of us, so they left us to it. At some point, they must have gone to bed.

Peter Gilbert

And so it came to pass that Joff and I were left with a VHS tape of the TV ad, a home video player, an alphabetically arranged CD collection, a cassette tape deck, a CD player, and three bottles of red wine.

I had seen the thirty-second advert once before I had left the office. On the way home, I already had an idea of what would work. Exactly. Before I left the office car park, I had rummaged around in the glove box to find a tape of Hazel O'Connor's music to play on the way home.

In the early '80s, the punk scene was fading into new wave, but heavy-metal and pop albums maintained a high level of sales. A chart featuring the top thirty albums might include such diverse artists and groups as Cliff Richard, Billy Joel, Barry Manilow, UB40, Michael Jackson, Diana Ross, Yes, AC/DC, Ian Gillan, Saxon, the Police, Siouxsie and the Banshees, Judas Priest, and—more obscure—Sky.

In among the artists of that early crossover was Hazel O'Connor, a peroxide-blonde, post-punk 'queen' who had a relatively short career and limited chart success but who left us with one of the all-time greatest ballads and a film, *Breaking Glass,* bizarrely co-produced by Dodi Fayed, which charted youth's unrest at the time in the way that the film *Quadrophenia* had done the year before (1979) but having been set in 1965.

The soundtrack to the film *Breaking Glass* is ever present in my car. My kids regularly request 'Give Me an Inch' and 'Blackman'. They sing along, completely unaware of the lyrics' meanings depicting the racial and political unrest from more than three decades before. To them, the songs are simply great tunes. My kids also love the lyrics in the track 'Eighth Day', as the song is about robots that have taken over Earth. The song's story reflects the fear of the rise in technological advancement. My kids, ironically, take this technology for granted as they listen to the song on their iPods or iPhones.

In my opinion, every track on that soundtrack is great. Many still sound fresh and relevant today. Therefore, this album, to me, is always a treat, especially when I get to listen to it all the way through. This despite that I had bought it for only two songs, 'Will You' and 'Eighth Day'. It is definitely not a Nutsey Beach album.

I wish I could say the same about every album in my collection, although *London Calling* by the Clash, *Night at the Opera* by Queen, and

My Old Man's a Busman

Meatloaf's *Bat Out of Hell* are all, when played end-to-end on a long car journey, a treat.

The storyline for the All Gold TV ad went roughly like this: A woman walks out of a pool of molten gold. She is golden, shimmering, and holding a box of All Gold. Above her, from a large container, gold explodes and rains down on her, making her even more golden and covered in gold. Feel free to insert your own golden shower jokes here. We did.

There's a part in the song 'Will You' where, during the instrumental break, it pauses. Next comes one heavy drumbeat, which is followed by several others. It is a bit like the music at the start of *EastEnders,* if you're familiar with the opening to that particular TV soap opera.

With no word of a lie, this song had popped into my head the first time I had seen the golden explosion on the tape in the office. So, with that creative idea in the bag, it should have been a five-minute job to pull it together with Joff—and then we would be off to the lounge to discuss holidays, cushions, candles, and shopping with the women.

However, apart from the possibility that Joff and I were trying to avoid the above scenario, three major factors turned our brainstorming session into an all-nighter.

1. We didn't have the sophisticated equipment that an advertising agency would have.
2. We felt that we should offer some alternatives.
3. ... bottles of wine to drink.

After rerecording 'Will You' onto a cassette tape, Joff and I spent hours practising synchronising the tape to the VHS by playing the advert and working out the exact moment to push the 'Play' button on the tape recorder in order to make the whole thing work. I had no CD player at the time, so I had to use this slightly antiquated equipment for my 'big reveal'.

That night, my brother and I also read through pretty much every CD in my collection, which was quite large, to find any likely candidate tracks to use as alternatives.

Creating a large 'possible' pile, we then played the relevant tracks, sometimes over and over again, in order to determine whether or not they could or would work.

Peter Gilbert

Finally, with our list reduced to a final five (having hit on that number purely because we were slightly drunk and I'm quite a fan of alliteration), we had to go through the process of recording the songs and then practising cueing them up correctly in time to the video, which, of course, became more difficult and took longer as we consumed yet another bottle of wine.

On the following Monday, I found myself in front of Chris (who had been true to his word) and his slightly cynical boss, who must have been wondering why he was watching someone from sales walk in with a portable tape recorder. This was my big moment.

'Okay, let's see what you've got,' Chris said.

Having agonised for hours on the running order, I'd set 'Will You' to play first, but despite all of my practise over the weekend, it didn't quite go according to plan, as the VHS machine in the office had a slightly longer delay than the one on my home player. The sync was slightly off.

I was mortified. After all of the effort and planning, I thought that I'd totally stuffed up when, at the key moment in the ad, the gold did not quite explode in time to the drumbeat, as I had meticulously planned.

Thankfully, Chris and his boss got the idea and nodded approvingly to each other. Having gone through the others, which luckily didn't rely on precision timing, they liked 'Will You' the best—enough, in fact, that they set up a meeting to play it to the advertising agency the next day. I couldn't believe it. I'd done it. We'd done it. Well, at least I had gotten it past Alex. I left that office on one of the biggest highs I remember, with thoughts of setting up in business as a finder of tracks for TV ads.

And that, just as Chris had predicted the week before, was the end of my involvement with the process. I wasn't even invited to the meeting with the agency.

Chris and his boss said that I'd done a good job and thanked me for my input. They did present my idea to the advertising agency, and my music choice was used for the advert shown on TV, including the explosion to the drumbeat, the very first idea that had instinctively popped into my head. But I was gutted.

Deep down, I really did want some sort of recognition. Who wouldn't? Also, the agency had cut and chopped the music to fit both the thirty-second version of the ad that I had seen and an alternative ten-second version, so the final product did not reflect my original vision 100 per cent. Also, given these edits, the agency could now take all of the credit for the finished ad—which, I'm sure, they would have done anyway.

That said, in both versions of the final ad, the drumbeat does come in on the golden shower scene. The use of this particular piece of music was subsequently the subject of an article about the complexities of music rights in advertising, so I should feel proud of my accomplishment even though I was never actually acknowledged and, I'm sure, was forgotten by all of those involved.

Following is an excerpt from Joanne Fellows's dissertation 'Acquiring Music for TV Commercials':

> This purchasing of the publishing rights alone gives the advertising agency and composers the opportunity to reproduce a piece of music in any manner (license permitting) they anticipate will enhance and substantiate the message of a commercial.
>
> The license will specify how much of the music, in terms of time, may be used on an ad, and this will, more often than not, be thirty seconds. Within these thirty seconds an agency is permitted to use whichever fragments of the music it selects, providing that when the music is ready to be broadcast no more than the said amount has been employed.
>
> Matt Cox (1997:5) gave an example of this freedom of adaptation as the Terry's All Gold advert which engages an articulation of 'Will You' (Hazel O'Connor[,] 1981), noting that:
>
>> It starts with the drums[,] and then they've edited a bit of the saxophone from earlier on. Then there's a ten second cut down and it goes in to the very end bit. I'm sure that those edits they've done themselves were not officially sanctioned by the record company:

basically by getting their license with the ten second cut down[,] they're free to do what they will with it.

Once a license has been bought[,] there is no reason for a composer to object to any cuts made to the music.

The very nature of music in a commercial (i.e. its brevity of duration), will always make reduction of a pre-existing piece inevitable and, therefore, consenting to your music's use in a commercial must surely acknowledge that there is a necessity for cuts to be made. However, despite the way an agency choose[s] to treat a particular piece of music, the fact remains that licenses are there to be negotiated and can be extremely lucrative for composers, publishers and record companies.[1]

Given the above, I have no idea if Hazel O'Connor was involved in the process or even if she knew that the licence was being sold. Even if she did, most would argue that this was a fair transaction; after all, she was paid for the use of her song, and 'we' used her song to promote our product.

Of course, she may have hated the fact that her beloved song was sold out just to sell a few more chocolates at Christmas. She may have even been a Black Magic lover, like Mum.

In my mind, however, Hazel O'Connor loved that her song was used in the advert, as this meant that more people got to hear it and, maybe, subsequently purchased it. I believe that she would have been thrilled to know that this was all because of a true fan: me, an independent researcher who spent years working in dull offices trying to work my way into a position where I could exploit my passion for music and, on a whim and on my say-so, get my favourite artists and their songs used in ways that they could never do on their own, bringing them untold riches . . .

Maybe not, but I'd like to think that Hazel O'Connor at least saw the advert and, regardless of the way the music was cut, was pleased that

---

[1] Fellows, Joanne, 'Acquiring Music for TV Commercials', *Philip Tagg* (18 September 2000). <http://www.tagg.org/students/Liverpool/jofelldiss.pdf> accessed 4 April 2014.

her music was used (okay, deep down, I hope that she hated the way the music was cut).

And my reward?

Well, it must be worth at least a pint, maybe Spitfire or Doom Bar as a thank-you, if ever I meet her . . . and maybe a half of 'Old Badger's Arsehole' for Joff.

Peter Gilbert

My Top Ten Songs including Gold

'After the Gold Rush'—Neil Young
'Golden Years'—David Bowie
'Gold'—Spandau Ballet
'Silence Is Golden'—The Tremeloes
'Golden Touch'—Razorlight
'Goldfinger'—Shirley Bassey
'Golden Brown'—The Stranglers
'Gold on the Ceiling'—The Black Keys
'Fool's Gold'—Amy Winehouse
'Band of Gold'—Freda Payne

Things to Check Out

On YouTube:

- 'Will You'—Hazel O'Connor
- 'Eighth Day'—Hazel O'Connor

Elsewhere:
www.myoldmansabusman.com

My Second Radio Interview

'Well, that was "Telephone Thing" by the Fall, and this is Frank Skinner on Absolute Radio. If you want to text in to the show on your telephone, then the number to text is eight-twelve-fifteen, I say, eight-twelve-fifteen.

'Our first guest today is . . . Friend of the Show Pete, whose name may be familiar to regular Absolute Radio listeners, as he was here a while ago talking about the book that he was about to start writing. He promised to come back and talk to us when he was about halfway through.

'So, Pete, I'm guessing—well, I know, actually, because I've had the privilege of reading it—that you are indeed about halfway through. And what a half it was, to use a familiar footballing term and also one that is relevant to one of the first chapters in your book. Do you want to fill the Absolute Radio listeners in?'

'Thank you, Frank. Firstly, can I say what a pleasure it is to be back? Thanks for inviting me.'

'My pleasure. I could not help noticing a few references to yours truly in the book. Was that planned originally or inspiration from the day that you spent here at Absolute Radio?'

'Well, Frank, as I said at the time, I would probably use the interview as an homage to one of my favourite films, *The Commitments,* which I did. And, as the third chapter includes me meeting Bobby Moore in 1970, a World Cup year, and talking about the hit that the England team had back then, it seemed logical to reference your and David Baddiel's "Three Lions" song.'

'And by "England team hit," for the Absolute Radio listeners, you're referring to "Back Home" by the 1970 England World Cup Squad, which David and I—Baddiel, that is, not Beckham or the statue of—used as intro music to one of the *Fantasy Football* series.'

'Yes, that's right—and it was the first single that I ever owned. And, if I remember correctly from listening to you on *Desert Island Discs,* yours, too?'

'Crikey! I'd almost forgotten that I'd been on that, let alone the details of the interview itself, but, yes, you're absolutely correct. In *The Commitments,* though, if memory serves me right, and it is indeed a good film, was it not a series of fantasy interviews with Terry Wogan?'

'It was, Frank, but the cast of *The Commitments* were all Irish, and so I guess that Terry was most relevant for them, or Roddy Doyle, who wrote it. Also, it was set at the time when Terry would have been very high profile on Radio 1 and TV. I did think of using him to make the connection really obvious, but while I think he's great, and an institution, I don't really listen to him now. I've been a genuine fan of yours for ages, and so you were a more obvious choice than Terry to reflect my story.'

'Well, I'm flattered on all sorts of counts, as I'm sure everybody at Absolute Radio is to be held in the same regard as such a monolith of broadcasting as Sir Terry Wogan. So, without giving too much away, what can you tell our listeners about the book—which, while I have to say is very entertaining . . . have to ask again: Is it all true?'

'Every word, Frank. And by that, I mean that it's all written exactly the way that I remember it in my head. So, if it came to it, I believe that I would pass a lie detector test on everything.'

'Well, I hope it doesn't come to that. Before we carry on, I have to say at this point, for the benefit of the listeners, that this book is written as an autobiography but contains lots of other elements, too.'

'Well, Frank, the original idea was a novella based around the major events concerning celebrities like choosing Hazel O'Connor's song for a TV ad and stealing Robbie Williams's underpants that I mentioned last time that I was here. But as I was writing it, there were so many other things, which I hope are interesting or humorous, that went in, that it took a slightly different direction.'

'But it will still include Robbie's pants, surely?'

'Oh yes, it's just that not quite as many of those stories ended up in the first half, as I'd originally planned. I never intended to write about decimalisation or 1970s public information films, for instance, and I had no intention of pop cricket playing such a large part at the beginning of the

My Old Man's a Busman

second half—meaning that the only real celeb stories, other than getting Bobby Moore's autograph, are the Hazel O'Connor TV ad and meeting Roy Lynes and Sir Christopher Cockerell.'

'I'll leave the Absolute Radio listeners to find out for themselves who Roy Lynes and Sir Chris are, hopefully by buying your book. Choosing the music for that TV ad is a great story, but I'm glad that you did include those other bits. I had completely forgotten some of those classic TV ads and films that you mention, and I spent a happy hour or two reminiscing on YouTube, thanks to the references in the book, as I'm sure that our listeners will do, too, when it comes out.

'Also, again without giving too much away, I have to say that Cath and I are now devotees to playing your pop cricket game. And, if I'm not mistaken, the Fall track before this interview would get me twenty-four runs but also one wicket, so I'd be twenty-four for one?'

'Now I'm flattered, Frank. I could never have dared to dream that a celebrity would be talking about and playing something that I made up as a bit of fun for the family one Christmas. I hope that you played your "Three Lions" song, as that would also have got you twelve runs just for the title, and forty if you included you, David, and the Lightning Seeds, with no wickets.'

'Hang on a moment . . . you're right. Although why I should be surprised at that, I don't know. You invented it, after all. But if you think I'm allowed to play that record at home, you are much mistaken. Anyway, we digress, and the Absolute Radio listeners have no idea yet what we are talking about. But, basically, it's a cricket game that you can play when listening to music, where you get runs for legs and wickets for no legs—but I'll have to leave you in a state of antici . . . pation until you've bought the book . . . a *Rocky Horror Picture Show* reference for our listeners there.

'So, there's some celebrity bits, but it's also the story of your life and family told through anecdotes, general observations, and events of the time, such as the World Cup in 1970, decimalisation, and various TV ad campaigns. So, what can we expect from the rest?'

'Well, Frank, most of the ancient history stuff is done now, which fulfils the objective that this is partly a record of events for future family generations, so I think that the rest of the chapters will be more in line with the original plan.'

'So, what can we expect apart from the now almost eponymous Robbie story?'

'Well, other than that Robbie story, there's Lofty, or, as I'm sure he'd prefer now, Tom Watt from *EastEnders*; a story involving Lisa Snowdon and her dress on a yacht in Monaco; playing charades on Christmas Day with the drummer from Razorlight; getting shanghaied in Honduras; and my girlfriend's stepmum being taught to swim by Tarzan.'

'Blimey! It certainly sounds like the back end will be as interesting as the front . . . can we say that on Absolute Radio? Hang on, let me just consult the book . . . yes, it's okay, thank goodness for that. Well, I look forward to reading the completed tome. And, on behalf of myself and the listeners, will you come back to Absolute Radio when you've completed it?'

'Of course I will, Frank. It will be an honour. In the meantime, good luck with the pop cricket. But before I go, I must tell you a funny story. I gave my youngest son the beginning of the book to read, and after reading the opening interview, he looked up wide-eyed and asked if I'd really been on the radio and interviewed by you.'

'That's brilliant. Art imitating life, I think that's called. Well, that was Pete, and I'm delighted to tell you that we have another author, Ben Elton, as our main guest, who will be talking, amongst other things, about his collaboration with Richard Herring to bring to the London stage a new musical called *A'side,* based on Richard's *As It Occurs to Me* podcast series. But before that, talking of A-sides, here's the A-side to Elvis Presley's B-side "Don't Be Cruel": "Hound Dog."'

Pop Cricket

Back in the Reigate days, with the Austin Cambridge and elastic-band-driven DAF cars, we would spend a fair amount of time at weekends in the car, visiting relatives in and around Surrey and London.

These trips were not that long by today's standards. I regularly jump in the car to do 200-mile, 3.5-hour runs to visit family. In the early '70s, before portable cassette players, Discmans, iPods, iPhones, in-car DVD players, talking books, Kindle, or even half-decent car radios, there was very little to entertain bored children.

On a longer trip to the seaside during the summer holidays, we had the challenge of 'who can see the sea first?' This challenge always brought a thrill of excitement, as those words conjured up visions of the day ahead, hopefully filled with sun, paddling in the sea, building sandcastles, eating crunchy sandwiches (unfortunately, not sandwiches filled with Crunchie bars, but sandwiches that were crunchy in texture because sand always got into them), playing games of catch with Dad (who remained in his deckchair during), and playing the inevitable game of cricket (the only reason for which Dad got out of the deckchair, I remember). But this thrill was very short-lived, as it only really came into play about five minutes before we arrived in Bognor Regis, Brighton, or Littlehampton—despite Mum and Dad's attempts to drag out the challenge to last for the entire journey from Reigate. While we were still over a hundred miles away, they'd shout, 'Who can see the sea?'

Dad was an avid cricket watcher in the summer months. On Sunday afternoons at home, one would find him in the lounge, often with the curtains pulled—not because he was overexcited about the cricket, but because the sun was reflecting on the TV. This would infuriate Mum on a beautiful summer's day.

Most weeks, the TV showed only county matches. But the 'real deal' were the test matches that went on for days on end. I think that Mum would have happily moved out during those periods. She did like cricket, though. Her mum, my nanny, had actually been nanny to famous cricketer Colin Cowdrey when he was a child. But Mum just couldn't stand that the sun was shut out in order to see the TV better.

Dad's passion for cricket meant that our trips to the beach included taking along his beloved portable radio so that he could listen to the commentary all day.

In those early days, there was nothing more boring to me than cricket, as it meant either sitting in a dark room when it was sunny outside or that Dad would not leave his deckchair to play on the beach until the commentary had finished. Over the years, maybe through a process of attrition, I gradually became a bit more involved.

I had always caught snippets of the matches, watching with Dad for a bit and then running off to play when I got a bit bored, only to return when I thought it would be more exciting near the end of the match. 'Three overs to go, twenty-two runs to win,' the commentator would say, or some such similar score line, meaning that I'd see about twenty minutes of exciting play as the team chased the final few runs.

This got me interested enough to know who a few of the players were. I wanted to emulate them when playing. My first 'hero' was Tony Greig, a thick-accented South African who bowled (and batted) for England and who, for some reason, had caught my imagination. Maybe it was his exotic accent, which I heard when he was interviewed, or his large presence; he was 6'6" tall and stood out from all the other great players of the time. Whatever the reason, when playing cricket on the beach, I would always imagine that I was Tony Greig. That is, until 1976.

Other than featuring cricket, the summer of 1976 is best remembered, amongst those who can remember it, as one of the longest, hottest summers ever experienced in the British Isles. People now claim that it was hot and sunny from May until September. It did feel that way at the time: like one long, glorious, never-ending summer. And that is how we like to remember it. Factually, the temperature only reached 80°F (26.7°C, but we all used Fahrenheit back then) between 22 June and 16 July. Because it was hot every day, it was definitely a heat wave, judging by our usual summer standards.

Also, it remained seasonally sunny and warm until the end of August, when the first rain of late summer arrived, right at the end of the school holidays. For us kids, it was the first and last of the school holidays where we could go out and play every day without encountering rain.

What was true was that it was so hot that the ground everywhere was parched and cracked. Even the tar on the road was sticky and melting some days. The news was full of talk of drought—and, of course, we had the obligatory hosepipe ban.

Where we lived at the time, in Hythe, the unseasonal weather had also unleashed a plague of ladybirds, literally millions of them flying in swarms for days. As we walked or cycled through them, we'd have to cover our faces to avoid breathing them in. Still, to a twelve-year-old on school holidays, this was a small price to pay.

One upside was that our parents could plan trips out, picnics, BBQs, etc., without worrying that it might rain. That said, looking back, my family didn't do BBQs. I have no idea why, but for the entire time I lived at home, we never owned a barbecue grill—nor did we attend a BBQ at somebody else's house. Maybe it just wasn't a '70s thing, or maybe it was just a bit too avant-garde or 'continental' for the likes of us.

Another upside was that we got ice lollies every day, some from the corner shop or the ice-cream van. Our favourites were Fab, Zoom, Funny Feet, and Haunted House, but, because these were costly, they were supplemented with ice pops, a cheaper, shop-bought alternative, and homemade ice lollies, which were made in cups or beakers with diluted orange or lemon squash.

The excessive heat also made us inventive. Empty washing-up-liquid bottles and Jif lemon containers doubled as water pistols during the day and pillow dampeners at night. The latter was required if we were to get some relief from the balmy heat that kept us awake. We simply squirted cold water onto the pillow.

I don't know if the heat was getting to everyone, but musicians were producing some bizarre recordings, too. Good old prime-time *TOTPs* was still keeping Dad (and me) interested with Pan's People and Legs & Co. (although I think that my allegiance was moving from Babs of Pan's People to the 'dusky one', as Dad referred to her, from Legs & Co. This was a big sign of my maturing taste in women, I think!). We danced to the hits of the day, such as the novelty song 'Jungle Rock' from Hank Mizell or the latest from Showaddywaddy, Leo Sayer, and the Brotherhood of Man, with the literally odd interlude of an Alex Harvey or Noosha Fox track.

The older boys at school or my friends' older brothers ridiculed our musical influences and talked about the cool bands they'd seen on a strange programme called *The Old Grey Whistle Test*. That said, even this reputedly cool dude's *TOTPs* was, at the time, peddling prog rock and American West Coast music from the likes of CCR (Creedence Clear Water Revival) at a time when the Notting Hill riots were signalling the dawn of a new era in music: punk. It would, however, take a couple of years before punk rock's chart success made major inroads on *TOTPs*. When it did happen, such as when the Clash, the Sex Pistols, or Siouxsie Sioux made an appearance, it was great . . . and our parents hated it.

Another big feature of that summer, was that the West Indies, nicknamed the Windies, toured the United Kingdom for a test series (five five-day matches) and a series of five one-day matches. I, of course, like Dad, was patriotically watching the opening match as an England supporter, but as the first test developed, I remember being blown away by the thrilling and flamboyant way in which the Windies played their cricket. It was like nothing I'd seen before. Secretly (and shamefully), I started to support the opposition.

It wasn't simply that I wanted to support the winning side. At this stage, the first game, it was still anybody's series to win. It was simply that the Windies played a different cricket than I'd witnessed before. It was exciting to watch. I wanted to see it instead of going out to play.

The county matches on Sundays may have featured one fast bowler who livened things up a bit, but the Windies had a four-man fast-bowl attack, meaning that they could bowl at the English batsmen at speeds close to 100 mph all day long. Instead of making people wait hours (or maybe minutes) to see a few runs scored, the West Indian batsmen seemed to be able to reach a century (a hundred runs) on a whim.

Over that long hot summer, on and off, I did want to be out on my bike and eating ladybird-covered ice lollies, too. But I watched that West Indies side of cricketing greats—including Clive Lloyd, Viv Richards, Gordon

Greenidge, and Michael Holding—make a slow start. England managed to hold out. The first two tests were a draw. Then, the West Indies team systematically took England's batsmen and bowlers apart. They won the last three tests to win the series 3–0. They also won every one of the five-day matches. My favourite player became Joel Garner, the huge, 6'8" fast bowler. He was nicknamed Big Bird and seemed to bowl the fastest and have the most presence. Tony was history.

I was hooked. I loved watching the team play, and I was now a Windies fan. I even admitted it to Dad, who, while not entirely pleased by my chosen allegiance, was at least pleased that he had someone with whom to watch the game. Of course, there have been some great cricket tests since that time, with amazing performances by England, including the great players such as Botham, Gatting, and Flintoff. Arguably, no performance was better than when England won the Ashes against Australia in 2005. While as an adult who now quite rightly supports England, I still remember the thrill I felt when watching Clive Lloyd's Windies play in 1976.

That test series also allegedly gave us one of the best lines from a commentator in sports history. With Michael Holding in bat facing Peter Willey, with play about to resume after tea, commentator Brian Johnston spoke the immortal line, 'Welcome back to *Test Match Special,* where the batsman's holding the bowler's willy,' although there is much speculation about whether this actually happened, as no audio evidence exists.

In May 1976, the Olympic Games were held in Montreal, Canada. I remember Olga Corbett, the young darling of the Russian gymnastics team, winning gold medal after gold medal and being in the newspapers and on the news virtually every day. Still, my sporting allegiance that year went to the cricket.

That was probably the last time that a six-foot-tall West Indian bloke throwing a ball at 100 mph at some pieces of wood took priority over women dancing around while wearing next to nothing.

On our family's numerous car journeys and on trips where there was no sea involved, we would relieve the boredom by playing other games.

Throughout December, counting Christmas trees was a favourite. This was simple, but it was a big deal to Netty and me, as it signalled the run-up to the big day.

Peter Gilbert

We'd set off in the car and, looking out of our respective windows (i.e. each player only looked at his or her side of the road) counted the number of Christmas trees we could see in people's gardens or houses (through the windows). Whoever had counted the most by the time we reached home, or our other destination, was declared the winner! Strangely, this game has never caught on as a Winter Olympics event. Whilst we imagined at the time that it was only us who played, it turns out—I learned from listening to features on various radio programmes—that many other people did the same when they were kids.

On long motorway trips these days, counting Christmas trees would be an extremely dull game. But back then, when we travelled from relatives' houses in Sutton and Peckham to ours in Reigate, there were enough towns and villages along the route to keep the tree count high and to keep us children engaged and happy. It was unusual to see the big, flamboyant displays one sees today, the trees covered in lights and the giant Santas waving from rooftops. I'm eternally grateful to those people who simply put their Christmas trees in the window for other people's pleasure.

As was evident in many aspects of our lives, we were creatures of habit. From as early as I can remember, I always sat behind Dad in the car, whilst Netty sat behind Mum. I have no idea why. But this seating arrangement meant that the results of the counting Christmas trees game were sometimes the same when we travelled the same journey the next time, unless my sister or I cheated or spotted a new tree that had been put up since our last trip.

Habits follow one into adulthood. Ask most people who are part of a couple if they sleep on a set side of the bed and the answer will be yes, even though no one will be able to explain why. My side of the bed is on the right. That is to say, I'm on the right side when I'm lying down. If you were standing and looking at me from the end of the bed, which would be weird, I'd be on the left side.

One of my family's all-year-round favourite car games was pub cricket.

As an only child, Dad claimed to have invented all sorts of games to keep himself amused when he was growing up. 'The war was on, there just wasn't the money about for toys and games, and I didn't have anyone else to play with,' he told us when we asked why he had made up a certain game.

My Old Man's a Busman

I'm not certain what the difference really is between an inventor and a person who makes things up, but I do know that my dad was not the inventor type.

His story was that he invented pub cricket to pass away time on car journeys when he was a child. However, subsequent research shows that 'pub' or 'sign' cricket, which uses pub signs, appeared in one of the issues of the *AA Book of the Road, c.1966*. We did have those books in the house, so maybe Dad got the idea from one of those. Or maybe he did create the game and word spread.

The outcome of the game, for us, was again determined by our chosen side of the car, as each player, or team, earned points from the names of pubs we passed.

Runs were made by counting the number of legs apparent in a pub's name. For example, the Red Lion would earn four runs (as a lion has four legs), and the Happy Farmer would earn two runs (a farmer is a human and, therefore, has two legs).

To boost the number of runs to better reflect a real cricket score, a pub name with an indeterminate number of legs would count as twenty-four. The Coach & Horses (an indeterminate number of horses and, therefore, legs) or the Horse & Hounds (an indeterminate number of hounds) would each score twenty-four.

If the pub name had no legs (e.g. the Anchor), it counted as being out and therefore earned a wicket. Play continued until a contestant had ten wickets or until we arrived at our destination. Our parents considered this game educational as while it did relieve the boredom, having no calculators back then we also had to do all of the adding up.

We happily played this game for hours. To this day, I can't help but convert every pub name into runs and wickets. I also subject my kids to the game, even though they are now teenagers. ('Dad, I don't care how many runs that is. It's stupid.')

Another of Dad's 'inventions' was tiddlywinks football, which was similar to Subbuteo, but which preceded that game by decades and was therefore the forerunner and granddaddy to Subbuteo. Dad's version was played with tiddlywinks, which served as players and the ball; a pitch drawn onto a large, pink-material-covered board; and bicycle clips, which served as goals.

I have no idea why the board was not made of a green material, except to say that it was probably all that my grandma had available at the time. Remember, there was a war on. I never questioned the bicycle clips, though.

Then there was dice football. Players simply created leagues of teams, drew up a full season's worth of home and away matches, and then rolled a die to get the scores. Dice football was realistic, except lots of times the teams scored four, five, and six goals—and no one scored nil, let alone experienced a goal-less draw. Despite its flaws, Dad and I loved dice football and would play for hours.

Once we had played the leagues, Dad would draw up the new league tables, with the relevant teams moving up and down in the ranks, and then we would start again. Surprisingly, he didn't make me wait until the next season.

Dad's leagues always reflected the actual football league at the time, but sometimes he allowed me to include a team from a place we had visited, such as Bognor Regis. Places like this, which were outside of the real football league, were only allowed into our lower leagues. They never competed against Liverpool, Arsenal, or Dad's team, Tottenham Hotspur. Instead, they battled it out with the likes of Tranmere Rovers and Accrington Stanley.

I was always dissatisfied when a lowly Peckham United team I had been allowed to add had managed to work its way up a league at the end of the season. It was even worse if, after I made continued lucky throws of the dice, the team was elevated to play against what my dad perceived as the proper teams.

We also had dice cricket. This was much more involved than dice football. It realistically reflected the nuances of cricket by using four dice to score.

Various combinations of dice-throw totals could lead one to be bowled out, caught, stumped, caught and bowled, run out, etc. A batsman could score a realistic number of runs. All match scores were captured on a realistic cricket scorecard, each one hand drawn—with pencil and ruler—by Dad, who even drew up player stats.

Again, Dad preferred the realistic approach. A county match, such as Surrey vs. Yorkshire, was played out with the correct player names of the day, but I wasn't really engaged at the start. This was pre-1976, so I was not familiar with the players. To keep me interested, my dad agreed to use non-real player names. We made up teams from people we knew and people who were in the media so, begrudgingly, Dad would find himself playing a match with Bob Willis bowling to Elvis Presley or Suzi Quatro.

Once I had mastered the rules, I became my dad, playing for hours on my own and creating my fantasy teams. Ironically, in 1976, I didn't use a made-up team the likes of which I'd insisted on. I used that West Indian test team. I finally realised that I had really turned into my dad when I introduced my own kids to the game.

My children had no interest in real cricket, but they were intrigued by the stories about how the game came about. In a moment of complete role reversal, I tried to persuade them to play with the England and West Indies teams of 1976, but they, having listened to the stories, wanted to make up their own teams, just as their dad used to do to annoy their granddad. I therefore found myself begrudgingly forced to play with Mr Bean bowling to Steve Backshall. Now, that's just not cricket.

As an adult, I have spent (okay, wasted), many, many happy hours playing numerous made-up games with various family, friends, and colleagues. The people that I choose to play with depends on the game and, to some extent their degree of political correctness. I did not invent all of the following games, but did enhance some of them a bit, not wanting to be outdone by my peers when it came to legacy stakes.

Yellow Car, No Return

This game is as simplistic as counting Christmas trees, but it does not rely on the season or depend on one's being in a residential area. Therefore, it can be played on any journey.

The rules are these: Every time you see a yellow vehicle, you call, 'Yellow car' [or 'yellow truck'], no return,' and you win a point.

If you call it incorrectly (for example, if everybody else thinks it's gold, not yellow, or that it's dual-colour and, for instance, more white than yellow), then you lose a point.

The person with the most points at the end of the journey wins. This is safe and politically correct and, therefore, a family game. To extend the playability, we have since added orange, which is worth two points, and pink, which is worth five.

Motorway Fruit Machine

You simply score ten points by shouting 'Jackpot' first (possibly accompanied by banging your fist or flat palm on a seat back, steering wheel, or glove box—in the same way that you would hit the button on a real fruit machine) if you spot three vehicles of the same colour, aligned in the three lanes. You may include the vehicle you are travelling in. To extend play, you can award extra points for same vehicles (e.g. three cars and bonus points if they are the same make).

It goes without saying that you should never drive dangerously or erratically simply to achieve a jackpot.

Pig/Dog/Bird

I once read some research saying that the shape and features of all human female faces can be categorised into three animal types: pig, dog, and bird. That is to say that the features are similar, not to say that the animal is indicative of a female's attractiveness. I'm speaking specifically of the terms *pig* and *dog*.

To play, go about your normal business on your own (but preferably with friends or a partner) and categorise the people around you into the three types.

To increase playability, simply allocate points to each type.

As dog is the most common default and as the majority of the population falls into this category, this only gets one point.

Birdlike features are not uncommon, although they are easy to spot. Still, they are not as common as doglike features, so this gets two points.

A true pig—a female displaying obvious pig-like features—is the real prize and is therefore worth three points.

Please note:

1. This is not recommended for play where a person may be caught or overheard.
2. Especially, don't play this at work.

The 50/50 Game

Over the years, in every workplace and pub in the land, men (in the most non-PC of ways) discuss 'would you or wouldn't you?' or variations on that theme. For example, would you marry, go out with, or shag a female colleague, mate, partner, celebrity, etc.

Feminists, I'm sure, will be up in arms, but it happens. This is what men (or boys, as my girlfriend would contest) do. It's very childish, puerile, base, and degrading to women. It usually takes the form of 'Who'd *do* that new woman in accounts?' or 'Would you rather do the new woman in accounts or Laura from *I'm a Celebrity . . . Get Me Out of Here!?*'

This game usually has a relatively short shelf life, as it includes a couple of people whom everyone *would*. So, once it's established, for example, that the new woman in accounts is the 'fittest', the game dries up a bit.

Zadie Smith, author of *White Teeth* and other novels, told a great related story on Radio 4's *Desert Island Discs*. She said that at school, all of the girls wanted to be like the pop star Madonna—and not for the reasons you might think (her looks, body, voice, or success). Smith recalls that when she was a teenager, many of the boys at school would brag about what they'd do or like to do to some girl or female celebrity, but she remembers quite clearly that Madonna, even though massively popular and a sex symbol at the time, was never part of these conversations. She concluded that Madonna did not come across as someone who a boy would be doing anything to. Rather, if anybody was going to be doing the doing, then it would be Madonna. Respect.

Having grown bored with these conversations at work, we were delighted when, one day, a colleague introduced us to a twist on this.

According to the rules of 50/50, you have to name the person whom you think is a real 50/50 call (i.e. one about whom everyone else playing cannot quite decide). This indecision is often accompanied by phrases such as 'She's quite good-looking, but . . . ' and 'I know that age shouldn't come into it, but . . . '

If anyone playing definitely would or definitely wouldn't, the player scores no points and the next player takes a turn. If every person playing calls it as a 50/50, then the player scores a point. This is much more interesting and fun. The record for game play without scoring any points at all is about four hours.

Please note:

1. See instructions 1 and 2 for the pig/dog/bird game.
2. Don't play this if one of your group 'would' do anybody who has any three limbs and a pulse (there's always one) or if someone is worried that his wife or partner may find out that he was playing. This type of player votes 'no' for everybody, so you'll never score a point as long as you play.
3. Presume that women have equally derogatory conversations about men.

Lucky Dip

Another Dave (who happens to be a friend of Laura Catlow) introduced me to a variation of the 50/50 game. In this version, the player names a number of people (or recognised group), one of whom is an obvious 'wouldn't', and then everyone else takes it in turns to say whether or not he would risk the gamble (i.e. 'take' whichever name came up).

A great example was calling the Corrs. You may get one of four amazingly beautiful women, but, then again, you may get their brother Jim. Is it worth the risk? Will you take the odds?

I seem to recall that the Spice Girls and Girls Aloud were suggested along the way, which seems odd, given the people who suggested them. As if those men would turn down any of those women in real life.

A more recent addition to the game has been the female cast of *The Big Bang Theory*. A player may get Bernadette or Penny but could also end up with Amy or even Howard's mother.

My Old Man's a Busman

I once tried calling Sara Gilbert (no relation), who plays Leslie Winkle (in *The Big Bang Theory*), a 50/50. I remember having liked her and her character from *Roseanne*. But another player immediately said, 'No way!', so that round was over pretty quickly, leaving questions about my taste in women. Personally, I don't think that there's anything wrong with geek chic. Were my fellow players going to turn down Zooey Deschanel, too?

I don't think we've ever allocated points in this game. It's just a bit of fun.

Sooty

At various times in my career, I've been called upon to develop or simply run courses for teams of people. I cover topics such as presentation skills, team building, and leadership. I always enjoy the element of running lateral thinking exercises, which are designed to get people to think 'outside the box'. Sometimes, the exercise is about something commonplace, such as 'uses of a safety pin', but once people list the obvious, I can get them to think much more creatively. I also create scenarios where the participants have to come up with 'alternative' ways to solve a problem. The idea is that people will use lateral thinking when we get down to the actual course or problem that we're trying to solve.

One of these scenarios that is always fun to do and gets a great response is Sooty.

The Exercise, or 'Game'

In January 2009, a story about Prince Charles appeared in British newspapers. He was overheard calling his old school friend by a nickname, Sooty. As the friend was not a white Caucasian, the papers assumed that the nickname had something to do with the colour of his skin and that, therefore, it was a racist comment.

'Assume that this was not the case and then come up with alternative reasons why Sooty may have been Prince Charles's friend's nickname.'

This game has elicited some great responses over time, including the following:

- He (or his father) was a chimney sweep.
- His favourite toy/TV character was Sooty the bear.

Peter Gilbert

- At school/college/university, he was president of the Society Overseeing Tangy Orange Yoghurts.
- He is mute (like the TV puppet character Sooty the bear).
- He had a girlfriend called Sue (like the TV puppet).
- He uses fake tan (and looks 'orange', like the TV puppet).
- He's the father of Isy (Isy Suttie, the comedienne).

But, by far, the best one—and the one that still makes me laugh—is this:

- As a child, he was fisted by Harry H. Corbett (the puppeteer whose hand would have been inside Sooty).

Fantasy Movie Casts

This is another one that can be played in mixed company.

Take an old, existing film or forthcoming release and discuss your fantasy cast.

Points are awarded on the basis of nominations that receive widespread approval. This is not as strict as the 50/50 game. It can be based on a majority decision.

One that got a great response was the impending launch of the *Thunderbirds* movie in 2004, before the cast had been announced. Also, we have often discussed James Bond films with Michael Caine often nominated in the lead role.

The rationale for Caine is, that while he played a similar (albeit anti-hero) character, Harry Palmer, in the movie adaptations of Len Deighton's spy novels *The Ipcress File* (1962) and *Funeral in Berlin* (1964), his rougher, cockney approach—most evident in the character he played in *Alfie* (1966)—would liven up some of the more conservative Bond moments.

Imagine a Bond movie with the line, 'She's got a little ginger moustache, but I find I'm quite willing to overlook the odd blemish in a woman, providing she's got something to make up for it,' or, 'All right, Tinkerbelle. You're nicked,' or, 'Put your knickers back on and go and make us a cup of tea. There's a luv.'

Sean Connery always used to come out as our best Bond. More recently, however, it's become a close-run race between Connery, Pierce

Brosnan, and Daniel Craig, although we've often agreed that Brosnan's character in the remake of *The Thomas Crown Affair* (1999) is more Bond than his actual Bond.

Another movie/TV based game that I play, especially with the kids on long car journeys, involves taking the title of a film, programme, or character and using wordplay to create new versions. Like pub cricket, this game is fun, is vaguely educational, and (I claim) develops creative thinking.

One example is the TV programme *Cash in the Attic*, where experts in antiques (or junk) go around people's homes to see if they have anything of value to sell at auction in order to raise some cash. This presents great wordplay opportunities:

- Cash in the Attic: There is a surprise on the show when they actually discover Johnny Cash in the attic.
- Kashmir in the Attic: Presenters count how many woollen jumpers are lying around the house.
- Kardash in the Attic: Kim presents the show.
- Cardash in the Attic: Celebrities play Scalextric at the top of the house.
- Cashidy in the Attic: Sean Connery presents a one-off *Partridge Family* memorabilia special.

This inevitably leads to alphabetical wordplay:

- Dash in the Attic: Celebrities are timed racing around the loft.
- Pash in the Attic: Will the team discover any valuable pashminas?
- Hash in the Attic: The team discover cannabis plants.
- Bash in the Attic: Due to BBC cuts, the boxing this week is brought to you live from council worker Fred Blogg's house.
- Fash in the Attic: This week, the show is presented by Justin Fashanu.
- Flash in the Attic: This is a late-night version of the programme.
- Gash in the Attic: An even later-night version.

Peter Gilbert

Not all of these examples come from when I've played the game with my kids!

Following a discussion with friends of childhood film scary characters, we also came up with the following:

- Bitty Bitty Bang Bang: The biopic of David Walliams
- Clitty Clitty Bang Bang: The biopic of Vanessa Del Rio
- Ditty Ditty Bang Bang: The biopic of Nancy (from the musical *Oliver*)
- Hitty Hitty Bang Bang: The biopic of B.A. Robertson
- Nitty Nitty Bang Bang: The biopic of a Victorian nurse
- Pity Pity Bang Bang: The biopic of a manic-depressive
- Titty Titty Bang Bang: The biopic of Jordan
- Witty Witty Bang Bang: The biopic of Frank Skinner
- Zitty Zitty Bang Bang: The biopic of a teenager

Another favourite with the kids resulted in these rich pickings from *Star Wars*:

- Bar Wars: A reality show fronted by Ross Kemp and Danny Dyer
- Car Wars: The movie version of *Top Gear*
- Jar Wars: Behind the scenes of a Women's Institute fête with Kirstie Allsopp
- Jar Jar Wars: *Star Wars* fans argue over who is the shittiest character from the franchise
- Ma Wars: Members of Boney M argue about who really sang the male vocalist's part in their string of '70s hits
- Na Wars: A broadcast by Amnesty International

The characters are great fun, too. Here are a few Han Solo–related alternatives:

- 'An Solo: Where our hero is a cockney one-handed space pilot
- Ban Solo: Where we find that our hero has lost his licence because he had too many points

My Old Man's a Busman

- Can Solo: Where our hero is a DJ at the Mos Eisley Cantina
- Sans Solo: A director's cut wherein Han does not appear
- Tan Solo: Where the hero is played by David Dickinson

However, the richest vein to date, and also my kids' favourite, is the *Harry Potter* movies:

- 'Arry Potter: Harry uses magic to extricate himself from a complex fraud case.
- Barry Potter: The boy wizard gets a part in *EastEnders*.
- Carrie Potter: The boy wizard gets mad and uses his magic to throw knives at people—and ends up covered in pig's blood.
- Gary Potter: This is the tale of a cartoon wizard snail that lives under the sea.
- Larry Potter: Harry gets a part in the *Gavin & Stacey* Christmas special.
- Marry Potter: Harry takes Ginny Weasley up the aisle.
- Parry Potter: Harry becomes a fencing champion.

Along the way, we changed *Harry* to *Hairy,* and off we went again.

- Hairy Potter: Harry swaps roles with Professor Lupin by using the emulatus spell.
- Malari Potter: Harry visits Africa for Comic Relief.
- Dairy Potter: Harry leaves Hogwarts to run a farm with Ginny.
- Mary Potter: Harry's muggle cousin helps to revive ailing high street fashion outlets.
- Rary Potter: This is the yet unseen director's cut.
- Wary Potter: Harry smokes some dope and becomes paranoid.
- Hilari Potter: This is a remake by French and Saunders.
- Gwyngillgogery Potter: This is the Welsh language version. Hogwarts is situated in the hollow of a white hazel near the rapid whirlpool.

It must have been a long car journey, as *Hairy* then morphed into *Herry,* and we came up with the following:

Peter Gilbert

- Herry Potter: Giant puppet version of the film
- Berry Potter: In which Harry appears in a Ribena ad
- Very Potter: A documentary showcasing the best Harry Potter lookalikes
- Merry Potter: Hogwarts Christmas Special
- Cherry Potter: Harry and Ginny finally get it on

Having become bored with Harry, we moved onto Dumbledore:

- Bumbledore: The professor uses the dickensiatumus charm to transport himself into a character from his favourite novel.
- Crumbledore: Not to be outdone by Christopher Walken, the professor appears on a cookery show and bakes with apple, sugar, biscuits, and rhubarb.
- Fumbledore: The professor has had too many glasses of butter beer when Professor McGonagall appears in his study.
- Grumbledore: The professor is not happy when Professor McGonagall tells him where he can stick his old wand.
- Humbledore: The professor has to admit that Professor Snape is a better role.
- Jumbledore: The professor holds a car boot sale at Hogwarts.
- Mumbledore: 'Sorry, didn't get that one.'
- Stumbledore: This time, the professor has been knocking back the elderflower wine.
- Tumbledore: This is the sequel to *Stumbledore*.

With everything that happened before, it was almost inevitable that the following would come to pass:

1. I would want to invent a game.
2. It would probably involve music.
3. It may well involve cricket.
4. It would not be straightforward.

It finally happened in 2007.

Following a period of intense development, when I obviously had far too much time on my hands, my creation was 'showcased' as part of our family Christmas get-together. It was in the form of a music quiz. This was the birth of pop cricket.

In my family, a simple music quiz would have been nothing special, even laughed at if I'd tried to engage them with questions along the lines of, 'Who had a 1975 number-one hit with [this song]'? or, 'Fill in the missing word to the song title Dreadlock blank' or even if I'd gone to the effort of putting some tracks on a CD to create a *Name That Tune*–style quiz. So, this was a complex affair. I distributed the game two weeks before the event, providing a CD and an answer sheet. It was based broadly on the rules of pub cricket.

Never minding that it had been obviously influenced by and perhaps plagiarised pub cricket, I'm sure that I'd also been influenced by the body-parts game played throughout the film *Still Crazy* (1998). This is one of my favourite films. It stars Billy Nighy (at his best, in my opinion) as the lead singer of washed-up and out-of-date '70s rock band Strange Fruit. The cast also includes Jimmy Nail, Billy Connolly, Timothy Spall, and Stephen Rea.

During the film, to pass the time, the characters devise a game whereby they get a point for each body part they name that relates to a band.

When the game is first announced, points are awarded for the Faces, the Small Faces, and Little Feat. Later, Beano (played by Timothy Spall) phones up and interrupts Hughie (played by Billy Connolly), who is being 'pleasured' by a groupie, to shout, 'Cockney rebel. Cock, knee. That's two points, that is.'

The best scene for me, however, is when Beano tries to claim Dr Hook.

> Beano: *Dr Hook & the Medicine Show.*
> Clare: Objection, Your Honour.
> Hughie: Objection sustained.
> Beano: Well, some people 'ave hooks instead of hands.
> Les: Yeah, but it's not part of the body. It's not . . . anatomical.
> Beano: It is if you haven't got a fuckin' hand.

Peter Gilbert

I spent hours, over the course of many days, on the quiz, ploughing through my collection to get the right mix of songs that people knew, liked, loved, and hadn't heard before, or that perhaps was a different version. Finally, all the tracks had to work well towards making a realistic cricket score.

Having completed it, I posted a CD to all my family members who would be there. I provided the following quiz description and rules:

With rules similar to those of pub cricket, this is my version of the game: pop cricket. Where in pub cricket runs are scored by counting the legs on pub signs, in pop cricket, runs are scored by the number of legs that can be attributed in any way to the artist, group, persons, or song title. Also, as in pub cricket, if no legs at all can be attributed, then it counts as a wicket.

Note: For an indeterminate number of legs (e.g. the Travelling Wilburys), award twenty-four points (even if you know how many people are in the group). If it happens to be a group but sounds like one person (e.g. Milli Vanilli), then count it as two legs (i.e. it sounds like a person's name, and a person has two legs).

If the group is preceded by 'The', hence denoting a group—and even if the name does not appear to have legs—then it counts as twenty-four (e.g. the Tremeloes), but if the group name is simply inanimate (e.g. Take That), then it has no legs (and is a wicket).

A clue to this cunning and dastardly (although not Mutley) quiz is that it was designed to be tough.

Things to watch out for include a song or group name that sounds like something that does have a determinable number of legs. When you encounter this scenario, you have to go with that (e.g. if the group is the Black Crow, then it counts as two legs (a crow has two legs), not twenty-four for the group, although the Black Crowes would score twenty-four. Simple.

So, work out from the songs on the CD what the cricket score is.

I chose each track on the CD for one or all of the following reasons:

- The song is fun.
- The song is good.

- I think someone will appreciate the song's being on the CD (I've had to appeal to all ages).
- You may not have heard the song for ages.
- You may have never heard the song ever.
- I like the song.
- I had to find something to fit.

Enjoy!

Despite the perplexing set of rules and guidelines, and despite Dad's claim that he didn't remember ever teaching us pub cricket (which elicited much protesting and astonishment), everyone threw themselves into pub cricket over the weeks leading up to Christmas.

Questions were asked, rules clarified, and phone calls received.

'Just to check if I'm on the right lines . . . Should I count . . . ?'

On the big day, prizes—wine, chocolate, etc.—were awarded. I think that Netty and Joff tied, probably because they were more Internet-savvy than the others and so were more easily able to identify all of the artists and titles in the first place. But the highlight of the proceedings was Mum's guess at the title of one of the tracks. We have never let her live this down.

Okay, so I'll admit that it's not that clear when you listen to the song. But Mum had told us that she'd listened to it, literally dozens of times, and even played it to 'Auntie' Pauline to get her view. Mum's guess at the song 'Identity' was 'I Want to Dance'.

What?

Of course, she had no idea that the song was sung by Poly Styrene of X-Ray Spex. If she had, she could have looked it up on YouTube.

The actual CD playlist that I had put together and over which my family had poured for days and weeks is the following:

1. 'Rock Around with Ollie Vee'—Buddy Holly and the Crickets
2. 'Love Me Like a Rock'—Paul Simon
3. 'Young Parisians'—Adam and the Ants
4. 'Whole Lotta Rosie'—AC/DC
5. 'I Will'—Ruby Winters
6. 'I Would Rather Go Blind'—Ruby Turner
7. 'I Believe in the Man in the Sky'—Elvis Presley

Peter Gilbert

8. 'All I Want for Christmas Is You'—Mariah Carey
9. 'Sheena Is a Punk Rocker'—The Ramones
10. 'Identity'—X-Ray Spex
11. 'Please, Please Me'—David Cassidy
12. 'Too Much, Too Little, Too Late'—Silversun
13. 'We Love to Boogie'—T-Rex
14. 'It's a Shame'—Monie Love
15. 'Ça Plane pour Moi'—Plastic Bertrand
16. 'Lilac Wine'—Katie Melua
17. 'John Wayne Is Big-Leggy'—Haysi Fantayzee
18. 'Shangri-La'—The Kinks

The correct pop cricket score is 199 for 7.

Clues:

- If you check out Monie Love's version of 'It's a Shame', you will find that its full title is 'It's a Shame (Little Sister)'.
- *T-Rex* is short for *Tyrannosaurus rex.*
- Haysi Fantayzee and Monie Love sound like people.

Another reason why I came up with this eclectic mix was for the second part. Pub cricket contestants had to work out the correct titles and artists and then use the first letters of each, which were not in the right order, to unscramble the Christmas message. It was great fun to put it together, but it is harder than it looks when you're trying to play and earn a reasonable cricket score.

It was also harder for my family than it looked, as this was just before the likes of Shazam. Therefore, they had to do a bit of good old-fashioned research.

Because I am British and because this is cricket, I created more formal versions and variations on the theme. They are as follows.

Pop Cricket

Compile lists of your favourite songs onto a playlist, and then challenge a friend.

Pop Test Cricket

Play using your iTunes, Xbox music, or equivalent playlists, or on a long journey listening to the radio. As with real cricket, play until you have lost ten wickets each. Then, count up the runs and see who wins. You can even have two 'innings' each.

If there are two or more players, you can do one of the following:

- Take alternate songs (most relevant if playing while listening to the radio).
- Swap as each wicket falls.
- Get to ten wickets and then swap over.

20/20 Pop Cricket

As per test cricket, but limit to twenty songs for each player. The highest score wins.

One more rule: If 'Swords of a Thousand Men' (or something similar) is played, then the match is abandoned. Either that, or apply the maximum number of runs (i.e. twenty-four).

Some good examples of songs to use when playing pop cricket are found in the top-ten lists in this book so far. So, if you want to play—or if you are wondering what the songs are, or if you want to check—*my* answers are as follows (listed by chapter title):

'Scary Quo': Pop cricket score—201 for 2
'My Old Man's a Busman': Pop cricket score—248 for 7
'"Back Home" with Bobby Moore': Pop cricket score—341 for 5
'On the Radio': Pop cricket score—48 for 9

Peter Gilbert

'A Transport of Delight': Pop cricket score—124 for 2
'When Elvis Met My Auntie Margaret . . . Twice': Pop cricket score—148 for 2
'Getting Ahead in the Movies': Pop cricket score—86 for 6
'Nearly Shipwrecked': Pop cricket score—130 all out
'Hazel O'Connor Owes Me a Pint': Pop cricket score—108 all out

My Top Ten Cricket based Songs

'Soul Limbo'—Booker T. & the M.G.'s
'Cricket Bag'—David Frost
'Jiggery Pokery'—The Duckworth Lewis Method
'Dreadlock Holiday'—10cc
'Victor Trumper'—Locksmith
'My Cricket'—Rumer
'Shane Warne Song'—Kevin 'Bloody' Wilson
'Cricket'—The Kinks
'Fuckin' 'Ell, It's Fred Titmus'—Half Man Half Biscuit
'Howzat!'—Sherbet

Pop cricket score: 101 for 6

Things to Check Out

On YouTube:

- Funny cricketing commentating
- Joel Garner (Big Bird)
- 'Identity'—X-Ray Spex

Elsewhere:
www.myoldmansabusman.com

Ben Elton Made Me Write This Book

Another of my massive influences, apart from music, is the changing face of comedy.

I had been brought up in the '60s and '70s on Saturday-night variety shows like *Seaside Special* and *The Royal Variety Performance,* and on talent shows like *Opportunity Knocks* and *New Faces*—not to mention, in the late '60s, the weekly must-see show in our house, *The Golden Shot.*

The Golden Shot was a quiz show hosted by comedian Bob Monkhouse. Contestants competed for the chance to fire a crossbow at a golden apple, or whatever the target was that week, for the chance to win cash prizes. No Sunday was complete without hearing Bob say, 'Bernie, the bolt please,' as he instructed his sidekick, Bernie, to load the bolt into the crossbow. The contestant then had to tell the crossbow, manned by an invisible bowman, where to aim and when to fire by saying things like 'Left, right, up, down,' and, finally, 'Fire!'

The tension was heightened as, once Bernie had loaded his bolt, the action was shown in the first person. It was much like playing Halo or Call of Duty today. We, the viewers, looked down the target.

In our house, we would all be shouting 'Left!' or 'Up!' at the TV, as it was easy for us to see where the contestant should aim the crossbow in order to hit the golden apple. We thought that the contestants' instructions would not get them the prize: 'Left a bit, right a bit, up a bit . . .'

The word *tense* barely describes how we felt waiting to see what would happen when the contestant finally said, 'Fire!'

We were terribly disappointed if the contestant missed and didn't win the money—probably £20 back in the day—especially if he or she hadn't listened to our instructions.

Mum and Dad had deemed the variety and big comedy shows of the '70s to be safe for family viewing, even if the comedy was often a little risqué. So, my siblings and I were fed a comedy diet of shows like *The Two Ronnies* and *Cannon and Ball*. Also, Christmas Day was not complete until we had seen the Morecambe and Wise Christmas special.

Weekends—and, as we got older, evenings—were the time for sitcoms. We children were subjected to a wide range, as Dad, previously established as a bus driver, loved *On the Buses* in addition to other shows of the era, such as *Steptoe and Son*, *The Likely Lads,* and *Dad's Army*. But we also used to watch the current shows, which included *Man about the House; Terry and June; George and Mildred; The Good Life; Rising Damp; Some Mothers Do 'Ave 'Em; Porridge; It Ain't Half Hot Mum;* and *Mind Your Language,* to name but a few.

Naturally, some of these have aged better than others.

Mind Your Language, for example, which is a sitcom set in a language school, would not be shown on TV today because it presents an array of racial stereotypes, including an Arab man wearing a fez and a Japanese man who constantly bowed and said, 'Ah, so.' But to us at the time, it was simply funny.

One stereotype that the show did instil in adolescent boys (and their dads) was that French girls were very pretty and spoke in a very sexy accent.

So, whilst the programme would be considered extremely non-PC today, no schoolboy should be denied the vision that was Françoise Pascal, who played the very sexy French student.

This fact, clearly, was not lost on sitcom producers. In the early '80s, Vicki Michelle played another sexy French character, Yvette Carte-Blanche, in the sitcom *'Allo 'Allo,* which also gave us the character Madame Fanny La Fan, whose name is only bested by Kenny Everett's character Cupid Stunt. I can't believe that either of these got past the censors in those more conservative days, especially those shows airing before the watershed of nine o'clock, by which time children were presumed to be in bed, asleep, and out of harm's way. Now, of course, kids can enjoy full-on sexual innuendo and blatant references in shows like *The Big Bang Theory* and *How I Met Your Mother* at five o'clock in the afternoon.

Morecambe and Wise's 'Breakfast Sketch', however, looks as clever and brilliantly choreographed today as it did when it first aired. My kids enjoy watching it on YouTube. They also enjoy the classic episode 'Fork Handles' of *The Two Ronnies* because of its brilliant wordplay.

One lesser known episode, one of my favourites, is when Leonard Rossiter appears with Morecambe and Wise in 1978 for a parody of the 1940s wartime group the Andrews Sisters. Rossiter is very funny in everything I've seen him in, from the Cinzano ads with Joan Collins of the late '70s and early '80s to his brilliant, and probably best known, character Rigsby in the sitcom *Rising Damp*.

Generally, the guests on *The Morecambe and Wise Show* were upstaged by Eric and Ernie (the Ant and Dec of their day), as the viewer would focus on them (but especially on Eric) as they hammed it up. However, in this particular sketch, whilst they are all singing the Andrew Sisters' big hit 'Boogie Woogie Bugle Boy from Company B', Rossiter takes front and centre with his performance. Eric and Ernie don't really get a look in.

Then, in 1979, something happened to change all of that, blowing it out of the water. That something was *Not the Nine o'Clock News,* a television comedy sketch show that ran from 1979 to 1982 and which was originally shown on BBC Two as an alternative to the news, which aired at the same time on BBC One.

NTNON, as it was sometimes known, featured up and coming stars Rowan Atkinson, Pamela Stephenson, Mel Smith, and Griff Rhys Jones. It featured satirical sketches based on current news stories and popular culture; parody songs; comedy sketches; re-edited videos; and spoof television formats. Most important to us, it was a bit rude. The closest we'd had to this before was *The Goodies,* which could be equally non-PC, risqué, and anarchic at times, but which, because of its slapstick nature, managed to avoid being categorised as not suitable for viewing—even in our house.

Fifteen at the time, I was deemed old enough to watch the show. Unfortunately, however, it was not quite rude or anarchic enough for Mum and Dad to refrain from watching it. Therefore, I'd experience some toe-curling and excruciatingly embarrassing teenage moments when I'd want the ground to open up and swallow me. This was never more apparent than when my whole family watched in silence as the team sang the song 'Kinda Lingers', which, yes, was a cunning linguistic reference to oral sex.

At the beginning of the song, the team, playing pop stars in full pop-video style, seem to be holding back and keeping things reasonably

My Old Man's a Busman

ambiguous by making an effort to pronounce the phrase as 'Kinda Lingers'. As the song progresses, however, they just go for it.

We could all enjoy some sketches together, such as 'Gerald the Talking Gorilla', but what made the show must-see viewing for me and my generation was that it also included sketches and songs for us, ones that our parents hated, such as 'Gob on You!', which was a parody of punk rock and its culture of spitting—or gobbing, as it was known—at concerts.

We kids couldn't get enough of this. Whilst Mum and Dad would tut, huff, and harrumph when these sketches were aired, I'd be desperately trying to learn the words because, after episodes like this appeared, everybody at school would be singing the song the next day.

The songs and sketches were even released on records and tapes, which meant that we could listen to them over and over again and learn the rudest bits.

As we entered the 1980s, comedy changed. Old-school comedy and comedians were out of vogue. The new breed of alternative comics, as they were known, filled our screens with shows like *A Kick Up the Eighties,* a sketch show that introduced us to Rik Mayall as the Brummie character Kevin Turvey, and *The Comic Strip Presents* series, with its ensemble cast, again including Rik Mayall—along with Ade Edmondson, Dawn French, Jennifer Saunders, and Robbie Coltrane, all of whom went on to become famous in many other shows. All of these shows were brought to us by the first new TV channel in decades. Up to that point, we had only had three. Now, finally, we had four with the imaginatively named Channel 4.

Rik Mayall went on to appear in other new comedy shows such as *The Young Ones,* a sitcom based on four students in the same digs. For no reason, a contemporary band (e.g. Madness) would suddenly appear and play their latest release on the show. Mayall also starred in *Bottom*. Both of these shows also featured Ade Edmondson and brilliantly showed off Rik and Ade's anarchic style, which they had previously honed in their double act the Dangerous Brothers.

One of these shows' writers was Ben Elton, a stand-up comedian who also wrote and presented *Friday Night Live* and *Saturday Night Live,* which showcased new and emerging talent and launched the careers of comedians such as Harry Enfield (with his catchphrase-speaking characters Stavros and Loadsamoney).

Elton, who has since produced many TV series and West End shows, including *We Will Rock You,* which is based on the music of Queen, has sometimes been accused (by other comedians) of selling out. I can only presume that this is because he started out as a young, alternative comedian spouting very left-wing, anti–Maggie Thatcher, conservative views, but he became very rich and is associated with the likes of Bryan May and Roger Taylor of Queen, with whom he co-wrote 'We Will Rock You' and who are now seen as very much part of the establishment. For me, though, anyone who gave us *The Young Ones* and then the best comedy series ever (well, all except for the first series), *Blackadder,* deserves a few quid in his pocket and a lot of respect.

I got into *Blackadder* about halfway through series two in the mid '80s. I'd watched a couple of episodes of the first series and didn't really like it, especially the Blackadder character played by Rowan Atkinson. Because everyone was talking about series two then, especially about the character Queenie played by Miranda Richardson, I gave it another go and was immediately hooked. I still love it and enjoy it with my sons, too. Our favourite episode is 'Bells', which again features Rik Mayall. He steals every scene from Atkinson's character Blackadder as the completely over-the-top Lord Flashheart.

Ben Elton has written many books. I have read them all, some late into the night because I am unable to put them down. This takes me back to childhood, when I'd read in bed with a torch long after I was supposed to be asleep.

I've been a voracious reader ever since discovering Enid Blyton's series *The Famous Five* and *Secret Seven* at an early age. I'd buy the latest *Secret Seven* adventure with my weekly pocket money and devour it in one sitting, even if that meant breaking our very strict bedtime and lights-out rules.

I remember when I was seven or eight and Netty and I lied to our friends at school every Friday, telling them that we'd seen the previous night's episode of *Top of the Pops*. Had we admitted that we hadn't seen it, we'd be regarded, quite simply, as social lepers. Even though Mum and Dad were well aware of this fact (we told them every single week), they did their best to ignore us and insisted that we go to bed at 7.30 p.m. after *Tomorrow's World* and before *TOTPs*.

Lying in bed and being able to hear Led Zeppelin's 'Whole Lotta Love', which signified the programme's start, was torture the magnitude of which I cannot describe, as there is no modern equivalent, given our hundred-channel, twenty-four-hour TV. Missing *Big Brother*, *The X Factor*, or *Britain's Got Talent* doesn't even come close.

The first Ben Elton novel, *Stark*, was published in 1989. I can't put my finger on just what it was that made this book so great. Maybe it was the way in which he verbalised observations and built subtle links into the text for people to find or work out. Or perhaps it was the fact that Elton went off on musing and amusing tangents. Whatever it was, it was when I read it that I first thought that I would like to write a book like his. The seed was sown.

Choosing a favourite of his novels is difficult for me. I've enjoyed them all. Still, one of the elements from *Gridlock* always amused me. It's about marketing—more specifically, the global marketing of products, which has become even more relevant (and amusing) to me as my career progressed and I have been exposed to marketing techniques. Think Jif to Cif, Marathon to Snickers, or the Norwich Union Building Society to Aviva.

In Elton's book *Gridlock,* the British member of a European committee set up to name the next pan-European Ford car is berated by his bosses for agreeing to launch the new model as the Ford Crapé. It's obvious to the British reader why this is an issue, but not to the characters' European counterparts. It seems a bit silly to think that this could actually happen in real life, but it comes about in the book this way: 'But everything café society is, it's very now and on trend.'[2] It is amusing and, trust me, very believable.

I was reminded of this recently, when an employee of the company I work for received his new company car. In the current (and confusing) vehicle registration system that England has adopted, every so often a combination of numbers and letters emerges that should ring the DVLA's alarm bells but which slips through the proverbial net. One such combo is the numeral 11 (e.g. in 2011), especially when combined with the 'prefix' *sh–*. This is to be avoided, as the publishing industry, for similar reasons, avoids magazines titled *FLICK*.

---

[2]   Elton, Ben, *Gridlock* (London: Black Swan, 2006).

Of course, some will always push the boundaries. The best example is Mark Millar's graphic novel magazine *CLINT*. How this wasn't remanded to the top shelf, its title covered by opaque plastic, I'll never know. Whether to avoid the censor's pen or to perform an audacious coup, Millar went one stage further by adding an apostrophe above and slightly to the left of a lower case letter *I*. Thus, the magazine title reads, *Mark Millar's CLiNT*.

Without going into the mechanics (excuse the pun) of company car processes, which could fill a chapter (but be extremely tedious and off-topic), I would like to mention the employee who had waited six months for a new car. On the day it was due to be delivered, he had waited all morning in eager anticipation. He had rushed to the door when he heard the delivery transporter driving down the road. From there, he waited patiently as the driver manoeuvred his shiny new vehicle off the lorry and into his drive. It was then that he was confronted with the number plate: 'SH11 YTE'.

Unsurprisingly, he asked that it be changed.

With visions of publishing this book, I would practise with my own observations, turning things I saw into mental vignettes, storing them away for later use, whenever that might be.

Whilst on a stag do in Margate in the early '90s, I and a group of friends were sitting in a grotty cliff top café on the morning after the night before. We were hung over, drinking coffee, and contemplating the three-plus-hour drive home to Gloucestershire. Whilst we were deciding who had drunk the least and would take first shift, I noticed that a woman in a long coat, who had been sitting in the corner of the café since we had arrived, was trying to leave. I say 'trying', as she could not quite get away. Every time she closed the door behind her, the wind, which was blowing off the sea, would catch her coat and blow it back inside. Each time she thought she'd closed the door to leave, she'd step forward and be pulled back again. Nobody else had noticed this. The fourth time it happened, I was in hysterics, even with my hangover.

I eventually did the gallant thing and went and held the door for her, much to the confusion of my mates—not because they wouldn't have done the same thing, but because they were amazed that I'd picked up on it, as none of them had. They would be equally astounded that, of all the things that happened that weekend, I'd remembered this story.

My Old Man's a Busman

Another event occurred at Barcelona Airport. On the day in question, the airport was not particularly busy, yet the service in all of the cafés and restaurants was particularly bad—so bad, in fact, that even we, a group of Brits, actually complained about the queues and waiting time, only to be told that there was nothing anyone could do since the café was short-staffed that day.

Having eventually gotten our four coffees and found a reasonably clean table, one not piled high with SH11 YTE, I noticed a 'please leave your comments' card on the table. Someone had written on it. I picked it up. It read, 'This service was crap.'

It was probably written by a disgruntled youth or some thirty-something like us who had nothing better to do at the airport. But I love to think that it was written by an elderly churchgoing woman who was not normally given to any form of expletive but who was absolutely at the end of her tether because of the usual stresses of travel and had been pushed totally over the edge by the appalling experience.

My favourite episode, though, involves an elderly woman. I'm not being cruel. It just seems that elderly women do funny things. Just watch any episode of *You've Been Framed* and tell me that elderly women falling over and off of things doesn't make you laugh out loud. The best of these scenes, in my opinion, involve water. You see an old woman, slightly off balance, tottering backwards. The camera pans back. A few feet behind her is a child's paddling pool full of water. The camera zooms back in on the woman, who is still stumbling backwards towards the pool. The outcome is inevitable, maybe even obvious in the first second of the clip, but when it happens, it can still make crisps (presuming that you're eating them, of course) spray out of your nose. Comedy gold.

This particular incident didn't involve water, but, again, it happened at an airport, Florence (or Firenze, to use its local and more sexy and exciting Italian name), I think.

I was waiting at baggage reclaim, as one does, and noticed an elderly woman making her way through the crowd of people whilst waiting for the conveyor to start. What got my attention was her way of pushing through. Only old people, especially old women, can get away with this without causing a riot. As the conveyor started and the baggage began to come around, I watched as she proceeded to pick up a number of black cases similar to my own and give them the once-over before dropping them back down.

Now, knowing how inventive elderly people (especially those who have lived through the war) can be and how regular travellers with dull suitcases try to do things to identify their baggage in just such an instance as this, I was surprised that she had not thought to tie a piece of ribbon around the handle or put stickers onto the bag—something that would have at least enabled her to easily recognise it. By now, the woman had picked up and discarded her fifth black case. My gob could not have been any more smacked, therefore, when out though the plastic flaps came a black case covered in bright pink ribbons and yellow stickers. She calmly plucked it off the belt before walking away.

Nearly bursting, I turned to my girlfriend and asked, 'Did you see that?'

'What?'

'That lady, she [blah de blah, blah].'

'No. How do you notice these things?'

'Don't know, but maybe I'll write a book about it one day.'

My Top Ten Comedy Songs

'D.I.V.O.R.C.E.'—Billy Connolly
'Boom Oo Yata-Ta-Ta'—Eric Morecambe and Ernie Wise
'The Bantam Cock'—Jake Thakray
'Magic Roundabout'—Jasper Carrot
'Living Next Door to Alan'—Kevin 'Bloody' Wilson
'Chocolate Salty Balls'—Chef (voiced by Isaac Hayes) of *South Park*
'My Old Man's a Dustman'—Lonnie Donegan
'Colt 45'—Afroman
'Bond Is a Four-Letter Word'—Billy Howard
'Black Pudding Bertha'—The Goodies

Pop cricket score: 56 for 5

Things to Check Out

On YouTube:

- Leonard Rossiter, the Andrews Sisters
- Nice Danielle legs, 1 of 1
- Lord Flashheart's grand entrance
- 'Kinda Lingers'

Elsewhere:
www.myoldmansabusman

I Stole Robbie Williams's Underpants

The second person who is the famous cousin of someone I know (Glen Gregory of Heaven 17 being the first) is by far the more famous. His identity is given away by the chapter title.

Robbie Williams's cousin is my friend Dave of the many 'best adverts ever' debates. Dave, having introduced me to the music of the Macc Lads, can claim to have saved my life.

For my proper job, I drive many miles in the car. As I'm sure is the case with most drivers, I occasionally hit the proverbial wall, which appears either late at night, early in the morning, or two hours into the drive on a wet, bleak day on a dull motorway stretch when your eyelids feel like lead.

I've turned up the music. No good.

I've changed the music. No good.

I've opened the driver's-side window to give myself a blast of fresh, cold air. No good.

I've opened both windows to create a cold, hurricane-force sensation, similar to the one a person might feel after jumping out of a plane . . . No good.

So, when I find myself driving along, I slap, hit, and pinch myself—not just the type of playful tap a person might land on a partner's knee or leg in time to the music whilst driving along (although, of course, you should keep two hands on the wheel at all times), but full-on punches that leave bruises. I do this to try to stay with it and keep from succumbing to sleep until the next junction or service station. No good.

Then, that voice inside my head starts, the one with soft, soothing, hypnotic, soporific tones . . . 'If you just close your eyes . . . just for a second . . . you'll feel so much better . . . Go on . . . you know you want to.'

Noooooooooooooooooooo!

At this point, many times over the years, I've reached for the ultimate lifesaver, the Macc Lads' CD.

A smile crosses my face as I hear Mutley's gruff tones launch into the Macc Lads' 'Sweaty Betty': 'She wore big knickers and she worked on't sewage farm.'

As I tune into their rude, crude, and ridiculous lyrics (rhyming 'Huddersfield' with 'getting your udders feel'd'), I don't even need to stop, let alone think that I'll fall asleep and crash.

Between us, Dave and I know more song lyrics than pretty much anyone else I know does. We can spend hours, much to the annoyance of Dave's lovely but long-suffering wife, going through our repertoire.

We know it's not cool, but we just don't care. We regularly lose hours, usually the early ones after a glass or three of wine, scouring YouTube, Amazon (other music download websites are available), or our music libraries for our favourite and forgotten tunes, past and present, but mostly past.

Many moons ago, far more than we care to admit, Dave and I worked for the same company and had the opportunity to indulge our passion for music and compilations as part of our job.

We both worked in sales but had been asked to work with the marketing team on the relaunch of a toffee brand. Our job was to come up with some ideas for engaging and motivating the sales force. I think it probably took less than a minute for us to decide that music had to be the answer. It would motivate us, so why wouldn't it motivate everybody else?

It took another minute to decide that we should produce a tape for the sales team to listen to in their cars; I said that this was many moons ago, back when cars had cassette tape players (as referenced in Eminem's song 'Stan'), although I think that this was probably only a couple of years before CD players took over.

Anyone who had a cassette tape player will remember being frustrated when trying to find the next track, as one had to keep forwarding and rewinding the tape to locate the song. Later versions would find the gap (if the tracks weren't recorded too close together). Worse, sometimes the tape wound around the spools and took hours to remove, an operation that normally required a variety of instruments, including tweezers, a screwdriver, and a pen. Even then, the tape would probably be ruined.

Peter Gilbert

After a final minute, Dave and I had worked out that we should convince the team to allow us that compile all of this amazing tape while they got on with the other elements of the launch.

The finished tape featured a person describing the key facts and phrases about the products so that the sales team could listen to and remember these details while they were driving around. It also included music to encourage them (the sales team) to listen to the tape in the first place.

Sadly, I no longer have a copy of the tape. If memory serves me, it included 'Sugar, Sugar' by the Archies (we'd gone for a sugar-themed compilation to complement the toffee product that we were selling; this was very intellectual marketing), 'Candy Man' by Sammy Davis Jr, and—at Dave's insistence, despite the fact that most people had never heard of it—'Pour Some Sugar on Me' by Def Leppard. This last, I think, was the first song we had come up with. It at least gave us a modicum of credibility.

Because I had a heavy workload, Dave—I seem to recall—ended up working on the tape more than I did. I say 'work', but it was a labour of love. To this day, of all the things we achieved back in the day, we still talk about and are proud of the tape. Other people who were around at the time still remember it. We did it just to try to sell a few more toffees. I keep looking, but I don't think one will ever turn up on eBay.

To be specific (and truthful), Robbie is Dave's second cousin, perhaps once removed (Dave's dad's cousin Janette is Robbie's aunty). But, yes, I'm speaking of *the* Robbie from the original band Take That and the re-formed Take That. This is the Robbie of 'Angels', 'Let Me Entertain You', 'United', 'Swing When You're Winning', and 'Swings Both Ways' fame.

Now, before you run away with yourself here, expecting stories about wild parties at Robbie's mansion in the United States, you should know that Dave has never actually met Robbie Williams, although his brothers and family have. At the particular time I'm talking about, my connection with Robbie was both a little tenuous and somewhat vicarious in nature.

By the late '90s, I'd left the company at which Dave and I had worked together and was working for a promotions and advertising agency based in London. Pepsi-Cola was one of their clients. We had previously used the Spice Girls and other music artists to promote the Pepsi brand across Europe, but in this particular year, because he was famous and had wide appeal, Pepsi had signed Robbie Williams.

When we'd worked together, Dave and I both lived in Cheltenham. He still does, and I often visit. Cheltenham is a beautiful spa town in the Cotswolds, home to its fair share of famous residents, although, unfortunately, being Robbie Williams's second cousin does not yet merit a blue plaque on Dave's property.

However, there are a good few blue plaques to be seen around the town, as it and the surrounding area has been, or is, home to the likes of Dr Edward Jenner (inventor of the vaccine), Beatrix Potter, Alfred Lord Tennyson, Laurie Lee, Gustav Holst, Dame Felicity Lott, Sir Ralph Richardson, Damien Hirst, Brian Jones (of the Rolling Stones), and Arthur Travers Harris (Bomber Harris, WWII hero).

There is even an official blue plaque commemorating the house of Gilbert Laid Jessop (1874–1975), captain of the Gloucestershire cricket club, so maybe there is hope for Dave yet.

Maybe it's the private schools, the world-renowned Cheltenham Ladies' College, or simply the stunning scenery, but, plaques aside, the area also boasts links to Kate Moss, Jeremy Clarkson, Stella McCartney, Alex James (*Blur*), Tom Waite (Lofty from *EastEnders*), Lily Allen, Jilly Cooper, Eddie 'the Eagle' Edwards, Richard O'Brien (of *The Rocky Horror Picture Show* and *The Crystal Maze* fame), Anne Robinson, Kristin Scott Thomas, Tamara Beckwith, Würzel from Motörhead, and—we cannot forget—actor Mike Grady, latterly of *Last of the Summer Wine* fame, wherein he played the character Barry.

Grady came to fame by way of the late '70s sitcom *Citizen Smith,* but before that he had appeared in the kids' shows *The Fenn Street Gang* and *Tightrope*. More important, he starred in Pepsi's early 1970s *Lipsmackin'* campaign, which was, at the time, one of the most talked about ads in the playground. One was either one of the kids who could, or one of the kids who couldn't, recite the tag line of the ad: 'Lipsmackin', thirstquenchin', acetastin', motivatin', goodbuzzin', cooltalkin', highwalkin', fastlivin', evergivin', coolfizzin' Pepsi.'

Part of my job at the agency, working alongside a creative partner, an American called Eric, was to come up with promotions that would sell Pepsi's products in shops around Europe.

On this particular job, rather than just come up with the usual 'Buy twenty cans of Pepsi and get a free CD/poster/widget/etc.', Eric had also

Peter Gilbert

come up with some great photography and artwork ideas and had been invited to attend the much talked about 'Robbie photo shoot' in London. As we worked closely together, he thought that I'd be interested, as Robbie was a big star. He asked if I wanted to see if he could swing it for me to go along with him.

I wouldn't say that I was a massive fan of Robbie Williams. It certainly wasn't cool for a guy, especially one of my age, to like Take That, as they were a band for young girls (the equivalent of the Osmonds or the Partridge Family in my day). But he'd done some decent solo stuff by then and was seen as a much more credible artist (even though his army of fans were still mostly teenage girls), so, because of that and because I knew his relative, I agreed to go.

The year was 2000, a new millennium. It was a year when the Manic Street Preachers, Oasis, Britney Spears, All Saints, Madonna, Westlife, Craig David, Eminem, and various ex–Spice Girls could be found topping the charts.

As Robbie was a big star at the time, the whole photo shoot was very 'The numbers are limited' and 'Do you have a pass?' But my name was on that all-important list as third assistant to the creative director or some such lowly title, too lowly given my relatively senior position in the company.

The venue was a trendy studio in London. It was full of photographs of the famous people who had used it, many of them taken by the celebrity photographer Rankin.

Our task, on this one day, was to get hundreds of pictures of Robbie in various scenarios and outfits. These were to be approved by Robbie and his team and could be used by all of the countries on their Pepsi promotional materials.

The creative team had come up with a number of ideas, such as an image of Robbie covered in gunge on some DJ's decks, Robbie jumping through glass, and Robbie standing in a white suit covered in paint (all of which had to be pre-approved by Robbie and his team).

Our team on that day, given that this was Pepsi's global marketing campaign, included creative directors from Pepsi's US agency and European agencies, Pepsi's talent agency, the PR agency, a DJ, the lead photographer (not quite Rankin, but one who clearly, judging by his entourage, had second billing only to the star himself), make-up artists, photographers' assistants, assistants to the photographers' assistants, and, of course, a third assistant to the European agency's creative director.

Surely, you have heard of events becoming a bit of a circus. This was one of those. Everyone who was remotely involved or connected to the project wanted to be at this 'gig'.

The gig was on a Sunday, due to start at 9.00 a.m. sharp in order to get it all done in a day. Lunch would be sushi, as Robbie had specifically requested it.

In a bid to make everything perfect for the star and ensure that he was relaxed and in the right state of mind, a moving sushi bar was erected in the area of the studio that would be used for lunch. Much running around was done in the morning to make sure that it was 'all good for Robbie' and working.

At 8.59 a.m., everything was set—the paper through which Robbie Williams would jump to simulate a glass window (the glass effect would be added afterwards), the white room for paint, the sushi conveyor, the sushi itself, the cameras, the film, the make-up, the DJ decks at which Robbie would stand, and the real decks with a real DJ—to get everyone into the vibe . . . At 9.00 on a Sunday morning?

We were all set and waiting for the big moment.

At around 11.30 a.m., the man himself, entourage in tow, finally arrived and asked if somebody would arrange a warm chicken salad for lunch, as that was what Robbie fancied today. He couldn't possibly start the session until he'd eaten.

The sandwich arrived quickly. As I hadn't been sent to fetch it, I assumed that there was somebody on the list with a title lowlier than mine. Dinner ladies' fourth assistant or sushi replacement lackey, maybe?

After the slow start and long lunch, which Robbie spent playing backgammon with his manager, surrounded by a large crowd watching his every move, the day's event started properly. We got some shots 'in the can', or whatever the photography equivalent to filming is—'on the roll', maybe?

Robbie really threw himself into things in the afternoon. He had been covered in gunge for some shots of him behind some record decks and had jumped through lots of paper (which would be replaced as glass in the final pictures), accompanied by much whooping, applauding, and calls of, 'Great shot, Robbie,' from the collected entourage. All of this, of course, happened to the sounds being mixed by the resident DJ. It's no wonder that celebrities become divas, although I'm not sure if Robbie is or is not a diva.

If you arrive for a photo shoot and your sushi is going around a track on a mini train, your every whim is catered to (in this case, literally), and the onlookers applaud the way in which you jump through a piece of paper, then it's likely that these things will affect your perspective on reality.

The final 'scene' of the day was to be a shot of Robbie dressed head to toe in a white suit and standing in a white room, which would be systematically sprayed with different colours of paints to achieve the creative director's vision.

As I write it, I'm aware that all of this sounds like a load of creative . . . hyperbole. 'Let's imagine a scene where the painted, sprayed suit is juxtaposed against the starkness of the white background and then slowly fades into it.' It is hyperbole, but the final shots were stunning. I still have a framed photo as a memento.

To achieve the desired effect, Robbie's friend Jonathan Wilkes (who made his own short-lived assault on the pop charts) was in the white room with him, firing paint from a large water-blaster gun which was refilled with a different colour until they achieved the desired multicolour effect.

By this time, early evening, the final shots had been taken. Robbie, clearly bored of the staged shots and the whole thing, grabbed the paint-filled gun from Jonathan and ran out of the room blasting everyone who was standing around with pink paint.

I managed to escape the worst of it. As third assistant, I wasn't standing near the front where Robbie was being photographed. I got off relatively light, with only a ruined pair of jeans and a watch that still has remnants of pink paint on it (I don't wear it anymore). One of the female assistants, clearly in a senior position, given her proximity to the onslaught, did not fare so well. She had ended up pretty well covered from head to foot in paint and was in tears.

As events were winding down and we were running behind, the woman had gone off to change into her glad rags, as she was now going to be very late for a friend's birthday bash in central London. She had to rush off the second that we finished . . . in her little black dress.

Robbie did apologise profusely, but I never found out if the woman actually went to the party.

My Old Man's a Busman

Nipping to the loo before I left for home, I bumped into Robbie, who was coming out as I was going in. He was wrapped in a towel, having just had a shower to get all the paint off.

As I went in, I noticed that the shower door was open. I don't know what made me look, but as I peered into the cubicle, I couldn't believe my eyes. There on the floor was a paint-splattered pair of Calvin Klein boxer shorts. Robbie had obviously gotten into the shower whilst wearing them. He had apparently stripped them off and either left them behind on purpose or else forgot to take them with him.

I didn't know what to do. A friend, Sally, was a mad Robbie Williams fan. I immediately thought how amazed she would be to receive a pair of her idol's underwear. It was a sort of reverse Tom Jones scenario.

To an onlooker, I must have looked like a rabbit on a busy road. Go, don't go, go, don't go . . . what if Robbie comes back in and sees me picking up his underpants? What if someone comes in? I had to make a decision—and fast.

In the end, the lure of the prize was too much for me to turn down. I darted in and picked up the boxer shorts. I gave them a quick squeeze out, shoved them into my jacket pocket, and went to do what I'd gone in for.

As I left the loo, a couple of other guys were just coming in. A minute earlier and I'd have been caught in the act . . . pink-handed.

I'd gotten away with it. I left hurriedly and walked back down the corridor. To my horror, I saw Robbie walking towards me but, more to the point, back towards the toilet and shower. He hadn't just left the undershorts behind on purpose. Even a rock star doesn't just leave his CKs behind. Perhaps they were new or his lucky boxers. Either way, I made a quick exit.

Months later, I read a magazine article where Robbie was talking about the price of fame and had made reference to this event, saying something along the lines of, 'People will even steal the most personal possessions, given half a chance. I've even had my underwear stolen from a studio.'

I can't say that I'm proud of my actions that day. If I ever have the privilege of meeting Robbie, I'll happily replace his Calvin Klein's. But I console myself with a couple of things:

1. Those paint-splattered Calvin Klein underpants, to this day, are on display in a place of pride at Sally's house. They are her most treasured possession.
2. I never have a problem when I'm on a course and the person running it says, 'Let's go around the table and say something interesting about ourselves that nobody else would know.' It's a good story to tell. Even my kids, who are too young to have known Robbie at the height of his fame, know that he was famous, and therefore they are awestruck when they hear me tell the story. You have to take it where you can when you're doing it for the kids.

My Top Ten Songs about Crime

'Carolina Drama'—The Raconteurs
'Ma Baker'—Boney M
'Stagger Lee'—Lloyd Price
'I Shot the Sheriff'—Eric Clapton
'Maxwell's Silver Hammer'—The Beatles
'The Killing of Georgie'—Rod Stewart
'Delilah'—The Sensational Alex Harvey Band
'Riot in Cell Block #9'—Dr Feelgood
'I Fought the Law'—The Clash
'Jailhouse Rock'—Elvis Presley

Pop cricket score: 74 for 4

Things to Check Out

On YouTube:

- 'United' (live)—Robbie Williams
- 'Sweaty Betty' and 'Lipsmackin''—The Macc Lads

Elsewhere:
www.myoldmansabusman.com

Les Adventures de Pierre le Wag à Monte Carlo

My first experience of France was when I went there on a family holiday in 1974. We weren't loaded or taken to swanning off around Europe each year. Nothing could be further from the truth. My grandma had inherited some money and decided to treat the family to a holiday. I can clearly remember the day when Netty and I found out.

Living in Hythe at the time, we were only a bus ride away from the local beaches of Calshot and Lepe. These were not quite on a par with Bondi—or even Bournemouth and Sandbanks a little farther down the coast. As local beaches often do, this one had pebbles, ice-cream huts, and the sea, and so it counted as being the seaside. Calshot and Lepe sit on the Solent, the stretch of water between the Isle of Wight and the mainland, at the end of Southampton Water, and they have stunning views across to the island, which is only a few miles away.

On this particular Saturday, Netty and I had decided that we were going to take the bus to Calshot. The bus fare was about 50 pence return each. But, when Dad found out our plans for the day, he said, 'You may want to think about saving that money.'

'Why?' we asked.

'Well, we may be going on a special holiday this year,' Mum added.

Holidays up to this point had included going to Bognor Regis and staying in a bed and breakfast. The first I vaguely remember, being just over three years of age at the time, was to Morecambe Bay, where we stayed in a bed and breakfast; Littlehampton, near Bognor, where we visited twice and stayed in a rented bungalow; and Poole, near Sandbanks, where we stayed in a rented house.

My Old Man's a Busman

So, where to next?

Logically, if you follow the pattern (excluding Morecambe), the mystery destination would have to be farther west than Bournemouth, and we would have to stay in a semi-detached house.

'Where are we going?' we asked.

'It's a surprise,' Dad said. 'We'll tell you nearer the time.'

When Dad had gone, probably to watch the cricket, we started pestering Mum.

'Give us a clue. Is it north, south, east, or west of here?'

'Um, I'm not sure, really,' Mum said.

We were a bit confused. How could she not know what direction it was? Netty and I went to the beach anyway and spent the afternoon trying to work out the location of our next holiday.

I think we concluded that the place might be as exotic, and as far away as, Devon, given that Dad had often talked about this as amongst one of the places he had visited in childhood. Also, Devon was where Mum and Dad had spent their honeymoon.

At some point, nearer the time, the secret was revealed. We were going to France.

Wow! This would be our first ever trip abroad, but it turned out that it was not just a hop across the Channel, as we were, in fact, going to the South of France. At the time, it was the equivalent of hearing today that one is going to the Maldives.

Then we found out that we were going to stay in a hotel. Forget the Maldives, Necker Island. We were going to stay in Menton, a small town in the south-west of France that is only a few miles from Monaco, very close to the Italian border. This trip was my first experience of foreign shores. It was also very exciting and memorable. Generally, a few things stick in my mind.

Firstly, we travelled to France by train, as Dad had always feared flying. It's a shame that he never had the experience of flying, since, given his love of maps, I think he'd have loved to get that perspective, especially if in the air over someplace familiar, where could determine over which town he was flying or which road junction was on the ground below.

Ironically, one of Dad's favourite jokes was this:

> Two men are sitting in a plane. One of them, pointing out the window, turns to other and says, 'Look down there. Those people milling around look like ants.'
>
> The other looks and says, 'You idiot, those *are* ants. We haven't taken off yet.'

Over the years, I've flown a lot for my job. I still get a thrill when I am able to see and identify features about which I learned in geography lessons, such as the paths of rivers, eroding coastlines, and the formation of the oxbow lakes. Flying over a large mountain range such as the Alps, I could really make out the details of Arêtes, Pyramidal Peaks, and *Roches Moutonnées*. It is amazing that I can remember these clearly now but not when I was sitting for my A-level geography exam.

The only thing I really remember about the train trip down through France, other than that it seemingly took forever, was that I was wakened to see Paris. It was night-time, but I think that Mum and Dad thought that my sister and I should see it, as it might be the highlight of the journey. But in my tired, bleary-eyed state, I just perceived it as some lights in the distance.

Whilst in the South of France, we also took the opportunity to travel over the border to Italy. It was only a day trip by train, but it felt very exciting to be visiting yet another country, especially one that was, at the time, beyond our wildest dreams. We visited San Remo, an unremarkable Italian large town. My only real memory of this place is of the police with their smart white uniforms. All carried guns, which was very unlike the local bobbies in Hythe.

Having travelled to that area since, I know that we must have passed through Monte Carlo, Beaulieu, and Villefranche on the train. Stunning as these places are to an adult, they didn't leave an impression on me as a ten-year-old boy. I was probably listening to Elvis on my tape recorder and imagining that it was me singing to the crowd instead of taking in the beautiful Mediterranean coastline.

Joff, just learning to speak, was only about two years old on this trip. At the hotel where we stayed—a modest but very nice, family-run place—we were served every morning by the same waitress. By the end of the holiday, Joff had taken to calling her Stefanie, although this was not her name. Because he was so young, we were unable to ask him why, yet every time he saw her, he'd point and say, 'Stephanie.'

Eventually, Mum worked it out. Every morning, when the waitress came to our table once we'd finished breakfast, she'd politely ask, 'C'est fini?'

As Joff was two, my parents put him to bed fairly early. Every evening, Dad took me off for a walk while Mum got Joff settled. Netty never came with us, so I guess that she preferred helping Mum rather than going for long walks around the streets of Menton. There was nothing remarkable, such as taking a trip to the beach or seeing a famous landmark, about these walks, but they were memorable.

Each evening, we'd take a different route, just to look-see, as Dad would say. We found places that other tourists normally wouldn't, such as little parks in amongst houses, frescos, statues, and fountains in little backstreets. While wandering, Dad and I chatted about family history, football, or whatever it was we had just come across. This was quality time and proper bonding.

I think that I hold a rather romanticised view, as I'm sure that I didn't appreciate my walks with Dad quite so much at the time, especially given that he'd drag me out to take one every night. In later life, however, I've taken the time to do go on walks with my own kids. I hope they will look back on these and value them, even if now they'd prefer to be playing on their xbox.

'But, Dad . . . '

'No, it's stopped raining. We're going for a wander to see what we can see.'

These are happy memories. Still, nothing would have prepared me for the next time I visited Monaco.

It was the late '90s. I was working for a promotions company based in Margate, Kent. I'm aware that there is little Kudos to be had in admitting that I worked in Margate, but this job had perks.

Peter Gilbert

We worked with Pepsi in the United States, and so I did a few business trips to New York. We'd opened an office near Pepsi in the United States, so I then made regular trips to the States. The company was nominated for, and won, a Queens Award for Enterprise, which was presented at our Kent offices by HRH Prince Andrew, Duke of York.

As we'd recently opened our US office, we decided to ask Prince Andrew if he would officially declare it open while on his visit. I say 'ask Prince Andrew'; obviously, we asked his people's people, who asked his people, who asked his advisors, who asked his senior advisor, who, I presume, asked his batman—and, to our surprise, we received a reply saying that he'd be delighted to. Given the distance, this was not going to be a Live Aid concert scenario, with the Prince's arriving in Kent and then hopping onto the Concorde to fly over to the States. No, this would be done remotely via webcam. As I had set up and held responsibility for running the US operation, my colleagues decided that I would be there, not in the United Kingdom, on the big day.

The build-up in the UK office consisted of numerous visits by various authorities and the Prince's people, checks by security staff, and what seemed like endless rehearsals of protocol and minute-by-minute run-throughs of the coming event. It reached the point where it almost seemed like too much hassle, as there were too many consequences if one put a foot wrong or said something unscripted. On the day, though, all went smoothly. Things were much more relaxed than we could ever have imagined, as we had been led to believe that things would not be relaxed at all. Prince Andrew enjoyed his time playing with the products and chatting to the staff so much that he overran. He waved off his PA each time she tried to get him to leave (although this may have been because our MD, Emma, bore more than a vague resemblance to Courteney Cox).

Also, Prince Andrew really got into the spirit of opening the new office.

We had set up a video link between the two offices and had placed a giant screen in the Margate building so that all staff members and visitors could watch us when it came to the big moment. On the other end of things, we were watching the proceedings on a small laptop.

We had had a small plaque made for the US office. It was inscribed, 'Officially opened by HRH Prince Andrew, Duke of York'. One of the women in the office had made some little curtains to cover it. We thought

My Old Man's a Busman

that it would be fun to try to coordinate the Prince's speech with the unveiling of our plaque. Having had this explained to him, HRH Prince Andrew insisted that *he* pretend to reveal the plaque.

As the broadcast was handed over to the US office and we appeared on the giant screen, I made a short speech, ensuring to thank and welcome the Prince according to the strict protocol guidelines. Then, when the moment came, we turned the camera on the curtain.

HRH Prince Andrew said a few congratulatory words, ending with something along the lines of, 'And I now declare this office officially open.'

With that, we saw him put his hand into the air and, laughing, pull at an imaginary cord. We in the US office had not been briefed on this. Quickly realising what was going on, somebody on our team reached over and pulled the cord. The curtains opened to reveal the plaque.

There had been a bit of a delay and the curtains moved none too smoothly, given that someone was yanking the cord in a panic, making our UK colleagues laugh, but HRH Prince Andrew took it in good humour and blamed the time difference.

For us, it was over really quickly. We had missed the buzz and excitement of being there with Prince Andrew, but we had still had a great experience. So, we shut up shop early and went out to celebrate in the traditional British way.

Another perk of my job was that, once a year, my company invited its top customers to Monaco, more specifically, to the Formula One Grand Prix in Monaco.

I'd previously been to Silverstone to see the British Grand Prix. It was exciting, but nothing compares to the atmosphere of Monaco. The racetrack itself is the streets of Monaco and Monte Carlo. Building the course takes six weeks. Another three weeks of work is required to remove it after the event. Because of its tight corners, the numerous elevation changes, and a tunnel, the racetrack at Monaco is viewed as the most difficult Formula One track in the world. The track's layout has many of the stands sitting literally trackside. People can also get a great view just by looking out of their windows.

So, whilst watching from a building would be great, we were on a boat, moored right against the tracks and literally a few feet from the cars, Formula One racing cars.

Peter Gilbert

Once again, I found myself on a boat thinking of backgammon, as the World Backgammon Championships have taken place in Monte Carlo for thirty years. If the tournament had been on when I was there, I may have been tempted to enter and see if those hundreds of games, played years before, had paid off. But, being that the backgammon championships weren't taking place, I asked myself what else there was to do apart from sightseeing, going to the casino, soaking up some rays, popping along to the Cannes Film Festival, people-watching, star-spotting, car-spotting, bar-hopping, Champagne-cork-popping, women-watching, and watching the event itself.

It's said that there are only two types of women in Monaco during the Grand Prix: those on boats and those who want to be on boats. Although the same can be said of the race cars.

Sitting outside the Rascas Bar one afternoon, I was watching the fabulous cars (although not Formula One cars) driving around the track. The bar is closed on race days since the seating is right on the track, but on non-race days, the locals and visitors can drive around the track and show off their flashy cars. While Ferraris are two a penny in Monaco, a particularly unusual one caught my eye.

This Ferrari, bright yellow, came past with music blaring and engine revving. It was driven by a man who had dark hair, was good-looking, and was probably Italian. Nothing unusual in any of that.

What was unusual was that he was on his own. This was extraordinarily unusual, so much so that I pointed it out to the guys I was with. However, when that the car came past again—music and engine revving alike even louder now, probably to ensure that everybody looked—the driver had been joined by not one but two very glamorous women. And remember, there's not much room in the front of a Ferrari.

As the week goes by, Monaco fills up. The film festival crowd decamps from Cannes a few miles up the coastline, the boats arrive, and everybody else descends, filling every available room for miles around.

On Friday, I appeared, mole-like, out of my cabin. It was late morning. As I made my way, bleary-eyed, up to the deck, I slowly realised that something was very different.

On the previous days, I was staring across the track at the empty stands (why are they called stands when they're designed for people to sit?), but now I was facing hundreds of people. These people had to have arrived early to get good seats in anticipation of the afternoon's events. They had nothing better to do than watch the people on the boats, often through binoculars.

It is the closet I have ever felt to being in a zoo or being a sideshow freak. It was made worse because I had stumbled up on deck in my pants. Most people make this mistake, but generally only once. After looking around to see what the people in the crowd were all pointing and cheering at, I realised, to my total embarrassment and horror, that it was me.

Come Saturday, the noise is deafening from both the crowds and the cars. Nothing really prepared me for seeing and hearing all of the engines start up together or for the first time when they whizzed past me, only a few feet away. It was incredible.

Sunday is the main race day. It is off the scale in terms of atmosphere. Every inch of space is covered with people and flags; giant screens show the race; the crowd roar throughout the main race; and, when it's all over, the boats all sound their horns in unison. This is a deafening noise, nearly drowning out the sound of Champagne corks popping.

I have so many Monaco stories that the topic probably deserves a book of its own. It was too easy to bump into famous people there, as Monaco is full of them. It is even easier, however, if you're with my friend Tony.

Tony, or Tone, was a Monaco regular. He was also a great asset in many ways, predominantly because he speaks fluent French and has no shame. Tone leverages these attributes to brilliant effect, blagging his way into places and situations into which nobody else could manage to get themselves.

He got us into a very posh, exclusive Orange phone network promotional party when we were dressed in T-shirts, shorts, and jeans. Minutes later, Tone exited from the gents' toilets with his arm around David Coulthard, having convinced him that he knew him from somewhere. Then, he proceeded to drag Coulthard over to where we were waiting.

'Come and get your picture taken with the boys,' he said.

Another time, Tone chatted for a few minutes with the 'doorman' who was guarding a huge boat that was the venue for a posh party, supposedly attended by some celebs from Cannes, and managed to get us on, even though the party was a ticket-only affair. Two minutes later, I was standing,

Peter Gilbert

sipping a nice cold beer, turned around, and found myself shoulder to shoulder with Matt Damon.

The next day, I was walking past a bar near the harbour and heard Tone's dulcet tones. 'Pete, come and join us.' He was sitting with a bunch of guys who were all wearing Jaguar Racing team clothing. I sat down, and Tone introduced me to the group one by one.

'This is Bob.'

'Hi.'

'This is Terry.'

'Hi.'

'This is Peter . . . ' I did a double take and almost spat my beer over him as Tone introduced me to Peter Phillips: HRH Princess Royal Anne's son, Peter Phillips, who worked for Jaguar Racing at the time.

On a more recent trip to Australia, I was chatting to a couple of Aussies about England. The woman in the group, in all seriousness, said, 'I must ask. Have you met the Queen?'

Trying not to laugh, I said no, but in hindsight I would have loved to have seen the look on her face if I'd said, 'No, but I've met both her son and her grandson.' But I knew that if I said that, I'd never have gotten away from her.

I have many other stories that are similar to the one of my meeting HRH Peter Phillips, such as the time when GMTV interviewed Damien Lewis on our boat. I got the chance to meet and shake hands with him. To remain true to the ethos I've established regarding the celebrity encounters mentioned in this book, I'll stick to the encounters that lasted for longer than a fleeting moment.

The first of these is my meeting Ali-Beth, or, as she is known to the rest of the world, Beth Chalmers. You may not have heard *of* her, but you have probably *heard* her, as she is an actress and voice-over artist. As such, she has appeared in hundreds of radio plays, talking books, and TV dramas and comedies. Hers was the voice in Laboratoires Garnier, Glade, and Piriton TV adverts and she has read a female part in too many *Doctor Who* audiobooks to mention.

I can't remember why, but when I first met her, she introduced herself as Ali. Maybe she has been unsure of my intentions and wanted to throw me off the scent. Later, she told me that her real name was Beth. From that moment on, I called her Ali-Beth—and it stuck.

Tone and I had been sitting watching the world go by when we overheard these two women, who turned out to be Ali-Beth and her friend, moaning about someone and saying that they were not having a great time. Tone commented to them that one should not be in Monaco and be anything but happy. After that, we all ended up chatting. It turned out that they were staying with a relative nearby but did not have tickets to see the race.

'Come and work on our boat and you can watch the race from there,' offered Tone.

'Really?' they said in unison.

Then, quickly, Ali-Beth said, 'Sounds a bit dodgy. You guys seem nice, but we've known you five minutes, and you're inviting us onto your boat? We know what goes on in Monaco, you know.'

'Look, come along later, meet the rest of the guys, have a drink, and see what you think. We've got loads of guests on the boat at the weekend and could do with some help serving drinks.'

'Maybe. Okay.'

We didn't really expect to see them again, but later that afternoon they turned up at the boat.

We had a drink, laughed, and mercilessly took the piss out of each other. Ali-Beth and her friend absolutely gave as good as they got. Within the hour, they were part of the gang.

After that, they rocked up every day to hang out and, of course, consume copious numbers of free drinks. Still, good as their word, they turned up on Saturday and Sunday, worked like Trojans, and made a real impression on the guests.

In addition, by being lovely, fun, hardworking women, not only did Ali-Beth and her friend get to see the big race from a closer spot than they ever imagined, but they were also the envy of all the wannabes who would have given a right arm (or more) to have been on a boat watching the Grand Prix.

I kept in touch with Ali-Beth for a while. I still have the promotional photo she sent me, which includes a handwritten message thanking me and saying that she and her friend had a lovely time. One website offering Beth

Chalmers's services describes her as 'Professional, bright, warm and sexy with slightly cheeky undertones'[3]—which is exactly how I remember her.

I included this story about Ali-Beth because, when I was first thinking about writing the book, I considered calling it, or at least this chapter, 'Making Ali-Beth Famous', which is a bit pretentious given that, at that point, I'd hardly put pen to paper. Also, she seems to be doing a rather good job on her own.

This particular year (I went to Monaco four years in a row), I bumped into someone who had previously worked part-time in my office and who was good friends with a couple of people in my group. She was friends with a producer at GMTV. They were both in Monaco covering various celebrity stories linked with both the film festival and the Grand Prix. Chatting over a coffee, she said, 'Do you know anyone that would let us do tomorrow's broadcast from their boat?'

The next day, we were joined on our boat by GMTV producers, make-up artists, film crew and presenters, and a guest presenter for the day, Lisa Snowdon, who was discussing, amongst other things, the big news: Kylie Minogue had been diagnosed with breast cancer.

Also, the aforementioned Damien Lewis was interviewed about his latest movie. This is why I met him briefly.

Having agreed to stay for lunch with us after the show, the producer said that she was supposed to be having lunch with Tom Watt, the actor most famous for playing the character Lofty in *EastEnders* in the 1980s. He was promoting a film. Would it be okay if she asked him to join us?

Of course, it was fine. The more the merrier, especially if they were TV stars and celebrities. Most of the rest of my group, I think, would have been ambivalent about Tom, however.

I had seen Tom before, when I stood behind him and his kids in the queue to see Santa that previous December at Clearwell Caves, a local attraction close to where he lived. I'd recognised him and almost said hi but decided that since he was with his family I should not disturb or call attention to him.

---

[3] *Voiceovers.co.*, 'Beth Chalmers'. <http://www.voiceovers.co.uk/beth.chalmers> accessed 5 April 2014.

My Old Man's a Busman

When chatting over lunch, I recalled this meeting with him. He said, 'Yeah, that'll be right. We did take the kids there. We live nearby. It's great, isn't it?'

For the next two hours, Tom and I, beneath glorious sunshine and over beers and a delicious lunch, chatted about kids, Clearwell, music, movies, and TV—on a yacht in Monte Carlo. Before he left, he thanked me for respecting his privacy that day in December.

Having been deep in conversation with Tom, I had been unaware that another celebrity guest, Lisa Snowdon, had joined us. She had finished her GMTV work and had then decided to join us for lunch. She had changed her plans because we 'looked to be having a great time'.

We started off the conversation a little reserved. To us, she was a famous celebrity in her own right, but according to the press reports, she had just broken up with George Clooney, who was a megastar.

We needn't have worried, though. She was lovely.

Lisa chatted openly with everyone, had a beer and a laugh, and seemed just to want to be treated as one of the boys.

She ended up staying for most of the afternoon. Before she left to go up to the villa in the hills where she was staying, she gladly had pictures taken with everybody who wanted them. Once she finally left, we men all agreed that we had secretly hoped she would choose us to participate in her 'get over George' shag. We should be so lucky.

About an hour after Lisa Snowdon left, one of our group, Andrew, appeared from the main cabin with a bag in his hand and announced, 'Look, she left her dress behind.'

It happened that Lisa had changed out of her GMTV dress for lunch and had left it in the cabin by mistake. Leaving articles of clothing behind must be a celebrity trait, as now the tally of those who have done this includes Robbie and Lisa.

'I'm going to put it on. We'll take some photos,' Andrew said.

I suddenly felt a rush of conscience.

She'd been lovely, giving of her time, relaxing, being one of the boys—and this was how we were going to repay her? By betraying her trust, defiling her clothing, and humiliating her, as, inevitably the images would end up on the Internet? In an uncharacteristic move, I made myself very unpopular by demanding that Andrew hand over the bag and not put on the dress.

Lisa got her dress back, undefiled. I'm still friends with Andrew, although he's never really forgiven me. To this day, he taunts me and says that it's all my fault. 'We don't have *that* shot, Gilbert,' he complains.

My Top Ten 'French' Songs

'La Vie en Rose'—Edith Piaf
'Theme to *Belle et Sébastien*'—Pierre Medhi
'Je T'aime'—Serge Gainsbourg and Jane Birkin
'Tour de France'—Kraftwerk
'Ça Plane pour Moi'—Plastic Bertrand
'Moi Je Joue'—Brigit Bardot
'Young Parisians'—Adam and the Ants
'Joe le Taxi'—Vanessa Paradis
'Bourgeois Shangri-La'—Miss Li
'J'ai Deux Amours'—Madeleine Peyroux

Pop cricket score: 88 for 4

Things to Check Out

On YouTube:

- Lofty asks Michelle to marry him
- Lisa Snowdon, Special K advert

Elsewhere:
www.myoldmansabusman.com

Shanghaied

Having been lucky enough to visit the Americas on numerous occasions, on business trips and holidays to New York, Florida, Mexico, and Las Vegas, I always assumed that I'd also visited the subcontinent of Central America twice. However, I recently learned that my holiday to Acapulco does not count as a trip to Mexico because Mexico is actually part of the continent of North America.

I was embarrassed not to have known this, although I do think that this makes for a good pub quiz question, as I'm sure that it would catch lots of other people out, too. This admission left me wide open to ridicule from surrogate in-laws, as my girlfriend's stepmother was born in Peru.

I've had two very eventful trips to Florida. The first was booked by an ex-girlfriend as a birthday treat.

As a surprise, she had booked a fly-drive holiday for us to take in Orlando and the parks—Epcot, SeaWorld, and Universal Studios, et al.—to be followed by a drive down to the Florida Keys, as I'd always wanted to visit Key West. Then, we'd travel back up to Florida's west coast beaches via Alligator Alley, the main highway where one can literally spot gators on the side of the road.

This would have been perfect were it not that, on the plane journey over, I realised that I'd forgotten my driving licence.

This, in itself, would have not been an absolute disaster. My girlfriend could drive and had her licence with her. However, unbeknown to me at the time, she feared heights. In addition, she didn't feel confident about driving in a foreign country and on the opposite side of the road.

It wasn't that we'd been together for a short time. It was simply that living in South-West London, the topic hadn't cropped up. She was able to tolerate the Westway, I assume. However, when driving over the Seven

Mile Bridge and all of the other bridges that span the Keys and back again, the subject *was* broached.

I quickly became intolerant of her screaming while she was driving; she became intolerant of my intolerance. After all, as she reminded me several times, it was me who had *'FORGOTTEN THE FUCKING LICENCE'*.

Having made it to Key West later than planned and after dark, we went straight to the hotel.

I suggested that we drive around and look for a nice restaurant or bar to hang out in, but my girlfriend didn't seem keen to drive us. Instead, she ordered a takeaway pizza and got into bed. I didn't follow.

Five minutes later, we found ourselves in the middle of a massive storm with thunder and lightning. Five minutes after that, all the lights went out, as the storm had caused a power cut. My girlfriend screamed more. It became clear to me that she was afraid of thunder and lightning, too, especially in the pitch-black.

At some point, we ate our pizza and went to bed.

The next day, I awoke to the sound of suitcases being packed. 'I hate it here. We're going.'

Having convinced my girlfriend to at least do a quick drive around the town, we headed back north, having seen very little of Key West. Mercifully, my girlfriend screamed a little less, but not by much. I was biding my time, waiting for the right moment to ask the question: 'Don't you think that being forced to drive over bridges has helped you?'

So, we retraced our steps north to Fort Lauderdale and then headed west along Alligator Alley. Herewith began the relative calm period of the journey, which was surprising, as we were passing man-eating reptiles along the way.

The obvious question did occur to me. 'So, alligators are okay, but . . . ?' I kept quiet.

All was good for a few hours until we hit Tampa and a very high toll bridge spanning the bay.

My girlfriend screamed all the way up the bridge.

I shouted.

She screamed more and cried.

I shouted more.

We stopped at the tollbooth.

'I don't know what to do. What shall I do? Oh God!'

'Just open the window and throw the money into the hopper,' I replied.

Maybe the instruction was too literal for a hysterical woman. In hindsight, maybe I hadn't used my calmest voice to respond. But the next thing I knew, she had opened the window and, screaming again, had literally thrown out the coins just as one would toss seeds to the pigeons in Trafalgar Square.

To be fair, one or two did go into the hopper. Others bounced off, while some landed nowhere near and simply rolled down the road or under the car.

As the cars behind started on their horns, the shouting got louder.

I think that point signalled the end of the holiday. And of the relationship.

The second visit I made to Florida was with my bother and our then-partners. Like big kids (this was before we had responsibility for any of our own), we did the whole Orlando theme parks thing and then headed west to the Gulf Coast beaches, this time with driving licences and without anyone along who was afraid of heights, thunder, lightning, or the dark.

It was out of season, which was great for relatively short queues at the attractions, but not so much for the atmosphere in the small resort on the coast where we had booked a room. To put it mildly, Fort Myers Beach was closed. There was a rundown Pizza Hut, which brought back memories of a previous trip, but all of the local restaurants were dead. Walking into them felt a bit like walking into the Slaughtered Lamb Pub in a scene from *An American Werewolf in London*. Also, they all closed at 9.00 p.m.

Party on.

Arriving at our hotel, I felt an odd vibe, not something that I could put my finger on, but something that was just strange. It had nothing to do with any other guest, as we were the only ones there. It was just the feeling you get sometimes when driving through or being in a strange place. In hindsight, the hotel's name, the Pink Passion (or something similar), should have made us wary. We joked that it was the type of place for swingers to come to at weekends and meet up for orgies.

Having divvied up the rooms, we started to unpack.

I opened the top drawer of the unit to put some T-shirts away and was confronted with some pornographic magazines.

'Look, we were right,' I said, laughing. I picked up the mags and headed to Joff's room. 'Look what I found in the drawer. Maybe we were right about this place.'

'I wonder if we've got any,' he said. 'What are the chances? Or maybe it's that sort of place and porn is their equivalent of the Gideon Bible.'

With that, he opened the drawer and burst out laughing.

'Bloody hell. I don't believe it!' Joff exclaimed.

'What?' we all asked, pretty much in unison.

'I'm not touching it.'

We rushed over. To our amazement and hilarity, there in the drawer was a huge pink dildo. It kept us amused for the rest of the trip. That and the Tan Fannie tanning salon across the road.

So having established that I've only been to Central America once, which was Honduras, that trip was equally as unforgettable, but for different reasons.

Following is the tale of what happened after we discovered the pink dildo. We enjoyed a night of tequila; we were offered waitresses for the night; we got the best seats in a crowded restaurant; the house band played my favourite songs; and then we received an offer to go to a club where anything goes. This is pretty much every guy's perfect night, if there were no girlfriends or partners on the trip. My recollection, though, more closely aligns to the events in the movie *The Hangover*.

At the time, I was working for the company in Margate, Kent, which is on the Isle of Thanet. Despite the name, it's not actually an isle or island. In Roman times, it was, and it was separated from the mainland by the 2,000-foot-wide Watsum Channel. Some say that it still should be. But the Watsum has subsequently silted up and been filled in.

Given the Roman invasion of Britain in 43 AD and the Roman army's subsequent 'visits', the area lays claim to the following inhabitants: Julius Caesar, Gordon Ramsey, Tracey Emin, Vincent Van Gogh, Lord Baden Powell, Edward Heath (the prime minister, not the band leader), Eric Morecombe, Hattie Jacques, John Le Mesurier, Manfred Mann, Joseph Mallord William Turner, T.S. Eliot, Prince Frederick (the original grand old duke of York), and Douglas Trendle (Buster Bloodvessel of Band Manners).

My company, as previously mentioned, sold promotional items. One of our main clients, Pepsi, was making a major launch of one of its big North

Peter Gilbert

American brands, Gatorade, at a conference in Honduras and wanted representation from our company. My name was on that ticket.

I travelled to Honduras with a colleague, Anthony. We'd worked closely together and I'd lived with him in his house for a while when I first moved to Kent, so we knew each other pretty well. Anthony had also been on the Monaco trips with me. We'd had plenty of nights out together, so this felt less like *Wall Street* and more like the *Only Fools and Horses* episode 'Jolly Boys' Outing', set to the tune of that Chas and Dave classic 'Down to Margate', of course. 'You can keep the Costa Brava. I'm telling you, mate, I'd rather have a day down Margate with all my family.'

That said, for the day job, we were very well prepared. We rehearsed, were immaculately turned out, and behaved like consummate professionals. We were the Bodie and Doyle of the widget industry.

Widget has a number of meanings, but it is most commonly used as an alternative to *gadget* or *item*. It is also often used to describe promotional bits and pieces. Since I was in a related industry, it's an everyday term, expression, or word for me. *Widgets*.

This always makes my girlfriend laugh, however. She and her daughter use the word in its lesser-known, definitely-not-in-a-dictionary definition. They use *widget* to describe a woman's front bottom. The widget is actually an unusually acceptable term for this part of a female's anatomy, as people find most the others offensive.

Using *widget* in this way did once get my girlfriend into trouble. As an adult (a mature student), she was in her economics class. The teacher was talking about manufacturing and had used the word in his example: a factory making widgets. This sent my girlfriend into uncontrollable laughter, so much so that she was eventually asked to leave the room.

On arrival at the Honduras hotel, knackered after a very long day of travelling, we checked in and were almost immediately ushered into the gardens, where a massive party was in full flow.

It was the Gatorade launch party.

As travellers from afar (most were from the various countries that make up the PepsiCo Central American region), we were treated as honoured guests, had drinks thrust in our hands, and were, for a short time, the centre of attention. We socialised with anyone who could speak reasonable

English, although these were few and far between. Typical of Brits, neither Anthony or I spoke a word of another language.

Very quickly realising that we didn't have a lot to offer and being ready to drop, we made our excuses and left after a couple of drinks.

The following morning, we were up bright and early, raring to go. We set up the room, ran through the presentation, and laid out our widgets for all to see.

Looking back, I think we did a pretty good job. We got some orders. This was no mean feat, given that we presented to a room of 150 people, most of whose grasp of English was limited.

We were used to dealing with Pepsi people from all over the world whose employees all spoke English. But here, the launch was for the local distribution companies, which clearly did not have English language skills as a recruitment requirement.

'We can supply you with footballs.'

'Again, please?'

'Footballs.'

'Eh?'

'Fooootbaaaalls. David Beckham?'

'Aaaaah, David Beckham. Soccer.'

Anthony and I spent that afternoon at the main event, the big launch of Gatorade to all the conference delegates. This lasted for three and a half hours and was presented entirely in Spanish. Come evening, we were ready for a drink.

We were in the bar early and were soon joined by four guys who had been at our table earlier at the presentation, one of whom spoke good English. His friend had a limited vocabulary (seemingly in any language), and the other two only spoke a few words of English.

The English-speaking guy took an immediate liking to us. 'I love you guys, my new friends. I want to show you my country. You will join me for dinner at my favourite place,' he said.

Having nothing better to do and being mildly flattered, we agreed. His friend, who had said nothing other than hello up to this point, was clearly coming, too. Realising that they'd be required to converse, or at least try to speak, in English for most of the night, the other two politely declined and went their own way.

And so we found ourselves in the back of a four-by-four, in the dark, heading... somewhere.

After about a thirty-minute drive, we arrived at what I can only describe as a cross between an authentic Mexican restaurant, a wooden shack in the middle of nowhere, and a *Coyote Ugly*–crowded bar with lots of people who were pushing and shoving. It was quite chaotic.

We were ushered through the crowd to the bar, given a beer, and taken to some stools at the other end of the bar that were, shockingly, free. The conversation between three of us flowed. The quiet one sat with his vodka and Coke.

The atmosphere was fantastic. It was busy and noisy, a band was playing, and we were sitting at a corner of the bar near the kitchen, so we enjoyed regular views of the hot waitresses going back and forth to the tables.

After a while, our host, who must have noticed this, turned to us and asked, 'You want one? Want a piece of ass? Which one you like? You can have her.'

We looked at each other.

'Ha-ha, no. You're okay. Just looking.'

'No, really. You are my new friends. I give you what you want.' He grabbed the waitress passing by and asked me, 'You like her? You want this one?'

I can't say that the woman looked delighted by this sudden interruption of her duties or that she was being manhandled, but, then again, she didn't run off screaming or to call the police.

'No, honestly, we don't want any of the waitresses. We're fine here. Just chatting. Thanks.'

We looked at each other. A 'What the hell is going on?' look passed between us.

'Okay, my friends, what are your favourite songs?'

We looked at each other again, this time relieved that he'd let the waitress go on her way and that a potential situation had been averted.

We chatted for a while about songs. Since we both had recently listened to the Rat Pack, we figured that we'd be on safe ground with some classics, so we went for Dean Martin's 'Volaré' and Frank Sinatra's 'Bad, Bad Leroy Brown'.

Before we knew what was happening he'd asked the barman for pen and paper, written down the song names, and accosted another waitress, telling this one, 'Take this note to the band and tell them to play these for my friends.'

Horrified, we exchanged looks again. Was he just showing off and pushing his luck? Or was he a regular? Friends with the owner, maybe?

'You want to be closer to the band to hear your songs?'

We were shaken from our musings.

'No, you're okay. We can hear from here.'

'It's no problem. I've asked them to announce that they are your songs and are for my friends from England. We should be nearer when they say that. It will be fun, no? We need the table right down the front by the band for this.'

I looked over to the large table in front of the band and saw that the people seated there, a group of about twelve, were clearly protesting, as they were only partway through their meal and had been asked to move to a table at the back of the room.

'Come, come, we go.' Our host beckoned us as he headed for the table. We saw no alternative but to follow, painfully aware of the bewildered and hostile glances on the faces of the now uprooted party.

Our host, though, seemed blissfully unaware as the four of us seated ourselves at the large table.

'Tequilas!' he shouted.

My heart sank. I don't like tequila and was about to try to decline politely when Anthony said, 'I can't drink tequila, but Pete will join you. I'll just have a beer.' If looks could kill.

So, two tequilas arrived, plus one girlie beer and a vodka and Coke.

After about the fourth round, still fairly sober, having drunk only bottled beer so far, Anthony piped up. He said, 'I'll get these.' At the same time, he got out his wallet and put it on the table.

Within a second, our host's hand slammed down on his wrist, pinning it and his wallet to the table, saying in a half-mocking but very convincing menacing tone, 'You disrespect me.'

'Oh, sorry!'

'You are my guests. This is my country and my place. I invited you and I pay for everything. Please do not insult me.'

'Sorry!'

Anthony and I again exchanged looks, but this time it was more of an 'Oh, shit!' look.

Our host smiled. 'Another round. This time, tequila for *all*.'

I seem to remember that Anthony forced that shot down.

There were some lighter moments during the now tense atmosphere. For example, at some point I said to Anthony, 'Have you seen how many vodkas that guy's drunk—and he's driving us home?'

To which Anthony, laughing in the way that only somebody realising the ridiculousness of the situation would laugh, and being pretty drunk at that stage of the evening, replied, 'It's okay. He is having Coke with it.'

I don't remember whether we ate or not. I don't think we did. But the band did play our songs, or at least attempt to, and we did get a name check—along the lines of, 'This is for our new English friends from Pepsi'—before each one.

Before we left, our embarrassment about the ousting of a family from their table apparently not enough, Anthony and I were personally introduced to each band member, none of whom spoke a word of English.

'Very nice song, thank you.'

With some trepidation, we got back into the car. Yes, our host had drunk at least ten vodkas, maybe more, but we had no idea where we were or who we were dealing with. He seemed in a state no better or worse than when we'd met him earlier. So, I guess, at that moment in time, getting into the car seemed the best viable option.

The journey back was, in retrospect, relatively incident-free, given the circumstances. We were drunk. Our host was drunk but chatty. Our driver was drunk but seemed to be getting us back alive.

Eventually, we returned to the city and even recognised where we were, which was not far from the hotel. I relaxed. We were going to be okay.

'Would you like to come to our club?' our host asked.

'Er.'

'Come to our club. We have more drinks, girls, anything you want.'

Now, looking back, I have to hand it to Anthony. Despite my having kept up round for round, I can only assume that those early free tequila rounds had rendered his senses slightly sharper than mine. Before I could utter a word, he blurted out, 'Sorry, I really must go to bed, but Pete will come with you.'

If the look earlier did not kill, then this one was an Excocet.

I'm not sure how I managed to extricate myself from the situation—by begging and crying, probably—but I'm glad that I did.

Of course, it could have been great—five whole chapters' worth of stories—but, then again, a Honduran jail? *I'd rather have a day down Margate with all my family.*

Peter Gilbert

My Top Ten Songs about America

'No Entry'—Sham 69
'New York City'—T-Rex
'America'—Razorlight
'American Pie'—Don McLean
'Winter in America'—Gil Scott-Heron
'Breakfast in America'—Supertramp
'Letter to America'—The Proclaimers
'American Idiot'—Green Day
'American Trilogy'—Elvis Presley
'We Speak No Americano'—Sophia Loren

Pop cricket score: 36 all out

Things to Check Out

On YouTube:

- American bridges—Seven Mile Bridge
- 'Margate' (1983)—Chas and Dave

Elsewhere:
www.myoldmansabusman.com

Tarzan Taught My Mother-in-Law to Swim

In order to be 100 per cent truthful, I must say that the lady in question is not officially my mother-in-law. She's actually my girlfriend's stepmum. But in our world of complicated relationships and complex family situations, and given the length of time that my girlfriend and I have been together, she's as good as my mother-in-law.

It's not that modern relations alone are complex. The whole family tree interrelationship can be really confusing, as well. Recently, I found myself frustrated because every conversation about family connections ended with people not being able to explain the whole cousin thing properly (i.e. the difference between second and third cousins versus those once or twice removed) and, worse, those removed by marriage.

At a recent dinner with my mother-in-law's husband's second cousins, the conversation inevitably came around to family connections. The unanswered question, this time from my girlfriend's stepmother, was, 'So, if you are David's [her husband's] second cousin, what relation is my step-granddaughter to your children?'

After about an hour of offering conflicting opinions and conjecture, we called it a draw, but we were no nearer to really working it out. After this, I decided that it was finally time for me to settle some of these debates. On a mission to conquer the alliterative cousin conundrum, off I went to visit the font of all knowledge on these matters: Mum.

Explaining my frustrating lack of knowledge in this area and my desire to be something of an expert, I was gobsmacked to discover that Mum was going to have to look it up, as she wasn't sure, either.

Peter Gilbert

It appears that it's just one of those things that frustrates many of us, even my mum. It doesn't matter how many times we look it up or how many times it's explained to us. It just doesn't stick. Well, this time it was going to. We both agreed.

We spent the next hour on the Internet, printing off charts, discussing, arguing, shouting, and scribbling on various pieces of paper. Using great-greats as the starting point, which for us was my kids, we finally got it. Well, we got the basics.

What didn't help was that both Mum and Dad, odd for their generation, had no brothers or sisters, which also means that they have no nieces or nephews and that I, therefore, have no cousins. Our living points of reference were therefore somewhat limited, but we somehow achieved our goal by posing hypothetical relations and skipping the odd generation. I can say with a relatively high degree of confidence that my dad's first cousin Pat's late husband Mike was my first cousin once removed by marriage and that their children are my second cousins. I think.

The Internet advises that there are also such things as double cousins and parallel cousins, which may reflect more complex scenarios. But I'm happy with this new, if somewhat basic, knowledge. My kids had asked what relation, if any, they had to their uncle's wife's sister's kids, whom they saw occasionally. We came up with the idea of referring to these people as my kids' couscous, pronounced 'kuzkuz' (and not the fluffy rice alternative) so as to avoid having the debate or spending hours working it out. Although, of course, this might be what a parallel cousin is.

In a similar way, I fondly refer to my girlfriend's daughter as my 'sorta', short for 'sort of', as in, She's my sorta daughter because she's neither my real daughter nor my stepdaughter. She, in return, refers to me as her 'afer' or 'aferfafer', short for 'half a father'.

The dinner party that had sparked this conversation was not populated by an unintelligent group of people. They were anything but. The cousin mentioned has his own very successful business. David, whilst now retired, back in the day earned more money a month than I now earn in a year. He was also, until recently, the seventy-ninth most travelled person in the world (as measured by the Official Travel Club). In addition, as part of the London-to-Beijing car rally, he was one of the few Westerners who visited China in the 1980s. He has now dropped to about 173 in the travel rankings. According to him, 'Young whippersnappers like you are taking my place.'

Of course, with each decade, if not with each year, travel does get a lot easier and relatively much more inexpensive. David's early forays to far-flung shores really did cost him the proverbial arm and leg.

The second cousin's wife is also very intelligent. My girlfriend attained a First in her degree programme (my 23 per cent in French and my two GSCE A-levels are not something I boast about at these get-togethers). My mother-in-law, however tempting it is at this juncture to insert a Les Dawson–inspired joke, is anything but archetypal. She recently celebrated a decade-starting birthday (between fifty and seventy) and, without having been anywhere near a surgeon's knife, is up there in the glamorous-granny stakes with Lulu, Twiggy, Emmylou Harris, Blythe Danner, Joan Collins, Suzi Quatro, and Helen Mirren, although technically she's not a granny yet. So, I guess she would fall into the 'yummy mummy' category, for those of a certain age. She claims that at her age she's like Margate: 'Everybody knows where it is, but nobody wants to go there.' But I'm not so sure!

The first time my boys met my mother-in-law, my eldest mentioned the age gap between her and her husband, David—although not in front of them, I'm glad to add. I couldn't help but tell her this. After I had, she asked my son how old he thought she was. He thought, went red, gave his dad dagger looks for embarrassing him in that way, and then shyly replied, 'Thirty-nine?'

He'll go far.

My mother-in-law owes her looks partly to her heritage. She is Peruvian by birth and therefore has a naturally exotic look. Although I've not yet met her mother, everyone says that she still looks great, too. Clearly, there are some genetics at work.

Spanish is my mother-in-law's first language. Her clipped upper-class English accent is a surprise when one first meets her. It is the reason why I gave her the nickname Lady P (*P* is for *Patricia*)—or the Lady P, if referring to her in third person. This caught on with various family members, including my girlfriend, my girlfriend's daughter, and my boys, who know her by no other name.

Allow me to paint a picture. In the last few years, the Lady P has been to university studying French literature at MA level and now, while

Peter Gilbert

studying for her doctorate, (does that mean that she will become Dr Lady P?), she lectures MA students in French. She doesn't teach students how to speak French; she lectures them entirely en Français. No Saga holiday or visit the Hop Farm Family Park in Kent for her.

She was brought up in Lima, Peru. As a child, she attended the city's swimming academy, which was owned and run by one Walter Ledgard, a local legend and once a Peruvian swimming champion. Here, when she was about eleven in the early '60s, a friend of Walter came to the academy and helped out with the swimming lessons.

On the day when my mother-in-law was telling me this story, she went on to say, 'Oh, by the way, you may have heard of him. He was quite famous for a while.'

'Really? What was his name?' I asked.

'Johnny Weissmuller. He used to play Tarzan. You may have heard of him.'

'*What?*'

This was another 'Did I tell you that Auntie Margaret met Elvis?' moment.

Tarzan was another of my boyhood heroes, along with Marine Boy, the Flashing Blade, Casey Jones, and Robin Hood, so this was absolutely amazing news to me.

When I was younger, Ron Ely of the 1960s TV series was my Tarzan. But, as a fan of the character, I also liked watching the old black-and-white movies. Johnny Weissmuller was the man. He had been a champion swimmer and had won five gold medals in the 1920s, including three at the 1924 Olympics, before he became an actor and appeared in a dozen *Tarzan* movies in the late '30s and early '40s. He defined the role for my parents' generation. His portrayal of Tarzan is acknowledged as the definitive screen depiction of the character.

I, after watching one of the old movies in which Jane, Boy, and Cheetah appeared or the Ron Ely TV series on a Sunday morning, would run around the house or garden pretending to be Tarzan. I didn't wear a loincloth, but I did tuck a wooden spoon—which served as my knife—into my trousers and call to my imaginary jungle friends to help me fight off the baddies.

I never did perfect that famous Tarzan call. It wasn't until years later when I realised why. Depending on which story you believe, the call was composed of either three voices, three recordings of one voice mixed together, or a voice mixed with some animal noises. It is such a shame that is wasn't Ron, bellowing it out while standing on top of the waterfall in the opening credits of the TV series.

About Johnny Weissmuller, Lady P recalls:

> I don't remember much about him. He was only there for a week, but we all knew who he was. I do remember that he seemed to fill the pool and make it look smaller than it had before. I also remember now that the water looked bluer somehow, like his fame was affecting the surroundings. Well, it seemed like it to us star-struck girls.

Perhaps ever since that day, she, too, hankered for her moment in the limelight. She also says that in the mid '70s, she worked as a bunny in the Playboy Club in Park Lane, London.

Lady P was living in Dulwich, a wealthy London suburb, at the time. Her friend was working in the gambling bar at the Playboy Club and was about to take an extended holiday. She suggested that Lady P (which was not her moniker at the time) apply to cover her leave.

With a place at university just secured, Lady P had been looking for some work to tide her over and thought that this job would be fun. She learned from her friend that it was safe, despite other people's perceptions. It was just a job waitressing to wealthy men while wearing a different outfit.

The gentleman who interviewed her was very polite. The whole process, far from being seedy, was quite stuffy and very proper. Definitely, no disrobing or lying on the casting couch was required.

In some ways, this story is quite disappointing to me, not because I want to hear debauched stories of Lady P, but because it did not align with my perception of the mid '70s, especially not of the events surrounding Playboy.

While my mother-in-law did wear the bunny costume, she tells that the job was very much one of simply serving drinks to wealthy gentlemen at the gambling tables and to club guests. She remembers that rules were very strict. People who were sitting at the tables could not drink alcoholic drinks, although other guests could. Also, there were no 'liaisons' allowed in the club. It was not a brothel. If the women wanted to earn extra cash, they could only ever do so outside of the club. Lady P, of course, survived on tips.

I recently read an interview with Meat Loaf. Before he became famous with *Bat Out of Hell*, was an actor. In the mid '70s, he was living in London and had the part of Eddie in the film version of *The Rocky Horror Picture Show*. During this time, the Playboy Club was one of his gambling haunts.

He says, 'You could gamble there [at the Playboy Club] in those days. I went in with forty pounds and came out with twenty-three thousand pounds. I was rich. Dude! Twenty-three thousand pounds. I went and bought an apartment.'

So, who knows—mid '70s, the Playboy Club . . . Perhaps Lady P actually served Mr Loaf?

My view of that era, the '70s, in London—and in relation to Playboy—is very different. The Swinging Sixties had been followed by the growth of the porn industry. The '70s have become known as the golden age of porn. This, I hasten to add, is a retrospective view. In 1974, when a more progressive United States was publicly screening movies such as the infamous *Deep Throat* and *The Devil in Miss Jones*, we ten-year-old English boys were watching Suzi Quatro on *Top of the Pops*. This was the closest thing to leather-clad women we had.

Suzi was a leather-clad goddess and the first crush of many an adolescent boy of a certain age in the early to mid '70s. Suzi, the lead singer, was cute, played guitar, and, most of the time, dressed in black leather. I didn't get the leather thing then, of course. She just looked great in it. I felt stirrings.

Suzi Quatro was part of the rock'n'roll revival known as glam rock. In the United Kingdom, Mud, Sweet, Slade, Gary Glitter, the Rubettes, Wizzard, and Alvin Stardust were glam rockers. Arguably, the movement started with T-Rex's 1971 appearance on *Top of the Pops*, when they performed 'Hot Love'. Lead singer Marc Bolan, covered in glitter and satin, looked very glam.

Whilst Bowie and his alter ego, Ziggy Stardust, appealed to an older audience, and whilst the New York Dolls, at the time, were unknown to me, the flamboyant Slade, Mud, and Rubettes appealed to my juvenile pop mind. However, it was Suzi, dressed in black and rockin' to 'Can the Can' and 'Devil Gate Drive' that stole my heart and fulfilled my young fantasies of . . . kissing her. It would still be a few years before we boys gathered around a stolen magazine to gaze upon leather-clad women of a different type. Some of them were stars in their own industry, riding on the back of a very different cultural revolution.

Back in the United States and making its way across the pond was the rise of mainstream pornography via magazines and movies.

The origins of the golden age of porn are associated with the massive success of and hype surrounding early movies, such as the 1971 film *Boys in the Sand*, 1972's *Behind the Green Door*, and—to this day, the most talked about of them all—*Deep Throat*, after which the industry really took off, producing thousands of movies over the next decades.

When *Deep Throat* reached my schoolboy consciousness in the late '70s, I just knew that it was rude. Really rude. Ruder than naked women and 'rubber johnnies' (as condoms were called) as this film was talked about in hushed tones, even by the adults.

I could never have grasped that just seven years earlier, *Deep Throat* was viewed, discussed, and reviewed as a mainstream film, much in the same way that *Star Wars* or *Close Encounters of the Third Kind* was. How times had changed! And how many of us were pretending to know what a clitoris was, anyway?

The late '70s gave us and the world the much discussed *Debbie Does . . .* franchise. The first, *Debbie Does Dallas*, is the most well remembered and most often quoted.

The '80s gave us high production values and DVDs, which led to mass distribution and awareness of porn films, despite the more conservative view and the laws surrounding pornography that were in force at the time.

Nowadays, of course, anyone with a laptop or a smartphone can access free porn, although this may not the best outcome of the stellar leap in technology. While this on-the-go quick fix has its place and eliminates the embarrassment (for many a businessman away from home) of purchasing top-shelf magazines from the young woman attendant at a motorway services shop, there is something missing, namely the Old World charm and the thrill of finding a discarded porn mag, even the odd page, in a hedge.

Today's adult movie actresses, with their enhanced looks and implants, have, in my opinion, no place next to the original and more natural stars of that golden era. Porn actresses such as Seka, Linda Lovelace, and Vanessa Del Rio gave us adolescent boys our first images of porn . . . and clitorises. And, however high in quality a free MPEG may be, it simply does not provide the same thrill as meeting up the woods with your mates to flick through the pages of an illicit copy of *Penthouse*, *Playboy*, or *Asian Babes* in order to get a very rare view of boobs and bush.

The other thing that has changed in the industry, and not for the better, are the actors' names. Even if they did use stage names, there was something honest about Ron Jeremy, John Holmes, and Peter North alongside Kay Parker, Linda Lovelace, and Nina Hartley. Today, it's all Crystal Goes, Randy Roxxx, Ruby Lips, April Orbs, and Honey Pot. I'm reliably informed.

I think that all porn stars today should follow the rules the rest of us play by. One takes the name of one's first pet and adds it to the name of the street where one first lived, and that's your porn name. My porn name would be Nelson St Mary, with which I'm really happy. This came about because the first pet I actually owned was a fish I had won at a fair. We later discovered that it had only one eye, hence the name Nelson. The fish was, of course, nearly called One-Eye (I was only ten at the time), which, in hindsight, would have been brilliant.

Our first family pet, however, predated the fish. It was a black cat named Sooty. So, I can also claim the porn name Sooty St Mary, which is potentially even better than Nelson.

Joff would be Marmaris Malwood. Any name including *wood* is a good porn name.

My girlfriend, who stretched the rules (any pet, anywhere one has lived), can claim Fishy Forstal, which, unfortunately, sounds more like the result of an STD than a porn star. Some of her alternate porn names are Lady Waldron and, my favourite, Yo-Yo Nakatindi.

If I did ever enter into the industry, however unlikely that may be, I'd have to move house. Despite the fact that Nelson St Mary is a good name, if we're using the more relaxed rules, I may also claim Sooty Malwood. Even better, in Canterbury, near where I live now, there is a genuine Humpty Dumpty Lane.

My Top Ten *Tarzan*-Inspired Songs

'Jungle Rock'—Hank Mizell
'Three Lions'—Frank Skinner and David Baddiel, featuring the Lightning Seeds
'I Go Ape'—Neil Sedaka
'See You Later, Alligator'—Bill Haley and the Comets
'Tiger Feet'—Mud
'Monkey Man'—The Specials
'The Elephant's Graveyard'—The Boomtown Rats
'Crocodile Rock'—Elton John
'The Snake'—Al Wilson
'Bare Necessities'—Phil Harris

Pop cricket score: 198 for 2

Things to Check Out

On YouTube:

- *Tarzan* intro, 1960s
- *Tarzan Finds a Son* official trailer
- '48 Crash'—Suzi Quatro

Elsewhere:
www.myoldmansabusman.com

Rocking Around the Christmas Tree

Since Lady P is Peruvian, she conjures up music-related images of pan pipes, Incas, and the groups in ponchos who play in high streets up and down the land, selling their CDs of authentic pan-pipe music as well as their cover versions of classic pop songs to the crowd. But for me, I always think of a Christmas song, Alma Cogan's oft-forgotten classic 'Never Do a Tango with an Eskimo', which includes the line, 'You can do it with a sailor from Peru to Venezuela.'

This song, bizarrely, is a staple on our annual 'Best Xmas Songs *Ever*' compilation playlist. It vies for top billing with Kirsty MacColl and the Pogues, Slade, Dean Martin, Darlene Love, and Wizzard.

We review and re-edit this playlist each year. We play it when putting up the Christmas tree, while wrapping presents, when in the car, during most mealtimes, and, generally, throughout the festive season when we want to hear background music. However, it is strictly played from 1 December until Boxing Day, since before and after that time is not Christmas. Retailers and TV channels, please take note.

I actually like seeing buskers in the high street, even if they are not very good ones or are just starting out. My kids' friends are an example. I think it takes real guts. If I'm honest, I have to say that I'm a bit jealous. Everyone has got to start somewhere. Singing or playing in your local high street on a Saturday, where your schoolmates can see you, is brave in my book. I don't think that I could have handled it. I can just hear my schoolmates saying, 'Did you see Gilbert outside Woolworth's on Saturday? What a tosser.'

My first experience of a live performance was when I saw a group called Quartz in the early '70s. We were visiting relations, and the band was playing in a park in Basingstoke. I recall them as a four-piece band. There was some sort of stage, so I presume that the concert was part of local event

My Old Man's a Busman

or festival. I remember that Netty and I were fairly impressed. Then again, we were fairly impressionable at that age. To us, Quartz was obviously an up and coming pop group, the next big thing that we would soon hear on the radio or see on *Top of the Pops*. Surely, that's how it worked?

If only that were true. If so, our futures would have been about to change when we formed our group in Mark's garage. But life's not like that. Unsurprisingly, even though I remember that Quartz were pretty good and attracted a large crowd of spectators, we never heard of them again.

These days, as a savvier adult, I understand that, despite the digital revolution's making it possible for YouTube to turn unknowns into overnight stars, there are literally thousands of great bands and singers that never make it and, therefore, never fulfil their potential or realise their dreams.

For example, my friend Mark is a very talented swing singer. He recorded lots of the classics—from the likes of Dean Martin, Frank Sinatra, and Bobby Darin—in a professional studio. Mark spent months working on the record and gained a record company's interest. Before his record was released, Robbie Williams brought out his CD *Swing When You're Winning*, which covered all the same songs. And that was that. I played Mark's tracks to the family one Christmas and asked if they knew who was singing on the tracks.

'Frank, Dean, and Bobby,' they replied.

Laura Catlow is a singer-songwriter from Blackpool. My friend Dave, who knows her well, introduced me to her. He put a couple of her tracks on a compilation CD he made for me. Dave and I often swap playlists of new things we've heard or stuff that the other might like. Laura works really hard promoting herself. She does gigs all around the country and has even done some in the United States. She has appeared on local radio and can easily be found on YouTube. While her music is a constant in my car, my kids often ask me to play her tracks. Her song 'Gorgeous' is as good as any pop song that's been in the charts. I am still very much in the minority, as Laura Catlow is unknown outside of her hard-core fan base.

First is a band close to my heart. My sort of stepbrother-in-law (he's my girlfriend's stepbrother and Lady P's son), Ben Fox Smith, is the lead singer. Ben previously fronted the band Serafin and has played in a number of other bands. Despite having enjoyed success in Serafin, playing festivals, making videos, having their song used for a video game (NFL 2004), and having, according to *Wikipedia,* Simon Pegg as a celebrity fan, Serafin didn't make it. That's how hard it is.

In a fit of romantic fervour, I penned a song for my girlfriend and asked Ben to record it (my angelic choirboy tones had disappeared). He did, so who knows? If he convinces First to record it and make a video, and if it thereby becomes a massive hit, all of my dreams may come true.

Even Ben's brother, Christian, who enjoyed success as the drummer for Razorlight on their first album, gave it all up, just like Roy Lynes from Status Quo did. Christian is now enjoying life as a teacher in Columbia, having left in his wake a string of bands that never realised success: Stony Sleep, French Car and the Bulimic Wizards, Genre 18, Flying Mango Attack, or Young Sawbones, anyone?

After that first Quartz concert in the park, it would be a number of years before I started going to proper gigs, unlike Dad, who would tell stories of cycling across London when he was about twelve to watch the likes of Aker Bilk and Kenny Ball.

I was probably fifteen when I went to my first concert, but I have seen a number of memorable ones over the years. Starting late, and not being prolific, I've missed loads of opportunities that I look back on now and regret.

Where was I when ELO (the Electric Light Orchestra) was on their *Out of the Blue* and *Discovery* tours, when Queen was performing *A Night at the Opera,* or when AC/DC was on their *Let There Be Rock* tour performing 'Whole Lotta Rosie' with Angus Young—in full school uniform, thrashing his guitar solo front and centre?

How did I miss the Clash touring *London Calling;* Pink Floyd, *The Wall;* or Dire Straits, *Alchemy*—or Jarvis Cocker belting out 'Common People'? And that's just the ones that were accessible to me. Forget seeing the Rat Pack playing the Sands Hotel in Vegas, Elvis in Hawaii, or the modern equivalents: Tom Jones in the Millennium Stadium, Robbie Williams at Slane Castle, Oasis at Knebworth, or Chas and Dave in Margate.

I have been to a few live gigs, though, some more worthy of note than others. My first gig was seeing Ted Nugent on the *Cat Scratch Fever* tour in

My Old Man's a Busman

1978, where lead singer Derek St Holmes came swinging across the stage dressed as Tarzan to make his grand entrance.

I also saw the following perform live:

- Sky, featuring John Williams and Herbie Flowers, mainly for their modern take on the classical piece 'Toccata', which got into the charts at a similar time
- Darts featuring Den Hegarty—a doo-wop–rock'n'roll crossover band
- Paul Young in that '80s period of pop when the new romantics ruled the charts and everybody appeared on the Band Aid single at Christmas in 1984
- Sade, who was simply the epitome of cool. Her first album, *Diamond Life,* was the soundtrack to every mid-'80s dinner party. I remember that she came on stage and hardly moved for the entire ninety-minute concert but had the audience mesmerised.
- Paul Simon (of Simon and Garfunkel fame) at Wembley Arena, backed by a full African gospel choir. Strangely, I read that he is credited as co-writer of the *H.R. Pufnstuff* theme tune, following his filing and winning a lawsuit claiming that it had been taken from 'The 59th Street Bridge Song'. In my humble opinion, the *H.R. Pufnstuff* theme song sounds nothing like 'The 59th Street Bridge Song'. I have not been able to find corroboration for this information, but I so hope that it's true.
- Robbie Williams, twice. Once at a small venue for competition winners, about a hundred of them, which was amazing because Robbie was at the height of his fame. Being at that intimate gig was incredible. The second time was at a live recording of the *Pepsi Chart* show in Leicester Square. He was singing 'United', which he'd written exclusively for a Pepsi advert and which is still one of my favourite Robbie tracks.
- Mark Knopfler in the Royal Albert Hall, post–Dire Straits. Thankfully, he performed lots of their hits. The opening notes to 'Romeo and Juliet' nearly brought the house down.

- The Proclaimers. I cannot explain my fandom, but I have every album they ever made. I saw them at the Hammersmith Apollo, where we wore the obligatory black-rimmed glasses.
- Hullabaloo, a Kent band full of very talented musicians who were playing on the harbour arm in Broadstairs the night I met my girlfriend. Whilst you will have probably not heard of Hullabaloo, they played at Jamie Oliver's wedding, as he is a big fan.
- Screw Loose (Bournemouth). Joff is the drummer. If you like covers of '70s and '80s rock delivered by people dressed in wigs and leggings who don't take themselves too seriously, then Screw Loose is the band to see.
- Gil Scott-Heron, twice. My girlfriend is a massive fan, although I'd only ever heard 'The Bottle'. Luckily, Gil Scott-Heron came to London, so we managed to see him before he sadly passed away.
- The Monkees, another close shave. We saw them a few months before lead singer Davy Jones passed away.
- Jools Holland, three times—probably with more to come. His tours with his Rhythm and Blues Orchestra, featuring the likes of Roland Gift, Sandie Shaw, and Ruby Turner, are fabulous.

Given the two near misses with Gil and Davy, my girlfriend and I had two in our sights that we've not yet ticked off our list: the B-52s, my girlfriend's favourite band ever, and Status Quo. It is clear that I would be seeing the latter without her.

We were a little worried about the B-52s, as they were getting on a bit, so we bought the DVD of their Amsterdam show from the previous year, which was excellent. Still, nothing could have prepared us for the live show, which was spectacular.

It was an evening of camp, Day-Glo fun. One audience member wore a full lobster costume. My girlfriend, having made her way to the front wearing a bright red Kate Pierson wig, screamed at the top of her voice, 'Kate I love you!' over and over again. I think that she'd have 'turned' for Kate that night!

Promising ourselves for the last three years that we'd see them, Dave and I (he with the Robbie Williams connection and of the PG Tips' chimpanzee debates) finally booked tickets and saw Status Quo. We spent the three-hour car journey listening to the Quo and debating how they'd come on stage, which tracks they'd play, what they'd play for an encore, and what we would do if the show was disappointing.

The band opened with 'Caroline' and then blasted out 'Paper Plane' and 'Big Fat Mama'. Job done.

I've also seen Chas and Dave twice, once in Margate, so I've ticked one off my fantasy list.

Finally, I list T.Rextasy. Even though they are a tribute band, many of which I've seen and none of which I've listed here, in my opinion, they are the closest to the real deal that you one get without seeing the artists live. That's not to say that there aren't other good tribute bands around, but I always feel that it's just people dressed up and singing the songs, even though I may well have a great night. With Danielz fronting T. Rextasy, however, I feel as if I've seen Marc Bolan, especially when five hundred diehard fans are singing every word to every song and are taking the roof off when he ends with 'Hot Love'.

Another way to see your favourite band or singer is to put on a show yourself. This is, of course, entirely possible with a couple of the groups that I've seen, for example, Screw Loose (a couple of beers each would secure them) and, at a push, Hullabaloo, for a very special occasion (if we could secure mates' rates). But what about somebody more famous?

On a trip to Taormina in Sicily a couple of years ago, my girlfriend and I visited, as most tourists do, the ruins of the famous Roman amphitheatre that sits perched on a cliff top overlooking the sea and which, according to the tourist guides, has amazing acoustics because of the prevailing sea breeze blowing onshore. The setting and ruins are stunning.

Knackered from the heat and wandering around the entire site for a couple of hours, we went and sat in what remains of the seating area. It looks down onto the stage area and out to sea, so we were enjoying the same view that members of the audience would have done more than a thousand years ago. As we soaked up the atmosphere and the April sunshine, I started to ponder the feasibility of holding a modern concert in the ruins. This led to one of those great flight-of-fancy conversations we occasionally enjoy.

It started with my comment about how many seats I thought would have been in the theatre. Over the course of the next hour, my girlfriend and I had booked Andrea Bocelli, as there could be no more perfect singer to perform in that setting.

Over the next hour, we had developed a marketing plan, done 'deals' with local hotels, discussed the obvious health and safety issues, worked out where the dressing rooms would be and what the catering possibilities were, developed merchandising ideas, hired security, factored in insurance, calculated ticket prices, and, presuming a full house, turned in a very healthy profit.

Of course, some of our figures may have been flawed. After all, we didn't even have the back of a fag packet to hand. I can't remember the figure we decided to pay Bocelli, but I do remember enough to say that if he's available and will accept less than $250K, we have a plan.

Being loosely related, as possible future stepbrother-in-law, to someone who was in a famous band does lead to some surreal moments. No moment was more surreal—to me, anyway—than the one a couple of Christmases ago when all the family were gathered and we were playing post-Christmas-lunch games.

In attendance were me, my girlfriend and her daughter, Ben, Christian, David, and Lady P, who is a lover of playing games, especially at Christmas. Her favourites are Trivial Pursuit and charades. She is highly competitive and a renowned (amongst the family) cheat.

Having finished 'lunch' at about 4.00 p.m., as you do, we were sitting around the blazing fire, wine in hand, feeling stuffed and chatting, when Lady P entered the room with an armful of board games. Everyone groaned.

'Don't be like that. You know it makes my Christmas and that I'll be upset and grumpy if you won't play with me.'

'Go on, then.'

So began a three-hour Trivial Pursuit marathon with the requisite squabbling and attempted cheating. 'I know that I said Kabul, but you know that I meant Kazakhstan, because you know that I know that answer. So, you must give me the piece.'

We then heard the dreaded words we thought we'd be able to avoid, given the length of the Trivial Pursuit game. 'Time for charades now.'

And so it came to pass, on that snowy, cold, wintry Christmas night, all deep and crisp and even, that I acted out, amongst other film titles, *Planet of the Apes*. I leapt around monkey-like, with my fists in my armpits, and pointed out the window at the moon indicating at the two musicians, one who had made bona fide music videos and another who had had a top-ten single and a top-three album and had played Glastonbury.

'Is it *Star Wars?*'

Peter Gilbert

My Top Ten Christmas Songs

'Please Come Home for Christmas'—The Eagles
'Do They Know It's Christmas?'—Band Aid
'All I Want for Christmas Is You'—Mariah Carey
'Merry Christmas, Everybody'—Slade
'I Wish It Could Be Christmas Every Day'—Wizzard
'You're All I Want for Christmas'—Caro Emerald and Brook Benton
'Blue Christmas'—Elvis Presley
'Fairytale of New York'—The Pogues and Kirsty MacColl
'Let It Snow, Let It Snow, Let It Snow'—Dean Martin
'In Dulci Jubilo'—Mike Oldfield

Pop cricket score: 148 for 5

Things to Check Out

On YouTube:

- 'If There's Anything More'—Laura Catlow
- 'Horror Show'—Laura Catlow
- 'Day by Day'—Serafin
- 'Things Fall Apart'—Serafin

Elsewhere:
www.myoldmansabusman.com

Pop Art

Given my love for music, and given that I am part of the LP generation, I began to be impacted, at some point, by the designs used on LP covers. But it wouldn't be until years later that I developed a passion for pop art.

The first LP (or album, if you prefer) in my collection was, not surprisingly, given the time, a *Top of the Pops* compilation of hits in the early '70s. These albums contained all of the biggest chart hits of the year and were a forerunner to today's *Now That's What I Call Music!* collections. Also, they were very cheap. This was because the songs were not recorded by the original artists.

Having saved up my pocket money or, more likely, my birthday money to buy the album, I was extremely disappointed when I got home and played it only to find that 'Telegram Sam' did not sound exactly like T-Rex and that 'Puppy Love', originally by Donny Osmond, was sung by two women.

What a con. In hindsight, this was probably my first Nutsey Beach moment, even thought it would still be years before I heard of Nutsey Beach. The only slight saving grace was that the record did have the licence to use images of the *TOTPs'* house dancers of the time, Pan's People, on the cover. So, at least I had an image of a scantily clad Babs, the busty blonde and every schoolboy's (and his dad's) favourite.

I remember that the Wings' *Band on the Run* LP inspired a lot of discussion in our house, as the cover artwork included some of Dad's favourite TV presenters. Obviously, Mum always liked the pictures of Elvis on his albums. But it was the artwork on the Beatles' *Sgt. Pepper's Lonely Hearts Club Band,* both then and now, that made a big impression on me. This LP was Dad's, not mine. It was very much 'look, but don't touch'. I remember thinking that the front cover was fun. Dad pointed out all

Peter Gilbert

the characters he recognised. But it was the Sergeant Pepper disguise kit inside that made the biggest impression on me. You could cut out a mask and a moustache, etc., and turn yourself into one of the characters. We children weren't allowed to touch the disguise kit, either, let alone get a pair of scissors near it.

This record is now framed and has a pride of place on my wall. It's not worth a lot of money, as it's not an early edition. But it does retain the cut-out disguise insert, still in pristine condition, which came as no surprise to any of us when the album became mine years later. Of course, my dad had filed the LP with the other *B* artists, nestled between those filed under *A* and *C*.

Dad would have probably had no idea who designed the cover. It would be decades I found out. I appreciated this artwork, as well as other work by Peter Blake.

Other than writing dreadful poetry and, earlier, plagiarised lyrics, I have not created much art. I did make a few collages from movie magazines to use for my bedroom décor and personal amusement. I'd also drawn a series of cartoons in the airport following my first trip to New York. These featured a character called Jim and were mainly based on movie and song titles, although, again in retrospect, they would not have gotten me through an art GCSE unless the teacher was into irony.

My love for creating art, which had been virtually dead since I took dull art-appreciation classes at college, was rekindled when I met my girlfriend. When I first went to her house, I was amazed by the colourful art on her walls and how eclectically she had put it together. She was also very much into photography and had several arty projects on the go. This very quickly brought my latent Pisces creativity to the fore.

The Jim sketches that I had tucked away in a file, having regarded them as childish scribbles, could perhaps be framed and hung in my flat with pride as a quirky, personal art statement. I pined for the long since thrown away giant collage that I had made with cuttings from film magazines— the one that I had painstakingly put together, making sure that every visual reference was intertwined and explicable. On that collage, an image of William Shatner as T.J. Hooker is in the bottom left hand corner. Shatner is looking up at the USS *Enterprise*, which is floating around in the top right. The character Beetlejuice appears next to an image of John Lennon in his Sergeant Pepper costume.

I have been lucky enough to do a fair bit of travelling and visit a number of beautiful cities with a photographer (my girlfriend). One benefit is that I tend to see things I may not otherwise notice, as my companion is compelled to snap away at colour, perspective, angles, abstraction, and the oddities of life.

On these trips, my girlfriend has shown a consistent fascination with ornate door knockers, from the small and delicate shell to the large and ostentatious brass lion's head.

I can't remember exactly why it started. Maybe it was because we saw an outstanding door knocker when photographing thousand-year-old buildings in the piazzas of Venice. But once we'd cottoned on to it, we started to see door knockers everywhere, even much closer to home, on little crooked houses in Wingham, Canterbury, and Sandwich in Kent.

Yet again, I find myself playing the lowly photographer's assistant, holding the bag and passing the lenses. But while my girlfriend takes her photography fairly seriously, each time we take a new picture of a door knocker, or even pass or notice one, I can't help but smile, as I imagine publishing all of the photographs in a book entitled *Great Knockers* or *Amazing Knockers,* with two appropriately shaped door knockers placed strategically on the cover.

With this newfound love of all art, not just contemporary and pop, we always plan visits to galleries when we go on trips and holidays, whether these be the more famous museums throughout Europe or local artist exhibits. We've enjoyed seeing amazing work in both types of venue. We've been lucky enough to see some of the classics: *David, The Birth of Venus,* and the ceiling of Sistine Chapel. Whilst I can appreciate their beauty and splendour, for me, a pop art or Dadaist image can be just as engaging, if not awe-inspiring.

I can appreciate the wonder and detail of the likes of Da Vinci, but, honestly, I can only look at so many cherubs without getting bored. So, give me an exhibition of the work of Bansky, Mr Brainwash, Shepard Fairey, Eelus, Ben Allen, Lichtenstein, Warren Salter, Peter Blake, and, depending on your definition of *modern,* Vargas, and Peter Driben—plus vintage movie posters—if you really want to get me excited and inspire me to create something myself.

Peter Gilbert

Having already established that the Lady P's mother, at over eighty years old, is still a fine-looking woman, I should also note that she has a bit of a colourful past, which is highlighted in a story I recently heard about her. Some years ago, in order to finance her gambling 'hobby' in Lima, Peru, where she lives, she had to sell some original Vargas drawings, which she had come to her by way of family.

Alberto Vargas, himself born in Peru, is synonymous with pin-up-girl-style illustrations and art that was used in many mediums but which was mainly commissioned as commercial work for use in advertising and on calendars in the 1940s. Vargas's images adorned both *Esquire* and *Playboy* in the '60s and '70s.

At the time, other people copied, plagiarised, and paid homage to these works. The style is recognisable today in the women painted on the front of Virgin Airlines' planes and in the woman adorning the Fratteli's CDs.

I have a sketchbook and a calendar for my year of birth illustrated by one of Vargas's contemporaries, Peter Driben. I love the style. Given that it includes women in skimpy underwear, who wouldn't? But short of winning the lottery, I can't see myself ever owning an original Vargas. Today, his works are very rare and therefore bear high price tags. Some of his works easily fetch six figures.

I'm not sure if was these (more valuable) pieces or the slightly 'cheaper' five figure ones that my mother-in-laws mother used to pay off her debts, but her association with Vargas and with *Playboy* magazine is another example of a coincidence, given that her daughter, Lady P, ending up working at the Playboy Club for a while.

So, whilst we do have a notebook of sketches from a semi-famous artist, Driben, we don't have anything at home that is quite on the scale of the Sistine Chapel. We do have some large pieces in our growing collection; we need a mansion or a gallery in which to hang them all. The art my girlfriend and I own falls into a number of categories.

Cheap Reproductions

We try to avoid these, as we believe that an original is best. Still, I do have a *Kill Bill* poster that I love, although one day I may replace it with an original, cinema-size version.

Original or Vintage Movie Posters

These are more special. They are the original prints from the relevant eras, not reproductions. They were actually hung in a cinema somewhere to promote the film. Now, they look amazing hanging in our dining room. If we had more room and more money, I could get hooked. I recently saw an original *Barbarella*, featuring Jane Fonda in '60s psychedelic design, for about £7,000. Unfortunately, that one is not hanging on our wall . . . yet. However, posters for *It Started in Naples,* starring Sophia Loren, *Come September* and *Buona Serra, Mrs Campbell,* both starring Gina Lollobrigida, are, along with the poster of 1966's *Thunderbirds Are Go.* All of these, while still hard-earned, are available for a much lower price than the *Barbarella* poster.

Limited-Edition Art

The list of what I'd really like to own grows by the week: a Peter Blake here and a Peter Phillips, FAILE, or Eelus there. We do have the odd one or two, including a Jamie Reid. He is known for the album cover artwork for the Sex Pistols in the '70s.

The Unusual or Out of the Ordinary

We have an original commercial winegrowing map of Italy from the 1950s, which is both unusual and stunning. It also resides in our dining room, along with a large Victorian taxidermy pufferfish (called Spike). Given that I also love sci-fi B-movie imagery, I have an outsized limited-edition print of the *Attack of the 50 Foot Woman* poster, the scale of which is a conversation starter in and of itself. It is over five feet tall, which perfectly suits the movie's content. But while the poster's imagery is fantastic, the movie is dreadful.

If it sounds like our small, modest house is crammed with art and imagery, literally bursting at the seams, that's because it is. We need extra space to contain it all.

Peter Gilbert

For my birthday a couple of years ago, we decided to stay in the trendy Brick Lane area of London to visit some contemporary galleries and attend a couple of art exhibitions. We like the work of an artist who goes by the name of Eelus. His early work includes some amusing *Star Wars* prints. Recently, because I'd dithered for a day deciding whether or not to buy it, I missed out on a very limited-edition print of his, which is now out of reach, price-wise. By chance, Eelus was holding an exhibition in the area on the weekend when we were planning to go.

At the exhibition, the original canvas of the print I'd missed out on buying was hanging near the back of the room. Its price tag was way out of my league, and there were no limited-edition prints left. We were amazed to find that Eelus himself was there painting a huge replica of this artwork on the back wall of the exhibition space.

We introduced ourselves and quickly got to chatting about his work. I told him which pieces we owned and said that my girlfriend was working on some pieces, too. He was charming, having taken the time to chat with us for ages. He apologised because the piece in which we were interested was no longer available. Eelus explained that even he didn't have copies of some of his most prized images because, at the time, when he was struggling to make ends meet, he hadn't thought about it and had sold them all.

We jokingly asked about the giant image on the back wall, the huge replica of the image we coveted.

'I'll probably bin it after the exhibition—or maybe paint over it at the next one.'

'You are joking?' we said, almost in unison. 'It's fabulous.'

'No, it's far too big to store and transport around to other galleries. I've just done it for the show to create some interest and to stop me from getting bored.'

'So, if somebody wanted to buy it, how much would you sell it for?' I asked.

The price he names was considerably less than what we had expected him to say. Because the gallery was not particularly busy, we figured that we would not lose out this time, even if we allowed ourselves the luxury of a visit to a local café for a latte to think about it.

It didn't take long, probably two sips, before my girlfriend and I decided that the artwork was an absolute one-off. We had a rare opportunity to buy it, which seemed like fate, given that it was my birthday. We were going to get it.

And get it we did, but not before asking Eelus to sign it—well, one of the four giant panels that he had painted on.

He offered to let us have the exact colour matches so that we could repair it ourselves if it got damaged in transit if we wanted to, but we pointed out that this would be a little like taking a match-pot to the *Mona Lisa* when it was looking a bit tired. And anyway, if we did that, it would mean that we would not have an authentic Eelus. Therefore, he also agreed, once we hung it and learned if it was damaged in any way, to come and touch it up.

Unfortunately, magnificent though it is, our modest abode is far too small to house the painting. We put it in storage, where it waits for us to purchase a property big enough to show off its full potential. When we do buy a larger house, Mr Eelus will get the call if the screw heads we use on the panels need to be colour-matched with the painting.

Looking back, I realise that the first art to really register with me, apart from the cheap imitations of *The Hay Wain* on the walls of friends of my parents and relatives, was the art of Marvel.

Of course, I didn't know this then. At the time, they were just comics, but each one contained hundreds of pieces of art. If I'd realised this at the time, I would not have thrown away so much of Stan Lee's artwork.

Like Tarzan, Blue Peter, Crackerjack, Doctor Who, et al., a boy defines his Marvel era by his preferred images and recollections of his favourite characters.

For example, Thor, today, is not drawn the same way as the Thor in the 1980s. He has a different illustrator and has been developed. Today, we have not only a different-looking Spider-Man but also alternate versions of Spider-Man, which was unheard of in my day (the mid to late '70s unless the storyline was about cloning.

My preferred imagery is firmly that of the Stan Lee era of the '70s. My favourite comics were always those that featured Iron Man, Spider-Man, Thor, and the Sub-Mariner, with Captain America and the Hulk bringing up the rear. DC Comics did get a look-in, as I was also a fan of Batman and Plastic Man.

Seeing Stan Lee's distinctive style now takes me back to my huge collection of Spider-Man and Iron Man comics piled up at the bottom of my bed. I also recall those cherished Marvel annuals I had received at Christmas but had subsequently lost.

A few years ago, I bought my boys a large canvas of a repro Marvel comic cover from this era. It featured Spider-Man fighting the Green Goblin. I can't help but think that this and thousands of other images are just perfect. Artists may take, add to, change, or ape other, but these, in my opinion, cannot be bettered. They are complete works of art as they are.

A wave of nostalgia, brought about by the canvas, inspired me to want to create a Marvel piece of art. Instead of a collage, I wanted to make something more practical—saleable, even—and so I purchased a bookshelf with the intention of making it Marvellous. Of course, I no longer had the hundreds of comics I had owned when I was eleven years old. I turned to eBay and car boot sales in order to get hold of that original '70s imagery—which, I felt, was important to use.

The piece took ages to make, not because it was particularly technical, but because I was obsessed. *What picture would go best with that one? That one shows Spider-Man looking down, so I need the one next to it to show a character looking up.* I'd flick through a dozen comics, often getting sidetracked with the images and storyline before finding one that pleased me.

At least one of the sides of the unit was likely to show when displayed, so very strong portrait images were essential. These, however, were limited in the comics I'd bought, so I sourced even more. This doesn't even account for the hours I spent cutting, pasting and varnishing.

It took hours, days. But I was more than pleased with the result.

Eventually, not having room for the bookshelf, I put it up for sale on eBay. Incredibly, it sold for a reasonable price. I was over the moon. Whilst the money was not a great return for the hours I had invested, someone had liked it enough to pay good money for it. Was I now a selling artist, sculptor, or furniture designer? Could I make a living?

Before I got carried away with thoughts of workers and factories, though, I realised that I'd overlooked one important fact. The person who had bought it had done so on good faith, judging from images on a website. The person had not actually seen it in the flesh. Therefore, I waited very nervously to receive the buyer's feedback on eBay. When it finally popped up, I was so relieved! The feedback was good. I contacted the purchaser and asked for more specific feedback. It turned out that she had bought the bookshelf as a gift for her boyfriend, a Marvel fan who had loads of collectables, which she thought would be perfectly displayed on my shelves. She promised to contact me again after he had received the gift. I waited for ages before receiving an email telling me that he was absolutely delighted with the bookshelf. He couldn't believe that he owned such a unique piece.

I've made a couple more since, another Marvel and a Viz bookshelf, always with original materials. They've taken me just as long to complete. Would Sandra from the Fat Slags comic strip in Viz be looking at Spender's alarm clock?

Despite the fact that both of these items sold to famous musicians, my girlfriend reminds me exactly how long I spent on them. They represent 'therapeutic' labours of love, not a viable enterprise.

The first of these two, the Marvel, was for sale in a vintage shop in Margate. The owner told me that Newton Faulkner, a singer–songwriter who was in the town playing a concert in the nearby Winter Gardens, had popped into the shop and decided to buy it to put it in his studio. How cool is that? Now, one of my creations had been bought by a bona fide music artist.

A friend of my girlfriend purchased the Viz piece for her husband, John Harle. On first meeting, Harle doesn't fit the obvious Viz fan profile. He is an Ivor Novello Award–winning composer and has played with the London Symphony Orchestra at the Last Night of the Proms and with the likes of Marc Almond and Elvis Costello—but he is an avid Viz fan. I now consider myself not only a credible selling artist but also a furniture designer and maker for the stars. If only they still asked for your profession on your passport.

While you may not instantly recognise John Harle's name, it's very likely that you've heard his work, as he has composed music for TV and movies, including *Silent Witness* and Simon Schama's *A History of Britain*. He therefore joins a long line of famous people who were born or resided in Canterbury or the surrounding area. This list includes Charles Dickens, Ian Fleming, Arthur Wellesley (better known as the Duke of

Wellington), Orlando Bloom, Shaun Williamson (Barry from *EastEnders*), Joanna Lumley, and Vic Reeves.

Despite the fact that my girlfriend was right about my inability to pursue art making as anything other than a therapeutic distraction, however famous the buyers of my pieces may be, she has benefited from my newfound creativity. I made her a chair designed to resemble a Fiat 500 design.

A lover of all things '60s and Italian, my girlfriend loves the old Fiat Cinquecento and owns a modern Fiat 500 (with Italian branding).

For her Christmas present a few years ago, I purchased a '60s design wooden chair and dozens of original Fiat 500 adverts and calendars from the '60s and '70s. Then, I created the Fiat chair. I even bought a Fiat 500 badge and stuck it on the back.

If you're reading this and thinking about replicating this individual and romantic gesture, please note that it's a bugger to wrap up.

Also, once you give the gift, you're a bit buggered for the following year. It's pretty hard to beat. A bottle of expensive perfume is just not quite the same as a gift anymore. Of course, my girlfriend appreciated the chair very much. She cried genuine tears of amazement and joy. One of her plaudits was, 'This is one of the best pressies ever.'

The chair has a place of pride in the dining room. We use it every day in the dining room, thanks to about twenty layers of varnish.

Only *one* of the best pressies ever?

Marvel's artwork lead one to pose the question 'What is art?' Boy, have we had that discussion many a time, but never so much as when in a modern art gallery. While art is, of course, individual, sometimes it's just bloody ridiculous.

I'm not sure where this first started, but it may well have been on a visit to the Tate Modern in London. More recently, we've seen a pot of paint on a chair labelled as 'art', as well as various bundles of sticks tied together and placed on the floor to represent 'the textures and features of landscape that I saw as I travelled around Australia' (or something similar). No, it's a pile of sticks. If a pile of sticks is art to you, then that's fine, but call it what it is instead of pretending that it's anything else. Take a leaf out of Damien Hirst's book, *Cow in Formaldehyde*. It is what it is, and at least you know what you're getting, unlike with, perhaps, *The Myriad of Textures* (a multimedia art installation).

One of my 'favourites' was a square canvas painted purple, or perhaps magenta, and featuring a white stripe down the centre. According to the wall sign, this painting represents something like 'the Jews struggle against oppression'. Excuse me?

And the sheet with the rip in it? I can't remember what the description said, although maybe that was the one about oppression, its stripe representing humankind's desire to find an alien race on a distant planet.

Then there was the time at the Tate Modern when my girlfriend and I walked through to a room we had thought was empty—as, in it, there was a single hanging light bulb—only to discover that the light bulb was, in fact, the art installation.

Bring on the cherubs.

Our never-ending quest to find the most pretentious bollocks continues, although we now adopt this style, ironically, for describing our work on websites or at exhibitions. We especially like to use the word *juxtaposition*, as we think that it takes the pretentiousness to another level. We described one of my girlfriend's recent pieces as 'The lone (black) butterfly is a metaphor for modern living. Its juxtaposition with the white canvas symbolises unobtainable virtuousness', or some such similar nonsense.

No wonder, then, that the world-famous street artist Banksy likes to takes the piss out of the art world of which he is part. Yet, even from his slightly separated and anonymous position, he cannot avoid controversy and conjuncture. His film *Exit through the Gift Shop* inspired almost as many conspiracy theories as the moon landings and Area 51 put together.

I recently read an article in a magazine that listed someone's top ten pieces of art. Being a lover of top tens and art, I decided to do the same, although I soon realised that, despite my protestations and leanings towards the contemporary, I quite liked some classic art, too.

The Statue of Boadicea in London's Hyde Park Corner

Ever since I was a child, I've found the scale of this work to be amazing. For the giant Boadicea in her chariot pulled by two rearing horses, I have wanted a house large enough to house it, maybe as a garden ornament.

Also, I don't care what historians say about her name. It's not pronounced 'Boo-dick-er'; it's 'Bow-dess-ear'. That's what I learnt at school.

The Painting *Tribuna of the Uffizi* by Johan Zoffany

This is a fun image of English gentlemen studying the paintings of the Uffizi Gallery in Florence. For me, it gets all the cherub and religious stuff out of the way in one painting.

The Trevi Fountain, Rome

Not only did my girlfriend and I feel compelled to visit the Trevi Fountain six times during our three-day trip to Rome, but we were also lucky enough to be there for the once-a-month emptying of the fountain and bagging up all the money that was thrown into it. This was a unique and unforgettable tourist experience.

Icarus by Eelus

This is a one-off, an original on four boards. It's huge, beautiful, and mine.

Today's Home by Richard Hamilton

Its full title is actually *Just what is it that makes today's homes so different, so appealing?* An early example of contemporary pop art, *Today's Home* by Richard Hamilton uses magazine images in a collage-style work. It's simple but effective, and it always inspires me to create stuff whenever I'm reminded of it.

The London Underground Map

I've always loved maps—another Dad trait, I guess—but the London Underground map continues to engage and fascinate me. There have been many interpretations and mimics. Recently, my girlfriend and I produced one centring on food and proudly hung it in our kitchen. Each line bears the name of our favourite or an unusual fish, plus the names of meats, desserts, wine, chefs, etc. We're now working on another version using beers. Each line represents ales from different counties or parts of the country, so I'm enjoying researching beer names like Big Todgers Tuplin and Old Badger's Arsehole.

Wine Producers' Map of Italy, 1953

I searched for hours for this unique gift for my half-Italian girlfriend. I wasn't sure how it would go down, as, ostensibly, it's an old promotion poster. I shouldn't have worried, though; my girlfriend adores it. Like her, it is beautiful and unique and demands a place of pride in our house.

Falling from Grace by David Choe

I love David Choe's work and especially this piece, maybe because it's of a half-naked woman with her knickers pulled halfway down her bum.

Wink by Peter Blake

Choosing one Peter Blake image is a bit like choosing a favourite song. Give me at least ten so I have half a chance. Because this image is very similar to the '40s and '50s style of Vargas and Driben, it's the one I'm going for (that, plus I already have the *Sgt. Pepper's Lonely Hearts Club Band* album on the wall).

Marvel by Stan Lee

Any original artwork would be treasured. I'd like my girlfriend to note that Stan has now issued limited-edition prints (available through high street gallery chains).

Whilst I can dream of filling our house and garden with priceless art, not even the biggest lottery win would make me able to purchase everything on this list. Still, I hope to have established, all pretentiousness aside, that art can be simple and inexpensive and yet still elicit smiles and comments. Take most kitchen walls or fridges upon which are hung scribbles done by your kids or photos of your kids covered in chocolate or with buckets on their heads. That's your art, so go and get out that box of LPs from the loft or go online and order some albums for the cover designs alone. Buy some inexpensive frames and brighten up those empty spaces with fun, memories, and nostalgia.

If, like me, you decide that album cover art, with its wide spectrum of designs, is able to fill your every art requirement or simply that space in the kitchen, be careful and take your time. You may want to avoid *Heino* by Liebe Mutter and *Livin' in the New Wave* by André Cymone. Check them out! But *Fuzzy Duck* by Fuzzy Duck would be fun. Also consider *Some Girls* by the Rolling Stones, which is pop arty; *Crazy Elephant* by Crazy Elephant, which is psychedelic; and *Sorrow's Children* by the Pretty Things, which is . . . interesting. On the other hand, the Hurriganes' *Use No Hooks* and Jane's Addiction's *Ritual de lo Habitual* would definitely be conversation pieces when you have the rellies round for tea!

My Top Ten Art Songs

'Sisters of Art'—French Car and the Bulimic Wizards
'Art for Art's Sake'—10cc
'Matchstalk Men'—Brian and Michael
'Andy Warhol'—David Bowie
'Vincent'—Don McLean
'Magritte'—John Cale
'Goodbye, Toulouse'—The Stranglers
'Kodachrome'—Paul Simon
'Taking Pictures of Each Other'—The Kinks
'Kevin Carter'—The Manic Street Preachers

Pop cricket score: 172 for 3

Things to Check Out

On YouTube:

- *Attack of the 50 Foot Woman* trailer
- John Harle—composer and saxophonist

Elsewhere:
- www.artybollocks.com
- www.myoldmansabusman.com

Marine Boy

Marine Boy, despite being a two-dimensional 1960s Japanese cartoon character, was one of my earliest childhood heroes.

He lived in an amazing submarine and his friends were a dolphin called Splasher and a mermaid called Neptina. He had underwater boomerangs that gave off electric shocks powerful enough to destroy his enemies' submarines and hyper-powered propeller packs in his heels, which enabled him to fly through the water and he could breathe for hours under water by using oxy-gum.

In 1969, what five-year-old would not think that this was cool?

As a kid, I would pretend to be Marine Boy, running around with my imaginary friends and either pretending to throw my boomerangs or using sticks as a poor substitute, often at the washing whilst it flapped on the line and represented giant sea creatures I had to defeat. This was always in the garden, though. At the time, I couldn't swim very well, and therefore I didn't fulfil my boyhood fantasy of actually being Marine Boy.

Over the years, I learnt to swim and snorkel competently. Recently, I enjoyed my first diving experience whilst on holiday in Sharm el-Sheikh, Egypt.

This holiday, whilst fabulous in many ways, including the diving, was notable for a number of reasons.

The hotel in which we stayed was frequented predominantly by Russians, who, to the casual male viewer, were an attractive group of guests. However, I discovered from my well-informed girlfriend, that most of the female bodies were in some way enhanced, some in both the boob and booty departments. Therefore, I had a great excuse to openly study them (my girlfriend would argue that I ogled them) more closely so that

My Old Man's a Busman

I could spot them myself. I did this purely in the name of research and to gain the ability to provide input to conversations, of course.

When encountering a group of these enhanced bodies on the beach or in the foyer, along with those at the other end of the scale, who had clearly taken advantage of too many all-inclusive buffets over the years, it was like wandering around a hall of mirrors. The glamorous Russians displayed a penchant for browning their booties by wearing their bikini bottoms *à l'intérieur derrière,* which created a more all-over tanned look. My girlfriend was becoming a bit jealous, but was not sure she was brave enough to emulate the Russian women.

This led to an ongoing *Fast Show*–inspired running joke: 'Does my bum look brown in this?'

Our people-watching, a regular pastime, inevitably leads us to name individuals, couples, or families by that which first strikes us about them. The names tend to stick for the duration of our stay in any one place.

On this trip, we had, amongst many others, Doughnut Boy, so called because on our first morning, he devoured five doughnuts smothered in chocolate sauce at breakfast. He went on to become part of the Doughnut Couple, as his girlfriend (God knows where she put it, as she had a model's figure) followed his lead and had four doughnuts herself on day two ... and on every day after that.

Then there was the Peacock family, who pranced, preening and paraded up and down the beach. The mother changed her bikini three times in an hour on our first morning there. Then there were (I'm ashamed to say) the Fatties ... but they were.

We also named one group the Foo Fighters, as the male half of one of the two couples looked remarkably like Dave Grohl. One day, when we noticed the members of the group lying on sunbeds, three of them forming a *U* shape at the front, with 'Dave' at the back sitting up, we called them, collectively, Nirvana.

Then, finally, there was the Rusty Knots (or RKs, as they were fondly known). We named them this because one day, the mother had taken the bikini bottoms *à l'intérieur* too far and had given my girlfriend an eyeful of her RK while she bent over the sunbed.

Of course, we did wonder what the other hotel guests were calling us. We hoped that it was 'the English Couple', due to our fair skin and my holiday panamaesque hat, but that presupposes that we looked normal to everyone else. We could just as easily have been the Stupid Hat Couple or the White Bum Couple. We do feel a bit blasé when we are around so many of our continental cousins. Possibly, we may be called something much worse if we ever misjudge and are overheard by what we believe is an Italian-looking male and female couple who do not understand English but who turn out to be very tanned people from Margate.

This trip was also the first time that my girlfriend had read any of my book. I had initially said that I wanted to get to ten thousand words before she read any of it. After that, we both got really busy. I had just kept writing. So, she actually ended up reading the first draft of about half of this book. I had been worried that she'd get to page three and say something like, 'I can't read any more of this self-indulgent twaddle.'

She actually read it all through, twice, and then gave me very insightful feedback, having heavily marked the manuscript in black pen.

The problem was that for the rest of the holiday, I was on a mental safari, consumed with re-editing the text and layout of the book so I was ready to revise when we got back home.

Back home to the dreaded routine. Work, breakfast, work, lunch, work, dinner, bed, breakfast, work, and then, once a week, to break the monotony, breakfast, put the bins out, work, lunch, work, etc. This is the dreaded daily routine about which many of us complain and which many hate.

So, how did we so easily slip into a routine on hols? Wake up, coffee on balcony, beach, snorkelling, breakfast, snorkelling, sunbathing, snorkelling, lunch, snorkelling, dinner, drinks, bed, wake up, coffee on balcony, beach, etc. No putting bins out, though. Funnily enough, we didn't miss having to do that.

The snorkelling was amazing. Our hotel was extremely well situated on a coral reef. From a pontoon which extended from the man-made beach, we simply got in the water and were swimming, at close range, with rays, puffers, parrots, zebras, butterfly fish, and clown fish.

I'm sure that if we'd more closely studied the numerous fish-spotting charts for sale in the shops, we'd have also been looking for the donkey, camel, moth, worm, tarantula, chair, sideboard, cocoa, coffee, bluebottle, mongoose, meerkat, duvet, and vulture fish, as the names and varieties seemed to be endless.

In addition to observing the fabulous fish, I also wandered around the hotel, observing things and people-watching (my girlfriend calls it being nosy). It struck me that there was a plethora of would-be band or artist names available. Having made a list over the course of the week, I now offer up the following to anyone who is an aspiring Beatles, Oasis, Shire Horses, Serafin, Pulp, Little Man Tate, Elvis Presley, Buddy Holly, or Laura Catlow:

The Land Pirates, the Cornets, Parrotfish, the Lifeguards, Lifeguard Station, the Sandy Flips, Damp Pages, Grog and the Contrabands, Oleg and the Preachers, PADI, Assembly Point, Gene Ral, the Mares, Mousse Booty, the Flashers, the RK Band, and Fire Escape.

There's more: Stella Del Mare, the Sharm, Kardom and the Lecturers, the Dysfunctionals, Savage and the Doctors, Kids Akimbo, the Professors, and the Mighty Malbecs.

If you've purchased my book and are thinking of using one of these names to launch your multimillion-pound career, then, as the Tammy Wynette (or J.J. Barrie, if you prefer his version) 1970s song says, 'No charge.' Otherwise, just like Hazel O'Connor, you owe me a pint.

If you are a budding singer or part of a budding group but are thinking of straying away from the above list and thinking of a name on your own, then please heed the following. There is a type of bird, a kestrel, which is also known, genuinely, as a windfucker (because of the posture it assumes when hovering in the air).

I'd love to think that Dave Brock and Mick Slattery, in their early days, wrestled long and hard over the decision to go with this more shocking alternative before finally settling on Hawkwind. Had that (imaginary) flip of the coin gone the other way, then I expect that they would not still be reaping the rewards from their 1970s youth club floor-filler success, 'Silver Machine'.

How fabulous would it have been if the Tweets had gone for it, too—or if they had gotten away with calling their 1981 wedding reception floor-filler 'The Windfucker Song' instead of 'The Birdie Song' (imagine the dance)? What if other bands whose names are bird-inspired, such as the

Housemartins and Counting Crows, had taken this idea and spiced it up a bit?

Arguably, Wayne County applied this principle when he came up with the brilliant *double-entendre* Flaming Lips, although I wonder if he rejected the name of the eighteenth-century British novelist Fanny Burney as a viable alternative. Also, had Patsy Cline's son gone into the music business, who knows what would have come to pass? She married Charles Dick. They named their son Randy.

I also came to the conclusion on that trip that beer was not necessarily humankind's greatest invention. Don't get me wrong. After snorkelling for hours (which is tough) and then sunbathing in forty-five-degree heat, an ice cold beer seems to be the best invention ever. But my well-informed girlfriend revealed to me that some Ann Summers stores had once introduced a peephole system whereby guys (or girls) could spy on their partners whilst they tried on their sexy gear. This, quite frankly is absolute bloody genius.

I'm not sure exactly how the system was policed, but apparently one could only spy on his or her own partner.

So, when not people-watching, finding band names, learning about body enhancements, and hearing revelations about Ann Summers stores, I was snorkelling. Despite the amazing array of colours and types of marine life on offer, I often found myself on a mental safari, thinking about content for my chapters and deciding where it would go—or just daydreaming.

Was the New Vaudeville Band's 'I Was Lord Kitchener's Valet' written before or after Whistling Jack's 'I Was Kaiser Bill's Batman'? Did one inspire the other? Was it worth mentioning in the first place? Should the Elvis chapter go before or after the Hazel O'Connor, or vice versa?

Also, how, in that other underwater-based boyhood TV programme of my childhood, *Stingray,* given that it was made in the '60s and included so many marine based and alliterative names; The main characters were based in Marineville, there was a character called Atlanta, the mermaid was Marina, there was a Sam Shore and the hero was Troy Tempest, had they not thought to include the singer Sandie Shaw (sandy shore) especially as she sang *Puppet on a String?*

At one point, though, I was floating towards an enormous shoal of glassfish—and by 'enormous' I mean literally tens of thousands, if not millions, of glassfish swimming in a ribbon formation within metres of the coral reef. Spotting them, I tried to slow everything down to a bare minimum in order not to frighten them or give them reason to swim away. I stopped swimming and just hung in the water, arm and legs splayed so that I needed no movement to stay afloat.

I consciously slowed my breathing, as if even breathing hard through my snorkel would alarm the fish. Then, as they slowly moved away from the coral shelf and towards me, I found myself completely engulfed in the shoal. I was actually part of it.

So, for a few moments, I was completely at home in the sea. I was breathing under water, not even thinking about the mechanics of swimming or how to stay afloat. My total consciousness was consumed in this amazing spectacle.

It had taken forty years to relive my childhood fantasy, but here I was, accepted by and completely at home with the fish in my temporary underwater world. I was, for a few brief but unforgettable moments, Marine Boy.

Then the shoal, probably realising en masse that I was not a 10 cm glassfish, disappeared. They were gone, totally out of sight, every single one of them, literally within two seconds.

I looked around, but there was no Splasher to swim with or ride on, no Neptina to play with, and no cool submarine to swim back to. In addition to that, my utility belt did not contain any boomerangs to throw at evil underwater menaces. My Marine Boy fantasy bubble had truly been burst.

There was nothing else for it. I went back to the sunbed, grabbed a cold beer, and settled down to check out some more of those female body enhancements—just to make sure . . . Marine who?

Peter Gilbert

My Top Ten Marine Songs

'Rock Lobster'—The B-52s
'Too Many Fish in the Sea'—The Commitments
'Octopus's Garden'—The Beatles
'Little Black Submarine'—The Black Keys
'I Am the Walrus'—The Beatles
'Theme from *Stingray*'—The Barry Gray Orchestra
'Moby Dick'—Led Zeppelin
'Puff the Magic Dragon'—Peter, Paul, and Mary
'Dolphin's Smile'—The Byrds
'A Merman I Should Turn to Be'—Jimi Hendrix

Pop cricket score: 238 for 5

Things to Check Out

On YouTube:

- Marine Boy
- 'Silver Machine'—Hawkwind, on *Top of the Pops*

Elsewhere:
www.myoldmansabusman.com

My Final Interview

'That was "I'm Frank" by the Fall, and this is Frank, Frank Skinner, on Absolute Radio. Apologies for the self-indulgent nom de plume, but I genuinely love that record and thought that I would share it with you all today.

'Talking of loving records, I'm really pleased to tell all of you Absolute Radio listeners that today we're welcoming back Friend of the Show Pete, who, regular listeners may remember, was writing a book that included lots of his favourite records and that we had him on the show when he'd written a few chapters, including some about yours truly, hence the opening song, and again when he was halfway through, But I'm pleased to announce that he's finally finished it. So, Pete, well done. How does it feel?'

'Well, Frank, thank you, both for your praise and for inviting me back. It's been nearly three years in the making—and it feels great. Working full-time as well has meant that it's taken a lot longer than I intended, and I'm sure there will be rewrites and edits for any prospective publishers to come, but I'm very happy with it as an accomplishment, if nothing else.'

'Just to remind the listeners, especially any new ones, this book is about your life but also your, and I have to say, somewhat fantastic and amazing interactions with celebrities as well as amusing anecdotes and commentary on all things popular culture over the last few decades. And given that we're not a dissimilar age, I associated with pretty much everything in the book, as I'm sure that many of our Absolute listeners will, too.'

'Thank you, Frank. As I think I've said before, the book is written as something that I'd think that I'd enjoy reading, so if anybody else gets something from it, then that's a bonus. And I hope that any publishers that I send it to will do so, too.'

'I'm sure that they will. So, do you have any offers so far?'

'No, I've just finished it, so I'm in the process of sending it out to see what response I get. But I do want it to be published as a physical book.'

'Why's that? Might I be so bold to suggest that, as I'm oft accused of, that it may be seen as a little old-fashioned?'

'Maybe, Frank, but that's how I've always pictured it over the years in my head. And in some ways, that's more important than any monetary return.'

'So, more of a vision, a dream?'

'I guess so, Frank. Also that my mum would love to see it in the *Mail on Sunday*'s *Live* magazine's 'Top Ten Nonfiction Books' list and even if it sold a million online or digital copies, Dad would not have understood that this meant that it was a proper book.'

'And I assume that those things are important to you?'

'Yes, Frank. The book is partly about the family, so it's important to me that, if it's successful, it's in a way that they understand, however old-fashioned that may be.'

'Well, good for you. I must say that when I've had a book out, there's nothing more satisfying than seeing it displayed in all its glory on a high street shelf. I hate to admit that I've even been known to wander into a bookshop with a partner in order to act surprised when they point it out on the shelf. But I hope you're not that vain. It's a terrible curse.'

'Well, Frank, we'll see. But I wouldn't put it past myself.'

'Talking of vanity, having shared the book with my co-presenters, they were a bit miffed not to be part of the interview sections. Any reason?'

'Well, Frank, firstly, part way through writing it, one of your presenters changed, Gareth to Alun, so I was worried that if I included them and they changed again, it would date the text and maybe confuse the reader. I appreciate that other references date the text, too. But, as I believe that the radio interviews are integral to the text, I wanted to avoid this. And secondly, writing the interview dialogue with two other people, Gareth or Alun and Emily, was, frankly, excuse the pun, too much of an effort. I hate to mention it, but it was also the reason for not going with my other option, Radcliffe and Maconie, although I probably shouldn't mention presenters from another station.'

'No, you probably shouldn't. But we'll let you off just this once, as you didn't go with them and did manage to include my co-presenters, anyway.'

'Yes, Frank. The thought of Emily's wrath in being left out was too much to bear, and so I included her in the chapter about me appearing in a dreadful movie. But, unfortunately, Alun and Gareth only got a mention in the final interview section.'

'Oh, well. I'm sure they'll get over it. And, it left more words on the page for me. During the break, you were telling me a bit about the writing process and a few other bits that got left out. Would you like to share them with the Absolute Radio listeners?'

'Certainly Frank. I think that I may have said it last time, or maybe it's in the book, but most of the first nine thousand words that I wrote, and was so proud of initially, ended up on the cutting-room floor, so to speak, during the many edits that I've already done. Also, along the way, I've written, either physically or in my head, sections that have ended up as a couple of paragraphs or just a few lines.'

'Can you give us any examples?'

'Well, Frank, given the music content, I'd planned a whole section on prog rock, which ended up as a throwaway line about "Hocus Pocus" by Focus in the chapter on Elvis. Also, as I now live close to Canterbury, there were a few paragraphs on the so-called Canterbury scene of the late '60s and early '70s which I ended up taking out completely.'

'Soft Machine and Caravan would no doubt have been mentioned had they stayed in?'

'Indeed, Frank, but that level of detail is probably best left to the experts like Stuart Maconie and Mark Radcliffe.'

'You've mentioned Mark a couple of times. He really does know his onions.'

'He does, Frank. I loved his book *Reelin' in the Years,* where he picks a song from every year of his life and talks about songs, music, culture, etc., from those years. I was going to do mine a bit like that until I read his. One of my favourite anecdotes from the book was that he once met someone who had been in a latter-day line-up of Dave Dee, Dozy, Beaky, Mick, and Titch of *Bend It!* and *The Legend of Xanadu* fame from the mid '60s, but I can't remember who it was. He [Mark Radcliffe] says, "I naturally enquired, 'So, which one was you?' To which he replied, 'Dunno, I never asked, although I'm pretty sure that I wasn't Dave Dee.'"'

'Yes, that's a great rock'n'roll story. He has many to tell.'

'He does, Frank. It also reminded me of my childhood because when my dad talked about the group, Dave Dee et al., I loved the quirky name, which made them interesting. I also always used to think that there were six of them in the group in the same way that I thought that the TV series *Alias Smith and Jones* was about three cowboys.'

'That's brilliant, and I could talk about this stuff all day, but back to your book. I have to say that I found it very amusing—funny, even, in places—although it pains me to say that on air. And I love the way that certain themes and thoughts popped up throughout the book. Was that intentional?'

'Well, Frank, not from day one, but it evolved. When I started, there were a number of things that I knew that I wanted to put in later chapters. And so, when a relevant opportunity arose, I couldn't resist giving it a mention or nod towards it.'

'Any examples to help the Absolute Radio listeners find them?'

'Well, an early one was that I'd noted down the bus lyric from the Macc Lads, which, given that we're on live radio, I can't quote in full, but it ends with "on a twenty-nine bus" for use in the "My Old Man's a Busman" chapter. And then I used that as a quote in my first interview with you. Also, I mentioned people or groups in the main text that I knew would also appear in the top-ten lists or vice versa, like Robbie and Elvis.'

'A bit like a linguistic or novelistic join-the-dots, then?'

'Yes, I guess so. And whether everybody gets them all or not doesn't really matter, as I enjoyed putting them in. And even if I thought that one person found one and thought, *Ah, I get it,* then I'd think it was worth the effort.'

'All that effort for one person? Surely not. I think that I'd want to spell it out.'

'Well, Frank, as I say in the book, I'm a bit of a fantasist, so, if I'm honest, I'd really like thousands of websites and Twitter feeds discussing all of the songs, topics, and places in the book—and, of course, joining the dots.'

'Wouldn't we all. And your ultimate fantasy? Can we say that at Absolute Radio at this time of the morning? Let me check . . . yes we can, good. To clarify, your ultimate fantasy concerning the book?'

'Well, Frank, apart from blue plaques or statues in all the relevant places mentioned, pretty much everything else is mentioned in the book, so listeners will need to read it for themselves.'

'Nicely done. And as a "friend of the show", I'm sure that all our Absolute Radio listeners will be queuing on day one to get a copy.'

'Outside of Waterstones Poole, please, as my nephew works there, so I've promised to do a signing if it ever gets published.'

'I'm sure it will. Frank Skinner says, "It's the autobiography that most celebrities will wish that they had written." I'd let you use that, but you may need to go through my manager. So, Pete, to wrap up, it's been great talking with you over the past couple of years, as I'm sure the Absolute Radio listeners will agree. And will you please come back and talk to us again once your book has been published and is on the shelves?'

'Of course, Frank. I'd love to.'

'Final question: With all of the great stories in the book, have you left anything out?'

'It's funny you should ask that, Frank. I did realise the other day that there's no mention of when I lived in Margate, where we had pole dancers practise in our lounge, that Ronnie Biggs's father-in-law was the headmaster at my first school, or that my girlfriend photographed a dominatrix as part of her photography degree.'

'Ronnie Biggs, the great train robber? That's amazing. You definitely need to come back and tell us about that, but maybe not the other two. I take it that you mean dancers from Poland and someone that does tricks with dominoes? Thanks, Pete, and good luck. We look forward to it.

'Coming up, we have a guest that I've wanted on the show for nearly as many years as I've fancied her, Suzi Quatro, who will be telling us, amongst other things, about what it's like on the GMTV sofa and about her forthcoming tour of Kent with Status Quo, *Rocking All Over the Weald*. But before that, let me take you back to the late '60s, when Gerry Anderson's supermarionation ruled the TV and we all loved watching *Thunderbirds, Stingray, Captain Scarlet,* and *Joe 90, his* puppets on a string. And here, with *her* puppet on a string, is the delightfully alliterative Sandie Shaw.'

Praise for *My Old Man's a Busman*

What Pete Gilbert has achieved with his first book is to have produced a very well-observed trip down his own amusing and, at times, downright funny memory lane.

Whilst there are enough celebrity connections and anecdotes not to be out of place in an A-list autobiography—Elvis Presley, Robbie Williams, Bobby Moore, Status Quo, and Tarzan, to name but a few—the real hook of this well-crafted book is that the author isn't remotely famous.

The endearing appeal of *My Old Man's a Busman* is that it is told through the eyes of the 'everyman', but one who has had enough light brushes with celebrity along the way to have given him some great tales to tell. These stories, amusing anecdotes, and musings are seamlessly woven into what, for many of us, will be a memory-jogging, laughter-inducing remembrance of some of the major as well as some of the quainter, stranger, and more trivial moments of pop culture over the last few decades.

If you love pop music, pop culture, top-ten lists, and Elvis; if you feared the Daleks from *Doctor Who* and the child catcher from *Chitty Chitty Bang Bang;* if you mourn the demise of Pez Cresta; if you see 'conkers' as a rite of passage; if you like jokes about lolly sticks; and if you liked *Top of the Pops,* and bubble-gum-pink, limited-edition LPs—then you may well enjoy this.

Please beware! This book may waste days (if not weeks) of your life, as almost every paragraph will have you frantically typing into your search engine and getting lost on what may turn out to be an endless 'Internet safari'.

This book contains some adult humour.

—Ben Elton

Lightning Source UK Ltd.
Milton Keynes UK
UKOW03f0107280514

232422UK00001B/69/P